THE LIFE OF IVY COMPTON-BURNETT

THE LIFE OF
IVY
COMPTON-BURNETT

by

ELIZABETH SPRIGGE

George Braziller
New York

Published in the United States in 1973 by George Braziller, Inc.
Copyright © 1973 by Elizabeth Sprigge
Originally published in England by Victor Gollancz Ltd.

Standard Book Number: 0–8076–0685–5
Library of Congress Catalog Card Number: 72–96072

First Printing 1973
Printed in Great Britain

To the Memory of
MARGARET JOURDAIN

also of
BASIL MARSDEN-SMEDLEY
for so long friend of the friends

And with warm thanks to
HESTER MARSDEN-SMEDLEY
whose generous help with the preparation of
this biography cannot be over-stressed.

E. S.

ACKNOWLEDGEMENTS

MY WARM GRATITUDE goes to the following for their generous help with this biography, for allowing me to quote from letters and other writings and for giving me invaluable insight into the life and works of Ivy Compton-Burnett:

Lady Ashton, Dr Edith Batho, Mrs Sybille Bedford, Dr Phyllis Bentley, Mrs Janet Beresford, Mr and Mrs Benedict Beresford, Miss Katharine Blackie, Miss Elizabeth Bowen, Mr James Brandreth, Mr and Mrs Michael Browne, Bryher, Professor Charles Burkhart, Mr A. Calder-Marshall, the staff of Chelsea Public Library, Mr Anthony Compton-Burnett, Miss Vera Compton-Burnett, Miss Juliet Compton-Burnett, Miss Lettice Cooper, Mrs Spencer Curtis Brown, Mrs W. K. Davin, the late Dr Cecil Day-Lewis, Miss Kay Dick, Mr Ralph Edwards, Mrs Joyce Felkin, Miss Eva Fox, Dr George Furlong, Mr David Garnett, Mr Cecil Gould, Miss Rosalie Glynn Grylls (Lady Mander), Miss Cicely Greig, Miss Pamela Hansford Johnson, Mr Soame Jenyns, Mr and Mrs Dennis Jell, Mrs Maria Jolas, Mr Michael Joliffe, Mr Richard Kennedy, Mrs Alan Kidd, Mr Roger Kidd, Mr Denys Kilham Roberts, Mr Francis King, Miss Rosamond Lehmann, Mr Robert Liddell, Miss Mary McCarthy, Miss Olivia Manning, Mr Luke Marsden-Smedley, Mr Christopher Marsden-Smedley, Mr Peter Mellors, Miss Esther Miller, Mr Julian Mitchell, Mrs Mary Moorman, Mr Raisley Moorsom, Mr Raymond Mortimer, Mr Wilfred Mowll, Mr Ivo Pakenham, Lady Paskin, Dr Pasmore, Mr Vere Pilkington, Mr Michael Pinney, Mr William Plomer, Mr Anthony Powell, Miss Carol Rygate, Madame Nathalie Sarraute, the late Mr Herman Schrijver, Mrs Hilary Spurling, Mr Christopher Sykes, Mrs Alison Grant Waley, Miss Antonia White.

CONTENTS

LIST OF ILLUSTRATIONS

FOREWORD

IVY COMPTON-BURNETT (Burnett with the stress on the first syllable) was one of the most original and fascinating literary figures of our time. I was fortunate enough to know her all my adult life, as my parents met Margaret Jourdain through Janette Ranken (later married to Ernest Thesiger) years before Ivy and Margaret knew one another. Ivy was always very kind to me, particularly when in the late twenties I began to write novels, and I greatly enjoyed and admired her books from 1925 when *Pastors and Masters* was published. I did not read *Dolores* until years later.

I became a closer friend of Ivy's after Margaret Jourdain's death. I was living abroad at the time and had recently suffered a sad bereavement myself. Ivy and I met again in the "awfulness" of our plight and at once became more intimate. She never forgave Margaret for "deserting" her.

As the years passed I saw her even more frequently, both with other friends and alone, at her flat or at mine. I used too to take her for drives—to Kew or Richmond or sometimes to the country, always to look at flowers. She was very appreciative. "I like driving with you, Elizabeth. You don't torture your car." She observed one closely, remarking "You look well" or "tired", and saying "poor you" very sympathetically if she heard of any small disaster. In big ones nobody could have been kinder. Ivy also noticed what one was wearing and often expressed approval. The appearance of her friends mattered very much to her. She spoke often of their looks and of the way they dressed—saying on occasion "if you can call it dressed". Sometimes she would ask me where some garment came from and to please her I might tell her how much it cost. Money was one of her favourite subjects.

A great deal of our conversation was about those of her friends whom I also knew and about which of them liked or disliked which. And she enjoyed discussing their private lives, usually with sympathy and tolerance and often with amusement. Sometimes there was a touch of criticism: "I don't know that I like people to be complete hedonists."

We talked about books, too, especially the new ones by her friends, usually stacked under the sofa, and the latest novels, which arrived frequently from Harrod's library. Her voice was very pleasant, an Edwardian lady's voice, and she had a way of quietly repeating her words, particularly the last ones of a sentence, in a way that was entirely characteristic and not in the least irritating—rather endearing, in fact.

We did not talk about Ivy's own books except on one or two occasions when I was going to lecture about her work. Then I told her what I proposed to say about certain of her novels, and she smiled and nodded and murmured "Yes, yes, yes". But I was coward enough not to tell her that I should be mentioning *Dolores*, as by this time Ivy all but disowned this work of her youth.

In the last months of her life I was with her much of the time. Her illness never interfered with her interest in her friends. Quite simply she cared about us.

I shall always feel that I was overbold in agreeing to write a biography of Ivy, who had little wish to reveal her life and believed that all she had to offer the world was contained in her books. Charles Burkhart has not made me feel better with those terrible words in his preface to the recent edition of her first novel, *Dolores*.

When a writer dies, he loses his privacy, all but his essential, his irremediable privacy; and critics, disciples, the rare book dealers and the bibliographer would not leave him that, if they could help it.

I do not belong to any of these categories. Simply I am a writer who was privileged to know Ivy well for a very long time, and it is as a friend that I have written this biography.

E. S.

THE LIFE OF
IVY
COMPTON-BURNETT

CHAPTER I

Double Family

"IT IS SOMETIMES not without interest to trace the heredity of talent," wrote Dr J. H. Clarke in 1904, when compiling the short volume *Life and Work of James Compton Burnett, M.D.*,* and accordingly this biography begins with Dr Clarke's description of Ivy Compton-Burnett's father.

"James Compton Burnett descended from an old Scottish family, the younger branch of which came south. A notable member of this branch was Gilbert Burnet, Bishop of Salisbury, a well-known writer of ecclesiastical history who flourished from 1643 to 1715. From him James Compton directly descended."

Bishop Gilbert Burnet, his name also appearing as Burnard or Burnett, the last form soon to be permanently adopted by the family, was like his novelist descendant an indefatigable writer. Unlike her he was also what she might have described as a "deedy" person. His activities, ecclesiastical, domestic and regal, were innumerable. He married three times, had nine children, travelled, became a naturalised Dutch subject and returned to England with his friends William and Mary. His most important literary work was the *History of His Own Time*, which was published, according to his directions, six years after his death.

"The name Compton was taken about the year 1770, on the marriage of James's grandfather with a Miss Compton of

* Homœopathic Publishing Company, 1904.

Hampshire, a lady of large fortune, at whose desire the addition was made. There were several sons of this marriage, one of them, Charles by name, married a Miss Sarah Wilson, and James Compton Burnett was their son. On July 20, 1840, he first saw the light. His birthplace was Redlynch, near Salisbury, his father being a considerable landowner [James always described him as a farmer] in the neighbourhood.

"James was a dark-eyed, dreamy boy who grew rapidly, perhaps more rapidly than was consonant with strength of constitution. By the age of twenty-one he had attained the size and weight which he afterwards always maintained—both being above the average . . ."

In physique his daughter, Ivy, did not emulate her father, for she was small in build, but in certain other ways she undoubtedly took after him.

James Compton Burnett was educated in England and in France.

"After this he travelled for several years, principally on the Continent, studying philology, the love of which in him amounted almost to a passion. At one time he even had serious thoughts of devoting his life to this study. The effect of this is seen in the vivid literary style of which he is master. His unerring perception of the value of words is one of the many charms which make his books no less delightful reading than they are instructive and inspiring. . . . He commenced his studies in the great medical school of Vienna, being thoroughly at home with the German tongue."

In Vienna he took an M.B., and later a second M.B. at Glasgow University, receiving his M.D. four years later, the first thesis he submitted being rejected as it had too strong a homœopathic flavour to please the examiners.

Dr Clarke speaks of Dr Burnett, the name by which he was know, as "a man of wide culture and experience", with "great powers of perception", and this quality, besides his love of words, always distinguished his daughter's work. Dr Burnett had indeed a most unusual mind; his medical books were renowned for their originality, and "he could not rest content with ordinary methods". It was this trait which led to his becoming a homœopath, after much testing of this method against others, particularly with children suffering from diseases of the chest. This move he upheld in his apologia, *Fifty Reasons for becoming a Homœopath*,* than which, according to Dr Clarke, "no better propagandist booklet was ever published". It was written to refute a charge of quackery by a young allopath to whom Dr Burnett declared, "Your head is as full of scholastic conceit as an egg is full of meat, and you are therefore a doomed man, so far as scientific medicine is concerned."

Dr Clarke also emphasises another quality of Dr Burnett's which Ivy was to inherit. "There was no one better able to appreciate," he says, "or more ready to express generous appreciation of—his contemporaries." Many living writers, both young and old, bear witness to Ivy Compton-Burnett's unfailing interest in their work.

Another taste of her father's which she shared was his love of nature. Although he practised in London, Dr Burnett never lived there for any length of time. He had a special interest in trees and a wide knowledge of plants, deriving from his childhood in Wiltshire, which naturally had a strong influence on his work. But, apart from their medical value, he sincerely loved growing things and so did Ivy, particularly the minutest of flowers.

Dr Burnett married twice, first in 1874, when he was thirty-three, Agnes Thomas, who was twenty-one and by whom he had five children. She was the daughter of a homœopathic chemist, and it was generally considered that the well-born and brilliant doctor had married beneath him.

His first private practice, which soon grew very large, was in Chester. Thence he moved to Birkenhead, where he remained for some time. After this, in 1877, he started a homœopathic practice in London at 86 Wigmore Street which was to continue

* 1888.

successfully for the rest of his life. He also worked at the Homœopathic Hospital, treated needy patients without charge at 2 Fins-
bury Circus, and for several years was editor of the *Homœopathic
World*. According to his colleagues, one of the reasons for his
success was his insistence to his patients and their relatives on his
need of a great deal of time to effect a cure.

The first Mrs Compton Burnett died when Charles, the second
son and youngest child, named after his "farmer" grandfather,
was still a baby. A lady nurse called Miss Smith then came to
look after all the children, the older ones going away to boarding
school, and when at home gradually becoming independent.

The menage that Miss Smith joined was the kind of well-to-do
Victorian household in which Ivy Compton-Burnett was usually
to set her novels, a large house with enough servants to run it in
the style expected by their employers.

Two years after his first wife's death the doctor married
Katharine, the youngest daughter of Roland Rees, formerly a
Captain in the Royal Engineers stationed first at Gibraltar and
then in China, and by this time Consultant Engineer to the Dover
Board. Mr Rees was a Welshman and a Wesleyan, a man of
means and a considerable scholar, who was greatly respected and
had twice been mayor of Dover.

Ivy's mother, Katharine Rees, was a remarkable young woman.
To begin with, she was extraordinarily beautiful with a mane of
bright gold hair—such wonderful hair that at the mention of her
now a nephew in his eighties remembers how as a little boy he
was struck by "the glory of Aunt Katie's hair". She was well
aware of her good looks and far from indifferent to the appearance
of other women. She confessed to her sister Elizabeth, her children's Aunt Lizzie, that on social occasions she always had a
good look round to see if there were any female present as beautiful as herself.

Katharine also had great charm, and although not an intellectual
was extremely intelligent, with a fine sense of humour. She had
a good head for business and a lively interest in politics. Not that
she considered such matters part of a woman's sphere—the idea
of women's suffrage appalled her—but she enjoyed conversation

about politics. As one would expect, she was a staunch Conservative, regarding the new-fangled notion of socialism with horror. The doctor did not pay heed to the political scene, but he was heard to remark that if everyone were made equal today it would be a very short time before they found their proper levels again. Katharine also had a sharp temper, which in her last sad days was to become a sore trial to her family, but in the early years she was good at hiding her feelings from James, whom she loved and revered and from whom she took her cue, and with whom she was always at her best. She was good, too, with the servants; in spite of her tantrums they grew fond of her and stayed for years.

The fascinating Katharine had had many proposals of marriage and light-heartedly refused each suit. "You will do this once too often," Mater, her stepmother, used to tell her, and then one day, on the advice of a relative, Katharine went as a patient to the widowed Dr Burnett. They fell in love at first sight. James Compton Burnett was fifteen years older than the twenty-seven-year-old Katharine. He was entirely captivated by her. He was a man of a very loving nature; he had been devoted to his mother and also to his first wife, and now he gave his whole heart to Katharine. She needed no pressing to marry her splendid, great, bearded doctor, despite the responsibility this entailed of becoming the young stepmother of his five children. The doctor was tenderly aware of her youth, an awareness reflected in his chosen name for her of "Wifey".

James and Katharine were married on 11th September 1883 by her uncle Allan Rees, the Wesleyan Minister, in the Wesleyan Centenary Chapel at Dover. He took her to Paris for her honeymoon and lavished money upon her. At a later date he even showed her how much the trip had cost and impressed on her the need to run their home economically, as the expenses, with so many children to bring up, were heavy.

Although the doctor had cured Katharine of Bright's Disease and she had a great respect for everything that he did, from a social point of view she could not help regretting that he was a homœopath, for at this time such practitioners were apt to be regarded as charlatans, and her position as a homœopath's wife was therefore not as important as she would have wished. She was very conscious of her father's position and of her own superiority to the first Mrs Burnett, the daughter of the homœopathic chemist. Later, when the Royal Family appointed a homœopath as physician, Katharine felt happier about her husband's choice. All the same, Ivy's sister Vera remembers their mother saying on one occasion to the doctor, "Think where you would have been now, James, if you had remained an allopath", and his gently chiding reply, "Wifey, what about the Nazarene?" It was Katharine who introduced the hyphen to make the name sound grander, so that she and her children, but not the doctor or the children of the first marriage, became Compton-Burnett.

Although after her marriage Katharine still often attended a Wesleyan service, during all the years that the Compton Burnetts lived in Hove she and the children regularly occupied the family pew in St John's Church on the corner of Second Avenue, as befitted her social station. And after the service they paraded on The Lawns, all wearing their Sunday best. This was Katharine's social superficial religion, whereas her Wesleyan faith was entirely sincere.

Katharine proved a good manager and became—as a hobby— an excellent cook. Dressed anyhow but with her hair always immaculate, she would often go down to the kitchen to supervise the preparation of a dish, and it was she who generally carved the joints.

For their first home the doctor had chosen a charming country house at Pinner, then a very pretty Middlesex village, where Katharine's elder sister, Elizabeth, was living with her husband. Here he and Katharine settled down with the five children of his first marriage, ranging in age from eight to two, under the supervision of Miss Smith.

Ivy, the first of the seven children of James Compton Burnett's second marriage, was born at Pinner on 5th June 1884, followed by her brother Guy a year later. The doctor liked living in the country, but Katharine did not, so the Compton Burnetts shortly moved to Richmond, where Katharine's second son Noël and the second daughter Vera were born in quick succession. Although she was only there as such a small child, Ivy always remained interested in Pinner.

In 1892 came the most important of the family's moves—to Hove, which admirably suited Katharine's class consciousness. They lived for the first years at 30 First Avenue, where in 1893 their third daughter, Juliet, was born, followed in 1894 by Katharine, known as Topsy. In 1897 they took up residence at 20 The Drive, where the parents remained for the rest of their lives and where Stephanie Primrose, always known as "Baby", completed the family. Ivy was now ten years old, and 20 The Drive was Home.

This huge house of red brick, ornately faced with stone, still stands as a monument to mid-Victorian taste, although late-twentieth-century edifices of glass and cement now flank it. The place was suitably furnished in a slightly haphazard way, elegant period pieces cheek by jowl with nondescript furniture, and here and there a potted palm to lend distinction, what taste there was stemming rather from James than from Katharine.

Before long Mr Rees and the Mater also moved to Hove to be near the Compton Burnetts. Rowland Rees was by now a close friend of his son-in-law's, sharing with him in particular a great love of books. Mr Rees had a fine library, and Dr Compton Burnett was in the habit of buying whole libraries when any collection of books containing volumes that he wanted came up for sale, so his already large multi-lingual library continued to expand. Ivy's cousin Katie has childhood memories of her grandfather and Uncle Compton sitting together surrounded by beautiful books in an aroma of leather bindings, cigars and whisky. Katharine Compton-Burnett was not a serious reader, but she liked to have a pleasant book on hand and would often send members of the family with Miss Smith to fetch such volumes from the local library.

The double family caused complications from the start, for Olive, the eldest daughter of the first marriage, who had been eight years old when her mother died and had become a close companion of her father's in the intervening years, was bitterly jealous of her stepmother. And Katharine was not tactful with her stepchildren. She found them neither clever nor well-bred, although in fact Olive had plenty of brains. Katharine treated them as members of a different and inferior family from her own, and in consequence remained for them an intruder. Her stepdaughter Margaret, known as Daisy, was to become an exception to this feeling. To begin with she was religious, and used to accompany Katharine to the Wesleyan Chapel, and later also became something of a social companion to her. Even with her own children Katharine was somewhat aloof compared with their father and Miss Smith, now known as Minnie. This name arose through Guy, as a little boy, pining for Miss Smith in her temporary absence and being given a dressing-gown of hers to take to bed to comfort him. This idol he named "Minnie", and Minnie Miss Smith became, Mrs Compton-Burnett alone continuing to call her by her formal name.

Minnie was, as is well suggested by her portrait, a remarkable woman. She had the most beautiful dark eyes, but her looks were marred by a nose too large for her face and a sallow skin. Her appearance, however, was not the important factor, but her personality. She was a strong character and a born manager, but her management was rooted in love, and all the children of both families adored her. "She really was our mother," Ivy told a friend with tears in her eyes. She was also on excellent terms with the doctor, who trusted her implicitly and presented her with a brooch bearing the name Minnie inscribed in rubies and diamonds. Her relationship with Mrs Compton-Burnett was less easy, owing to the latter's uncertain and autocratic nature, but she remained her faithful helper always. In the early days Miss Smith had trays sent up to her and dined alone, but later she officiated at the schoolroom meals, this being the usual eating-place of the family, the enormous dining-room only coming into use when there were guests to entertain.

Minnie was also extremely good at Dumb Crambo, the mime game that all the children loved. She could impersonate a comic waiter or some such character to perfection. Acting games remained popular in the household right up to the time when

Noël brought his Cambridge friends on visits and he and Ivy organised sessions of witty highbrow charades. When she was little Ivy loved to play such games as hunt-the-thimble, often with her visiting cousin Katie, closer to her in age than her own sisters.

In order to attend to his practice the doctor spent several nights of the week at a hotel in High Holborn. Wednesdays and the weekends, which he spent at home, were festivals for the whole family, for he was a well-loved husband and an adored father. He spent more time with the children than their mother did—"she loved us, but she did not like us very much," Ivy explained—and the hours with their father were the highlights of their week.

He would appear in the schoolroom at breakfast time and exhort them to eat their porridge, "or else you will have nothing to put in your brain-boxes", and he played many delightful games with them. There was "Dippy", when the children dipped their hands into his pockets and kept the coins they caught to put in their money-boxes. And there was the spreading of sweets on the big table for each of the children, after much deliberation, to make a choice of three. Or he might order them from the room—"Hinaus!", for, lover of languages that he was, he liked to speak to them in German. And when in response to his "Herein!" the children came in again, they might find him wrapped in the hearthrug disguised as a bear. Her sisters remember how Ivy, when she was too old for these games, would stand aloof, watching—she was always watching—and winding the blind cord round her finger while, unlike her, the brothers went on playing with the younger children. Ivy did, however, as they grew older, regularly read aloud to them, particularly such favourite novels as *Vanity Fair* and Charlotte Yonge's *The Daisy Chain*.

Sometimes, early in the morning, their father took the children "fruiting", their word for visits to Mr Miles, the greengrocer, who had a great regard for the doctor and would talk to him about his health. Here the children were allowed to choose whatever fruit they wished.

"Wave to Mummy!" the doctor would say as they left the house, and Katharine would be standing at an upstairs window to wave back, haloed by her bright hair. Then after a "scramble" on the beach they would all return to 20 The Drive and the doctor would breakfast with his wife, before spending some hours at his writing and returning to London.

The doctor was not a church-goer but he was most definitely a Christian, and on Sunday evenings he always conducted family prayers himself. All the children who were at home and old enough were expected to attend, having first been inspected by Minnie to make sure that they were tidy. All the servants were present too, entering and leaving the dining-room in a formal procession. First came the butler, then the cook followed by the maids in their black dresses and white caps with long streamers, Buttons, the pageboy, and Leeny, the nursemaid, the under-servants, whom Ivy referred to as the "Squalors", bringing up the rear. One nursemaid having been called Leeny, to save trouble, this name was given by Katharine to all subsequent nursemaids, so over the years Minnie was supported by a girl known to the children as Fat Leeny, Thin Leeny, Dignified Leeny and so forth.

Olive, in her unhappy jealousy of her stepmother, whom she never called anything but Mrs Burnett, remained aloof from the second family. Ivy's closeness to her father was a further distress to Olive—indeed, from the time that she was quite small Ivy always considered herself the eldest daughter. She kept her distance from the first family, an aloofness that her brothers did not share. Olive was a clever girl, and as soon as she was old enough to earn her own living, which Katharine considered a social disgrace, she went away. Her father bought her a share in a girls' school, and later she became a journalist and edited a magazine. The elder son, Richard, also left as early as he could and trained as a solicitor. Charles, the younger son of the first family, who was only a few years older than Ivy, often spoke in his later days of not having had a happy home, and he too was swift to abandon it. The younger girls, Daisy and Iris, were very kind to their half-brothers and sisters and always remained close friends of Vera and Juliet. As soon as Iris grew up she trained as a nurse, and Daisy, after remaining at home for many years, eventually became a missionary. She went to West Africa, and on her return became the principal of the Carfax Home for Missionaries in Bristol, where she had trained. None of the Compton Burnett daughters ever married. But although the children of the first marriage had this difficult relationship with their stepmother they were all loyal to her and never let their father suspect that anything was amiss.

Ivy was a small child—not thin until much later—with grey-blue eyes and long fair hair which, although lacking her mother's brilliance of colour, was very pretty. Until her teens, when she began to tie it back, she wore it loose on her shoulders without band or bow. Her delicate hands and small feet were beautiful, as too were her teeth. She was not strong, being prone to coughs and attacks of quinsy and needing much care from Minnie. Guy, her elder brother, was also far from robust, with a tendency to bronchitis which possibly the sea air aggravated, and Noël early hurt his back in a fall and was unable to play any games for some years. Ivy and Guy were both exceptionally clever and were inseparable companions, having endless private conversations and jokes, too obscure for their relatives to understand. If Ivy chose to be scathing—and anyone might be the target for her irony—her shafts would certainly be witty but they could be wounding too.

The younger brother, Noël—Jim to his mother and Ivy and Noll to his younger sisters—was to become Ivy's other close companion, but, although he grew brilliant later and always had a vivid imagination, unlike Ivy and Guy he was a slow starter. For their early years these three were educated together. The fact of having had a boy's education always remained a source of satisfaction to Ivy. First they were taught by Miss Mills, the resident nursery governess, who also gave Charlie lessons and put the children through the examinations for the College of Preceptors. The next stage was Mr Salt, the visiting tutor, to teach Guy and Ivy Latin and Greek—and Noël too, when he was old enough to join in, although these subjects never really interested him. Ivy, on the other hand, at once became a keen classicist, and the tutor was enchanted by her. They were a closed circle, and the children hoped that they would never have to go to school.

When she was not with her brothers or her father Ivy was for the most part solitary. On country walks she would stroll by herself, gathering small flowers or perhaps picking up snail shells, which she did from earliest childhood. She had a fondness for minute objects, and collected whole families of little china animals. Also, when she was quite small she liked to do "real" things such as sweeping up rubbish with a diminutive dustpan and brush. And from early years she read, and not only read but studied. On holidays in the country, often in some farmhouse near Tunbridge Wells, she would sit through the long evenings with a candle on either side of her, working away at her classics. The one lesson which she did not enjoy was the piano, for she was entirely unmusical, whereas music was more important than any other subject for her sisters. They also liked painting, and to this too Ivy was indifferent. Words were her medium. She did not write stories in childhood, but used to compose little poems. The doctor would give a prize of one shilling for a good poem, but only sixpence for a hymn, as he considered this an easier form of composition.

All through these early years her brothers were Ivy's chosen companions. She never became close friends with other girls, even when she at length went daily to the Addiscombe College for the Daughters of Gentlemen, where her younger sisters, all but "Baby", also went in due course. As they grew older Ivy became more interested in her sisters, although this was not apparent to them.

In her first novel, *Dolores*, she describes the little stepsisters as "Sophia, a noble-looking girl of eight, and Evelyn, a fragile little damsel two years younger"—without doubt a picture of her own sisters, Vera and Juliet, nicknamed Judy.

Katharine was ambitious for her children and eager for them to excel. She was therefore not opposed to the notion of higher education for Ivy, and presently she was sent to a boarding-school for girls, run by her father's brother "Uncle Jack" and his wife, "Aunt Sarah", in preparation for entry to Royal Holloway College. Nor did Mrs Compton-Burnett object to Vera and Juliet going a little later to study with the famous master of music, Tobias Matthay, with a view to becoming professional musicians. She even suggested to her daughters, after their father's untimely death, that they might find themselves needing to earn a living. Although Ivy was disappointed that her sisters did not develop into intellectuals she was proud of their musical prowess. "We shall all bask in your glory," she wrote from Holloway College when she heard that Vera had passed an early examination. As an example of Katharine's class-consciousness—her relatives repudiate the term snobbery—Juliet was not permitted to invite her best friend, the daughter of her cello-master, to her parties.

The Christmas of 1900 was the last that Ivy and her whole family were to spend together. It was a happy occasion in their home with the traditional fare, Christmas tree and festivities, in which Dr Compton Burnett joined with his usual "playfulness of disposition", as Dr Clarke called it, although he was now not in good health. Some years before he had given considerable anxiety to his relatives and friends by being repeatedly indisposed, but of late these attacks had ceased. It had been noticed, however, that he had become unusually deliberate in climbing stairs, and one day after a walk he had mentioned a pain in his chest, although he countered uneasiness with the suggestion that this was only a little indigestion. When asked if seeing so many patients did not tire him, he replied: "No, I love it. It is my life. My only hope is that I may die in harness."

The death of a brother in 1901 affected him deeply, and in March of this year he made a new will. He had acquired certain pieces of land and farm buildings near Clacton in Essex which he bequeathed to the children of both marriages, hoping that this would give them independence. He left his personal effects to Katharine and the remainder of his property in trust, she to receive the income for life and this then to be divided between their children. He said to her, so she told them, "You see, Wifey, I can trust you to be fair." He also left several hundred pounds to Minnie on condition that she remained with the family to look after the children. Katharine's will was, however, not altogether fair, and it was left to her children later to adjust finances and help some of their father's first family.

Two weeks later the last patients whom Dr Compton Burnett saw noticed that his hands, usually warm in the coldest of weather, were icy. He dined as usual at his hotel that night and retired to his room where, on the following morning, he was found dead. He was only sixty-one, but he had lived and loved to the full.

The grief of his family—Ivy was now seventeen, and she came home from boarding-school—and of his friends, colleagues and patients was overwhelming. Vera, who was nine at the time, actually dreamt some nights before of her father's death, and the day after it Guy wrote a moving poem in round boyish script— he was sixteen—beginning:

> There is a velvet curtain drawn before
>   The eyes of men, concealing from their sight
> The hidden mysteries of the further shore,
>   Till they are taught to bear the fuller light.

The obituary notices all spoke of Dr Compton Burnett's extraordinary charm. The *American Homeopathist* remarked on "that magnetism, that witchery, that individuality which held his audience from the first moment", and the *Monthly Homœopathic Review* observed: "His personality and character were very uncommon, and we had almost said unique." Of Ivy Compton-Burnett we can quite say "unique", a uniqueness shown in all her attributes.

Life at 20 The Drive was never to be merry again after the death of James Compton Burnett. The brightness of Katharine's hair remained, but this was now her only brightness. The household was drastically reduced. There were no menservants, but simply the cook, two maids and of course Minnie.

Her sons afforded Katharine some comfort. She was proud when a few years later Guy went up to King's College, Cambridge, to read Classics, with ambitions to become a great headmaster, probably by way of the church. She was proud too when Ivy, having passed the London Matriculation in 1902, at the age of eighteen, went up to Royal Holloway College, also to read Classics. From here on 1st May she wrote to Katie:

"I have been back at college a fortnight now, and am quite settled down into work again. We have been having 'collections' at the beginning of the term. It is quite a new departure, and not altogether a pleasing one, for at the outset one's mind is painfully lacking in great ideas. After perusing my Roman History paper, which contained a map, showing as I thought considerable knowledge and artistic skill, the Principal impolitely informed me that it was evident that I had not much talent for drawing; would I do that map again please. I cannot say that she went up much in my estimation after that remark. To make matters worse, the only question she seemed to take satisfaction in, was one I had written in the exact words of the book. She praised my 'vivid description' and I discreetly refrained from telling her the sources of it. The swimming bath is open today for the first time; I have been watching a novice learning to swim; it is a most amusing exhibition. I believe I should be afraid to learn. The dramatic society are going to act a play. The dress rehearsal is to be tonight, and tonight the first-years are requested to attend. It is bad to be a first-year; I am looking forward to next term, when I shall be a second-year, and have about fifty whole first-years to sit upon. I trust that you will be able to interpret this scrawl, writing it is only by courtesy; I am in a hurry, writing in the quarter of an hour in which I should be dressing for dinner. I have been intending to write to you for the last three months, and I trust that you have also been intending to write to me, for intentions, when they are good, are better than nothing . . . Talking of intellectual subjects, does Aunt Lizzie still play those terrible games about the Kings of England and countries of Scotland, and writing down all the great authors you can remember beginning with K? The lists she used to produce, pages and pages

long, have made an indelible impression on my mind; I am
glad to feel that my mind is not absolutely a blank. I begin to
fear sometimes that it is. I must say goodbye now, and go and
endeavour in the short space of 6 minutes and 3/4 to arrange
my wig, an operation which Mother declares should occupy
every lady at least half an hour. Give my love to Auntie &
Uncle Robert, & to all the poor chicks who have just got rid
of the mumps.

    "With much love from
            "Your loving cousin
                    "Ivy."

    This "scrawl" is in fact easy to decipher, in a roundish script
oddly different from the scarcely legible handwriting Ivy was
soon to develop.
    Royal Holloway College, a branch of London University
since 1900, is a huge and ornate red-brick and stone edifice set in
extensive and beautiful grounds high on a hill above a reach of
the Thames twenty miles from London. This college had been
chosen for Ivy before her father's death as better for her health—
she and Guy still had weak chests—than the fens of Cambridge.
    Holloway is now a successful co-educational college, but it was
founded by Robert Holloway, the manufacturer of Holloway's
pills and ointments—popular remedies in their time—in memory
of his wife, in order to give women of the middle and upper
middle classes the educational advantages afforded by universities
to young men. The college had been opened by Queen Victoria
in 1886; a somewhat melancholy occasion this, as the Queen
was upset by the journey and refused to stay to tea. Consequently
the furniture which had been made in her honour was indignantly
dispersed about the building, and only at a later date reunited
as a Victorian collection.
    There had been few students in those days, but many of the
young ladies brought their maids with them, which helped to
fill the innumerable rooms. By the time Ivy arrived there were
one hundred and thirty-four students, but only a small number of
these was reading Classics. And although skirts still swept the

Dr James Compton Burnett

Katharine Compton-Burnett

20, The Drive, Hove

Ivy Compton-Burnett as a baby

ground and hair was piled high, no personal maids were in attendance, and Ivy was rather ashamed of being accompanied on her first arrival at the College. There was, however, a large and strictly disciplined domestic staff, and the standard of comfort was high. Each student had a study, on the walls of which were no pictures but one large mirror—a custom Ivy was to adopt. In none of her homes did she have pictures, but later a number of large and decorative mirrors appeared. There was also a bedroom for each student to which brass cans of hot water were carried twice a day. Everyone dressed for dinner, the Lady Principal wearing formal dress. She would receive members of the staff and students from time to time in her drawing-room, and etiquette, which included the segregation of students in their particular years, was strictly observed. Smoking was not permitted. The College was by the terms of its foundation non-denominational but required some religious observance, and Morning Chapel at eight was obligatory. Students were encouraged to be well-informed in current affairs and to have wide interests. Debates and amateur music and acting were in popular practice.

Lack of transport made the College on the whole a closed community. The railway station was miles away and could only be reached by bicycle or on foot, and students were forbidden to walk or bicycle alone outside the grounds and were required to be indoors by sunset. So even the occasional horse-bus lumbering down the hill did little to connect Royal Holloway College with the rest of the world. Incidentally, as Ivy had not then learned to swim, she was not permitted to join in the excursions on the river, so her outings were mainly in the well-kept grounds —the head gardener used to arrive on his pony, and the strawberry beds were famous. Royalty would sometimes attend the garden parties and enjoy the fruit. Ivy all her life was a great eater of fruit; even at afternoon tea, after toast with a scrape of butter and a variety of buns and cakes, she would eat grapes or pears and press such fare upon her guests.

She excelled at once in her work, and in 1903 passed the Intermediate examination.

B

In 1904, only three years after the death of the doctor, another tragic blow fell. Guy, now nineteen and still in his first year at Cambridge, was doing exceedingly well. Indeed, he had made a remarkable impression on both dons and undergraduates in this short time. Home for the vacation, on Easter Day he was taken ill and developed pneumonia. The rest of the family were just recovering from a severe epidemic of influenza. A few days later his brother and sisters were told that Guy was critically ill and were taken to his room for a glimpse of him. Early the next morning he died. He had been wonderfully patient and kindly to his mother, and from this tragedy Katharine really never recovered. She became increasingly difficult and critical, and the household was held together in a precarious fashion by the faithful Minnie. Noël, now a day boy at Brighton College and very good-looking, devoted himself to Katharine and took Guy's place as the centrepiece of Ivy's life. She always needed one special person to whom to devote herself, and this was to be Noël for the rest of his life. Nevertheless this was a lonely time for her; in spite of Katharine's preference for her own family she was ill at ease with Ivy, and Daisy now definitely had the position of the elder daughter. It was she who used to pay calls and leave cards with Mrs Compton-Burnett, and although Ivy did not enjoy such social activities she felt bitter at being supplanted by her stepsister.

In 1906 Ivy was awarded a Founder Scholarship in Classics amounting to £30 a year for two years. Later in the same year she gained her B.A., Class II, Honours Degree. A few months later her cousin Katie met one of Ivy's examiners on board a liner. The latter declared that all the examiners had been defeated by Miss Compton-Burnett's handwriting which was the reason for her not obtaining the "First" that everyone had expected of her.

It was not until 1907 that Ivy's time at the Royal Holloway College came to an end, and she was now required by her mother to devote several hours of each week-day to teaching her young sisters. She was not enthusiastic about this duty and her usual method was to set the children exercises—paraphrasing Shakespeare, writing essays, doing mathematical problems, at which Ivy herself was very good—and remotely supervise their labours while sitting at the end of the schoolroom table occupied with her own writing. By now she knew that she wanted to be a writer, and she soon set to work on *Dolores*. Before this she had written "only just childish things that everybody writes who is probably going to be a writer".

Absorbed as she was in her own interests and dissatisfied with her home life, Ivy showed considerable affection for some of her relatives at this period, including her cousin Katie and her sister Vera, although with the latter she was never demonstrative. Juliet, like Noël, was a slow starter and hampered by short sight. Ivy did not disguise her impatience with her, nor did her mother, who could not tolerate any imperfections in her family. "Don't peer, Judy," was a constant reprimand to the poor child. Vera, who was always devoted to Juliet, was now, to Ivy's pleasure, showing signs of developing into an intellectual. Ivy wrote a poem for her sixteenth birthday in September, 1907, of which the last of the three verses runs:

> Well has childhood done its duty.
> Steadfast at your side has stood;
> Faithfully its care has kept you
> Clasped you closely whilst it could.
> Never may it break the spell,
> Never bid a last farewell,
> Ever may its voices reach you
> Through your years of womanhood.

Noël enthusiastically helped his sister with her novel. "Meddled with it" was how she put it herself, so that in the end she felt that she scarcely knew what part of it was hers or what was not. It has sometimes been called a collaboration; nevertheless, on the proof copy is written "Noël Compton-Burnett with the author's love", not the usual inscription to a collaborator. The first chapters of this page proof copy are very much corrected in pencil and whole passages have been crossed out, but the book was printed in its original form without these alterations.

Noël had by now entirely conquered his backwardness. He had had to be crammed in order to pass the Little-go examination, but once he had begun reading history at King's College—he went up in 1907 and was a contemporary of Rupert Brooke—he carried on the tradition of Guy's brilliance. He was tutored by Oscar Browning, now an old man, who was both proud and fond of him, and he became the secretary of the Political Society, founded in the seventies by Oscar Browning to help him in his chosen task, "the training of statesmen by academical instruction". Papers were read and debates held, and Noël was in his element. He twice won the Gladstone prize and took a double first in History, but by temperament he was an artist and his personal ambition was to become a poet. Hearing Rupert Brooke read some of his early poems at the famous little "Carbonari" society at King's was one of his most valued experiences. During this period he also attended some courses at Göttingen University, went to Munich and made several German friends.

Ivy greatly enjoyed not only Noël's company, but also that of the young men whom he brought home on visits. She had by now become a witty conversationalist herself. It was the intellectual gifts of Noël's friends which she admired rather than any attractions of their sex, although she did at some point, so she told a few friends, have a proposal of marriage. One of these young men was Arthur Waley, who remained a friend of hers for the rest of his life, but the most important of them to the Compton-Burnett history was Jack Beresford, the closest of Noël's friends at King's, for not only did Noël marry Jack's sister Tertia, but the Beresford family had a far-reaching effect on Ivy's life and work.

CHAPTER II

Dolores

DOLORES IS OF the greatest interest to anyone studying Ivy Compton-Burnett's life and character. The heroine's milieu is an extraordinary distortion of Ivy's own background. In both there are two families: a father, the children of the first wife, and a stepmother and her offspring. Ivy was the eldest child of the second family, and Dolores is the elder of the two children by the first wife and her father's beloved companion, as had been Ivy's stepsister Olive. Dolores, like Ivy, is deeply attached to her scholarly brother, and there is plenty of irony about "that branch of dissent", the Wesleyanism, with the stepmother discovering, like Katharine, "how much higher a type church-people really were".

There is a take-off of the relationship between her mother and her aunt and of their family doctor. The word "homœopathically" is even used ironically when Ivy is referring to the way certain human beings react to one another, and one finds a lady (whom the father marries as his third wife) "whose foremost quality was a persistence in appending her husband's Christian name by a hyphen to his surname". She makes Dolores shortsighted, too, like her own sister Juliet, adding that this was said to be "a mark of high civilisation".

A woman's college (Holloway having moved in the book to Cambridge) and its staff, are described with an extremely amusing piece about the arrival there of Dolores and her encounter with another student.

"Oh, here is the name on a door." [Felicia gaily says, after admitting that she too is a newcomer and wishes that she had arranged to be something else.] "This is where I am kept, then. . . . Do you know, I believe all the people here have names? Is it not thoughtless when there are a hundred?"

The characters of the college staff in the novel are based on certain members of the Royal Holloway faculty during Ivy's time there. On the flyleaf of the copy of *Dolores* that is kept in the college archives, a contemporary of Ivy's has made a list of these characters, with the names of the lecturers from whom they derived. Even the protagonist, Claverhouse, the annotator suggests, was modelled on a visiting professor, although only in appearance. Dolores's return home to the duty imposed on her of teaching the younger children again stems from Ivy's life—her little sisters becoming in the book stepsisters.

Dolores, except for the dramatic emotional centre of the plot, is a gallery of caricatures, but Ivy's caricatures are not crude. They are sly and subtle and framed quietly in the skilful realism that was the result of her being so phenomenally observant. As Lettice Cooper aptly puts it, "unsparing in perception, sparing in judgment".

Apart from the ironic comedy of the book there is the intensely emotional core of the plot; the tragic passion of Dolores for the ageing and nearly blind playwright, Claverhouse, her love for whom she sacrifices to the demands of duty. It is surprising to find Ivy Compton-Burnett extolling duty, whatever unhappiness it entails, in her first book, when in later works her characters shy at the mere thought of it.

What comes through *Dolores* with indisputable clarity is the author's reverence for knowledge and her understanding of grief. No one without very deep feelings, who had not had vivid experience of suffering, could have written this book. People who only know her later work often assume that Ivy Compton-Burnett was heartless. In fact, although after *Dolores* she resolved not to wear her heart on her sleeve, no one who knew her well could doubt its existence.

Dolores is clearly not a self-portrait—Ivy would not have drawn herself as a "noble" character nor dwelt on her sufferings in this masochistic way, nor would she have given any later book such a title. Nevertheless it contains passages of self-revelation.

"There was that in Dolores which yielded to womanhood's spells. She hardly judged of women as a woman amongst them; but as something sterner and stronger, that owed them gentleness in judgment."

There is a true touch of Ivy here, and in the poignant allusions to the "creative spirit" attributed to Claverhouse, and his belief that the study of man was "the greatest thing that life offered to men" (a belief held by George Eliot), there must be something of Ivy's discovery of her own urge to write. When Claverhouse reads his play aloud to his friend, who exclaims: "It is wonderful. It is great," he responds with: "It is true, is it not? It is that that I strove for." And as an illustration of his play's truth he adds: "Listen! When Althea hears that her father is dead, she utters no sound, no word—that is true." This was certainly true of Ivy when she learnt of her own father's death. And one cannot over-emphasise her integrity and regard for the truth.

There are other episodes which may not echo Ivy's early life, but which certainly foreshadow events in her future books. A mother and an old servant listen, though in this case bene-volently, at keyholes, another mother, without benevolence, opens her daughter's correspondence, and Dolores' brother makes a clandestine marriage. The book also contains many character-istic observations, phrases and epigrams which might have appeared in any of the nineteen works to follow. Even the opening sentence, "It is a daily thing," reflects Ivy's way of looking at life. But there are many descriptions of people and a few of places such as were never to appear again, a clumsiness of syntax and an over-use of adjectives which seldom occur in the later novels.

Such descriptions and much else, such as the author's addresses to the reader, obviously derive from assiduous reading of the Victorians and particularly of George Eliot, though I. Compton-Burnett's descriptions lack the wealth of detail that the leisurely

pace of Victorian writers encouraged. However, even after Ivy
had developed her individual and original style an echo of George
Eliot remained. Oscar Browning had frequented the latter's
drawing-room in her later days, which made through Noël a
pleasant link with her. One thing that Ivy did not share was
George Eliot's love of music; little mention of music or of the
graphic arts appears in Ivy's books.

It is interesting to compare the agnosticism of the two novelists.
Mary Anne Evans was by nature pious, and even when she became
George Eliot and through her reading of critical philosophy
abandoned belief in evangelical Christianity, she remained sincerely interested in religion. Whereas to I. Compton-Burnett
it became man's most extraordinary aberration and an irresistible
invitation to mockery. In her earliest years she had taken Christianity for granted—"One believes what one's parents tell one"—
but even then she did not like it. "I thought it was a humiliating
religion."

It was not through any outside influence that she lost her faith.
Simply, in her teens, she suddenly found that it was not there.
Her mother's dual religious practices probably had something to
do with this. With her ruthless honesty Ivy despised the disguise
of social observances as divine ones. The whole thing appeared
a mockery, although it gave her a shock to discover, as she opined,
that there was no God caring for her and that she was therefore
of very little account.

Like George Eliot, Ivy, with Noël's approval, chose John
Blackwood as the publisher to whom to send her first novel,
and although it was not written under a pseudonym at least
I. Compton-Burnett did not announce her sex, although the
reviewers revealed it. The book was immediately accepted.

By the time *Dolores* was published, Katharine was mortally ill.
Vera remembers how in earlier days her father, having witnessed
one of Katharine's tantrums—considering the footman imperti-
nent she had boxed his ears—had begged her to control her
temper, saying that such rages might cause a cancer. In spite of her
illness, however, she was able to appreciate having an authoress
for a daughter. Nor did she take offence at the irony so closely

touching her own life. Indeed she found the book's humorous characterisations extremely entertaining.

The critics all acknowledged a new writer of importance. In a long article in *The Times Literary Supplement** a reviewer said:

"Miss Compton-Burnett's *Dolores* is in many respects an unusually original novel. It is written with restraint, and reveals a peculiarly steady and isolated outlook on life and shrewd observation of character."

This critic already finds in the characters "fairly ordinary types of people", other than the extraordinary dramatist and Dolores herself, and "a just perceptible flavour of Jane Austen". He praises "the talk" in *Dolores*, "quick and characteristic and often deftly satirical", but finds "the narrative style in general rather crabbed and wearisome". Perhaps Ivy did too, as she never again made use of it. The notice ends:

"Miss Compton-Burnett has written with intense seriousness, her book lights up for the reader a serene and independent mind."

Serious and independent indeed, but as one's imagination roams over 20 The Drive one questions the "serene".

Reading the notices one is struck by the fact that the reviewers of that first edition of *Dolores* think more highly of the novel than do critics of today. The *Daily Mail*† reviewed two other novels by women at the same time as *Dolores*, both of them about family life: *Mothers and Fathers* by Constance Smedley, this title far more appropriate to I. Compton-Burnett than her chosen one, and *The Limit* by Ada Leverson. After observing in general that women writers lacked style, the reviewer declared that, amusing though it was, "no one could call *The Limit* literature". Colin MacInnes is one of Ada Leverson's admirers who would do just this, and so surely would Robert Ross,‡ to

---

* 2nd March, 1911.   † 3rd March, 1911.
‡ A distinguished man of letters, friend of Oscar Wilde.

whom the novel is dedicated. Ada Leverson was Ivy Compton-Burnett's senior by twenty-two years, but she had not started to publish novels until middle-age—*The Limit* was her third—and her brilliance as a writer had tended to be dimmed in the glare surrounding her friendship with Oscar Wilde, whose "dear Sphinx" she was. She was an inveterate theatre-goer and many scenes in her books are largely developed in dialogue in which fiction form she was a direct forerunner of I. Compton-Burnett. She too wrote of Edwardian society, but without the other's grimness. Her wit, however, although of a brighter colour than Ivy's, does often bring the latter to mind;

"Charles, how nice of you to call and return your own visit the same day."

  Having finished with the other two novels the reviewer continued:

"And now by way of contrast, here is a book *Dolores* which does possess just those qualities which the novels of women nearly always lack. Who Ivy Compton-Burnett is, whether Mrs. or Miss, I know not, but I do know that she has style, atmosphere, distinction. Her work is not so 'readable' as Miss Smedley's. . . . Nor is there the same play of light over hers as over Mrs. Leverson's pages. But *Dolores* is literature; of that no competent critic can have any doubt."

He notes a George Eliot influence and "a whiff—strange juxtaposition—of Henry James", and continues:

"Her art is not

> Radiant, adorned outside, a hidden ground
> Of thought and austerity within.

It is austere without as well as within. But it is a noble, stimulating austerity, and there are some perfectly delightful interludes . . . which show a sense of humour not unworthy of comparison with the finest examples.

"Everyone in the book is alive. You think of them not as 'characters', but as people. Each has his or her atmosphere. And over the whole record of Dolores's sacrifice of self there is a veil of beauty. In that we have the essential difference between books and literature. It is only Beauty that can give the unmistakable stamp. That is a rare quality always. Let us haste to signal it whenever we can."

The other reviews of *Dolores*, and there were many, contain some criticism of the book's "greyness", but most speak of it as a work of great promise and praise the dramatic dialogue, although Ivy had not yet had the chance to develop the taste for theatregoing which she later shared with Ada Leverson.

Robert Ross reviewed *Dolores* in the *Bystander*, this in itself being an honour for a new and unknown author, and called the book "a work of incontestable merit".

"Miss Compton-Burnett is the fortunate possessor of the gift of epigram, but, what is more unusual in an untried author, she has a firm control over this dangerous propensity. . . .

"A noticeable feature is the many sly hits at the ultra-fervent portion of the Wesleyan community, and not infrequently the consciousness of the special grace bestowed upon priests of the Establishment, as expressed by the Rev. Cleveland Hutton, call to memory the unctuous sense of superiority held by Jane Austen's great prig, Mr. Collins. When Miss Compton-Burnett has learnt, as she will, to form a more harmonious design, to group her characters with greater distinctness, and to gather up the loose ends within the constructed circle, we may expect something really striking from the young author, who combines strength with sincerity and humour with truth."

Ivy was pleased with these notices but very modest about the success of her "little book". From first to last this was her way of referring, half-affectionately, half-deprecatingly, to her current work. She had not yet come to have the dislike of *Dolores* which later caused her to banish it from the lists of her novels and avoid all mention of it.

On 6th March Ivy wrote to Katie:

"Jimmie is still at Cambridge—leading the emancipated life of a B.A., but reading hard in pursuit of further achievements. He spent last summer in Germany, to learn the language. . . .

"It is nice of you to be interested in my little book. I must not send you a copy, as it is against my publisher's interest for me to do anything at all that checks the sale; but there is a special edition for the Colonies, bound in paper, and costing only 1/–. If you would get a copy, and ask all your friends to do likewise, you will earn my gratitude, and be acting in a cousinly manner. I am sending you two reviews—*The Times* and *The Mail*— the only ones I have seen as yet; but I am told that the other ones are equally good. You must bear in mind for my benefit, that it is something to be noticed in *The Times* at all. So you have had no love affairs. What a hiding of your talents in the earth!"

On 23rd May Ivy wrote to her cousin again:

"So many thanks for your letter. It was a great pleasure to me. I am very glad you like my book, and think it was so nice to write to me about it . . . it is true that I made use of your Father and Mother just to give a superficial touch to the personalities. That I intended no resemblance in character I should have thought was clear. Surely there is no real likeness? Jimmie and Grandma could not even see the surface suggestion. If people will insist that a cap fits, and further insist upon wearing it, it is not to be laid to my account. . . .

"Mother is not by any means nearly well, as you have heard. She is very delicate still, and we are most anxious about her. Just now she is suffering very much night and day with acute rheumatism and can get no rest at all. We are just hoping that a change for the better will come soon.

"I have no news. Vera sends her love and thanks for your

congratulations. She is a very young L.R.A.M., and we are quite proud of her. Judy hopes to follow her example at Christmas."

Nowadays it is widely assumed that Ivy is admired by a clique of self-satisfied intellectuals, and although her fame has grown steadily this misapprehension has damaged her reputation. In fact she has ardent followers in every walk of life. It is interesting to visualise her first readers buying Dolores or borrowing it from Mudies' lending library and discovering its gems of wit and wisdom. There was no cult, but "I. Compton-Burnett was on her way."*

* I apologise for not being able to remember what writer said this about *Dolores.* E.S.

CHAPTER III

Break-up

IVY WAS CONSIDERATE and patient with her mother during these last difficult years. Later in 1911 Katharine died. She was only fifty-six, and even in death had her aureole of bright hair. Those close to her were glad that her sufferings had ended and that she was free of the dreaded ordeal of growing old. Throughout her long illness Minnie faithfully tended her. Even in the last terrible months of her life no trained nurse was engaged; to the day of Katharine's death Minnie did everything for her.

With the good press and unusually big sales for a first novel, Ivy appeared to be launched on a career as a writer, but her mother's death brought a great change into her life. She and Noël and Mr Mowll, the solicitor and family friend, were made guardians of the younger children, and, the half-brothers and sisters having all by now left home, Ivy at the age of twenty-seven became the undisputed head of the household. She enjoyed this power and became something of a tyrant, which was difficult both for Minnie and for Ivy's sisters, particularly for Topsy and "Baby", who were still in their teens and far from happy. The house was more open now to visitors, for it had been impossible to entertain during Katharine's last years, and Ivy reigned as hostess. She also sometimes paid visits to relatives and the families of Noël's friends, and was ceasing to be a recluse. She took considerable pains over her appearance, buying well-cut coats and skirts and hand-made silk shirts. She was careful to display her figure to its best advantage, and told Vera that if her face was the more handsome she, Ivy, had the better figure.

Ivy and Noël now took riding lessons and used to go for rides together on the downs, Ivy side-saddle to begin with but before long riding astride, always in a well-tailored habit.

Now too, in spite of the fear expressed in her letter to Katie from Holloway College. Ivy learnt to swim. Noël and the younger girls used sometimes to plunge in from the steps of the pier, but Ivy's regime never varied. She would wade out from a bathing machine in her blue serge costume, then swim with a slow unchanging breast stroke straight and rather far out to sea and straight back again.

It was at about this time that she had her first trip abroad—to the Tyrol with Noël. She was excited at the prospect; it was part of the youthful zest which came with the new freedom. She was never to be an ardent sight-seer, for churches and museums soon bored her, but scenery she loved, and flowers were "the passion of my life".

"Noël," to quote his sisters Vera and Juliet, "had a warm, outgoing and very human personality. He was interested in life and in people and his outlook was forward-looking, whereas Ivy always tended to look back to what became her chosen period. His taste in literature was adventurous. He had on his bookshelves the works of Nietzsche, Ibsen and Strindberg." It is unlikely that Ivy's reading ever took this direction. Noël was also intensely interested in politics—influenced no doubt by Oscar Browning's profound radicalism. Ivy, although she took little interest in politics, was always a Conservative.

Noël was now an historical Fellow of King's, having won this distinction with an unfinished thesis on Palmerston, unfinished because, as he explained in a letter to a friend, "I have left scholarship for the present and am sowing—prodigal the spirit but arduous the labour—certain literary wild oats."

During this period he was very much occupied at Cambridge, and also in becoming engaged to be married to Tertia Beresford, the sister of his great friend Jack. Vera and Juliet remember her as a very striking girl with an ivory skin, large green eyes and straight blue-black hair with a fine sheen to it. Ivy does not appear to have regretted his engagement, but without Noël's benign influence she became more domineering than ever. She had never liked music, but now with four sisters immersed in it—Vera and Topsy had even given a couple of recitals at the Brighton Pavilion—it had become anathema to her. Although the house was so large she adamantly refused to allow instruments to be practised in it, so her sisters were forced to rent a studio for this purpose.

In August, 1914, the war came, and on 22nd September Ivy wrote from 20 The Drive to Katie:

"So many thanks for your letter—it was as good as a talk. I daresay you are depressed. We most of us are that. Indeed, if long faces were of any help to anyone, it would be refreshing to reflect how much good we should some of us be doing. However efforts in that line being no good, the other is the one to be taken. I suppose though economising & meeting folks with folks at war are things not to be welcomed by the most stoic. . . . Jimmie was home with Jack Beresford for some days last week and he returns again this afternoon. He has so enjoyed his taste of soldiering, & looks so strong and well—with a *cropped* head, quite in military style! Can you think of him? It does not alter him as much as you might think. . . . You have enough to depress you and no mistake. As for earning money, nobody is doing much of that as far as I can make out, just now—or spending it either, for the matter of that. For my part, I am quite dreading to see Mowll next week, & hear what effects the war may have on us. I have cut down the girls' musical expenses as far as I can without really interfering with their progress. And they are all very good and sensible about it.

"I don't think I must think of Amica's★ college while we are living in Brighton, though in some ways I should like very much to join the essay class. I daresay I shall some time . . . Both my nice maids leave this Saturday and two more to come."

By this time Vera and Juliet were convinced that if they were to have any lives of their own they must leave home. They agreed

★ Mme d'Esterre, a friend of the family's who organised classes of an original nature for the élite in Chelsea, known as the *House of Books*.

to share a house in Carlton Hill, London, with Myra Hess, who was also leaving home, and who had been their close friend ever since they met her at the Tobias Matthay School. She was now launched on her concert career and they had become her pupils. The plan was to take their young sisters with them and of course Minnie, although she persistently declared that they would never get away from 20 The Drive. Anticipating opposition from Ivy, although she certainly was not happy herself at home, Vera and Judy drew lots as to which of them should break the news to her. The ordeal fell to Vera, and the opposition was even stronger than the sisters had anticipated. Later in life Ivy used to declare that she had always disliked Hove—it was of course full of dark memories for her from the time of her father's death onward—but nevertheless the idea of leaving her home appalled her.

"There's a back staircase and a front staircase," she protested, "so we can all live here and yet be independent."

Vera and Judy, however, were determined to move, and when Noël, now with a commission in the 7th Leicestershire Regiment and training on Salisbury Plain, expressed his dismay at his sisters' choice of time—in war—to break up the home, they wrote and explained to him how impossible it was for them to live their own lives any longer at 20 The Drive. And for them, now that they were adult, the uneasy period of Ivy's and Noël's guardian-ship was over.

So, in 1915, Ivy dismissed the servants and sold what furniture would not be needed for the two establishments. The five girls went with Minnie to a hotel in Hove, and thence all but Ivy moved to their part of Myra Hess's house on Carlton Hill. Ivy went to a small hotel in Westbourne Terrace, and soon wrote announcing that she was coming to pay her sisters a visit and did not know how long she would be staying. They replied that they thought it would be better if she left them to themselves for the present.

From his camp, Noël wrote in one of his many moving letters to Elliott Felkin, a close friend of his and Jack Beresford's:

"I wonder if you would ask your sister . . . whether she would put my sister Ivy up for her club. I should like my sister to know yours as I think they are rather kindred—at once in their contempt of the human race (though perhaps not quite primitive Christians for all that!) Ivy is often wandering about in town; the foxes have holes and the birds nests, cabmen repose inside their hackneys but my sister has not, etc."

Contempt of human folly Ivy certainly had, but just as certainly compassion for human suffering. Noël was right to be concerned about her loneliness. She never wanted to live alone, hence her misery, in spite of imperfect relations with her sisters, at the break-up of the Hove household. She did not believe that human beings were suited for solitude, and she never became reconciled to this state.

Elliott Felkin duly introduced his sister Winifred to Ivy and they became friends. Later Winifred had a shocking accident, losing the sight of one eye through a mishap with a ginger beer bottle, which led to her having a complete mental breakdown. Felkin was presently to introduce Ivy to his great friend Margaret Jourdain and thus to alter the whole course of her life. After the war he worked for the League of Nations, and Margaret and Ivy often visited him and his wife in Geneva. According to Mrs. Felkin her husband was the model for several of Ivy's "gentle young men".

By this time Ivy knew the Beresfords well and used to stay at the great rambling rectory in Easton Grey, the Wiltshire village where Jack's and Tertia's father, the Reverend John Jervis Beresford of ancient lineage, had the living. John Jervis, as the result of an accident while as boys he and his twin brother were playing with a pair of scissors, was totally blind. His brother had stayed at his side throughout their boyhood, went up to King's College with him and helped him to pass his examinations and take orders. John Jervis and his wife, Margaret Holinshed, who wrote poems and stories which appeared in a church magazine, had moved to Easton Grey in the hope that the country air would improve Mr Beresford's asthma. Unfortunately this grew steadily worse, while Margaret, having borne him six children, most of them brilliant, had a mental breakdown and spent the remaining years in a Home, beloved of all for her gentleness.

Shortly before the first war Mr Beresford had a particularly acute attack of asthma and went for treatment to a nursing home in London. Eva Fox, the sister of one of the nurses looking after him, who had herself intended to become a nurse, came often to read to the blind parson, and when he returned to Easton Grey she went with him and carried on the work that his wife had once done for him—transcribing his sermons and the many poems that he wrote, reading aloud to him, as did all the family, and becoming the treasured companion of his daughters—Dorothy, Tertia and Mary. From time to time she left in order to be with her own father at her home in Northampton, but the latter understood that if Mr Beresford sent for her she would return, and indeed she was never away for more than a few weeks before a telegram summoned her. She faithfully returned to Easton Grey, as a friend, not an employee, for to quote Dorothy, the eldest daughter, the Beresfords were "as poor as church-mice and as proud as Lucifer". They used sometimes to go to Tenby, but holidays were scarce and outside life was mainly introduced by Noël's and Jack's Cambridge friends and by weekend visits of Henry Asquith, then Prime Minister, and "Margot" to the neighbouring Great House, where Margot's sister lived. On these occasions the Asquiths spent much time with the Beresfords.

Staying at Easton Grey was an exhilarating change for Ivy. Even before the break-up of the family, she had had little congenial company since the visits of Noël's friends to The Drive. She at once became a friend of every member of the Beresford family and also of their loved companion Eva Fox, who remembers her as very pretty and extremely good company. Although Mr Beresford was a clergyman and his sermons, according to Mr Asquith, were the finest in the country, Easton Grey was by no means a "churchy" household, and Ivy's irreligion did not appear to trouble any member of the family. The children were a fascinating lot, good-looking, high-spirited, egocentric, articulate and extremely well-informed, although the boys alone had received any formal schooling, Jack going from grammar school to King's, where he, like Noël, had taken a double first in History. He too wrote poetry and his elder brother, Richard, who went to South Africa as Curzon's secretary, both wrote and reviewed books. After Richard and a daughter who died in childhood came Dorothy, the acknowledged head of the family, beautiful, vivacious, and domineering, who was to become one of Ivy's closest friends, then Jack and after him Tertia, whom Noël Compton-Burnett was shortly to marry. Finally there was Mary, the baby, equally pretty and the pet of the family.

Ivy and Dorothy were perfect foils for one another and held endless conversations, battles of swift, witty repartee, Dorothy threshing the air as she talked and Ivy motionless except for the alert attention of her fine grey eyes fixed on the great black orbs of Dorothy Beresford.

Ivy talked, listened and—as always—watched. Her sisters remember this intense watchfulness as one of her chief character-istics. And there was so much of interest for her to observe in this unusual family, and so much to listen to of crisp assertive speech. Without any doubt the Beresfords, and Dorothy in particular, were an influence in the novels that would shortly pour from Ivy's pencil. Eva Fox remembers her in those days at Easton Grey sometimes seeming preoccupied, as if on the brink of accomplishing something she was eager to do.

Years later, after the second war, Jack and Janet Beresford's son Benedict married an Australian girl, who had discovered I. Compton-Burnett's novels in her home town and greatly admired them. When, soon after her arrival in England, she was introduced to Benedict Beresford's Aunt Dorothy, with-out knowing about the connection with I. Compton-Burnett, she at once thought that Dorothy had stepped out of one of the latter's books, and as she listened to the biting dialogue around her felt that they were all living an I. Compton-Burnett chapter.

After Jack Beresford married Janet Spicer, in February 1915, Ivy used to visit them at their lovely holiday home in Hertfordshire. She and Janet became devoted friends, although Mrs Beresford was never one of her literary fans. She remembers how, in later days, Ivy used to enjoy walking in the countryside and how she would talk aloud to herself, probably, her hostess thought, trying out the dialogue for her current book. Noël asked Jack to get him a ring for Tertia, "of silver not polished with a small diamond in it". and not long afterwards he and Tertia were married. After all too brief a time, in June 1915, Noël was drafted to France. Tertia, perhaps partly as a result of Noël's anxiety about Ivy, went to live with her in the hotel in Westbourne Terrace. At Christmas time they moved to a flat in Queen's Road, Bayswater, in order to have Jack and Janet Beresford as their neighbours.

In the summer of 1916 Tertia, not yet having had a notification of Noël's death, received a letter of condolence from his commanding officer. Ivy had gone to Easton Grey for a few days to help Dorothy with the packing up of the rectory after John Jervis's death. Because of the close family friendship with the Asquiths, Tertia persuaded Janet Beresford to go to 10, Downing Street and ask the Prime Minister if he could institute enquiries about Noël. When she returned to the flat she found Tertia unconscious, having taken an overdose of sleeping tablets.

It was to this tragic state of affairs that Ivy returned from Easton Grey. She arranged for Tertia to go to a nursing home in Bexhill and went with her. By August, however, they were both back at Easton Grey where Ivy, in spite of her own heartbreak, and Eva Fox together helped Tertia to regain her strength. As soon as she was well enough they used all three to go for long walks in the country.

In an obituary article in the *Cambridge Review*★ J.H.C. wrote:

"Noël Compton-Burnett was a man whose friends easily got into the habit of thinking, quite without rational warrant, that he must come back from the war because his vitality was so unquenchable. In turning over his letters from the front the irrational conviction is strengthened."

★ November 1916.

The notice spoke of Noël Compton-Burnett seeming, even as a freshman, "curiously mature", "partly, no doubt, because he was the only surviving son in a large family which had lost its father". It referred to his love of Germany and observed that:

"Within King's, his foremost loyalty was, I think, to the Political Society, which he more than any man helped in its transition from the care of Oscar Browning, its creator forty years ago, into the hands of its second President. During the first term of war, when he had not yet received a commission, and the society was maintaining a threatened existence, this record appears in its minutes:

"'565th Meeting, Nov. 1914. Mr. Compton-Burnett read a paper on "Peace". There was no division.'

"It was, as I remember it, a moving defence of the love of peace, because peace is life. He had already decided to take his risks in war."

From the Rectory Ivy wrote to Katie:

"Just a word to say that I *am* feeling braver, and that your letter *has* helped me to feel so.

"It is a sorrow with a great pride in it—a terrible bitterness too, and a disappointment one cannot face as yet—but a great pride—for as the Provost of King's College writes to me—the most complete and gallant sacrifice that any man has made.

"Exact news has come to us too, and that is comforting.

"He was killed instantaneously, hit on the head by a revolver bullet, and had no pain. He had led his men right up to the German line, and secured it, and he fell in the greatest excitement of the battle, and is buried on the battlefield. Well, one thinks how as a little boy, he always said he would be a soldier.

"It has haunted me to think that perhaps he suffered, and longed for people who loved him; now I am happier. Tertia is well again, but often very low spirited. What can one expect?

No, there is no prospect of a child, dearest. I did not mean to give you that idea. There is no ordinary comfort, you see."

1916 continued to be a year of tragedy. Topsy and Baby—the latter now nineteen and Topsy in her early twenties—had remained moody and depressed in their new home and showed little interest in anything. One day in the autumn of this year they announced that they were going to the country for a change. For several days nobody had occasion to go into their bedroom, then Iris, the half-sister who was a nurse, came on a visit to Carlton Hill. When she heard that the girls had not returned she went up to their room, found the door locked and discovered that the key was inside. The door was broken down and Topsy and Baby were found in bed, dead. The doctor stated that they had been dead for several days and had presumably died of an overdose of veronal, of which they had a supply. Sir Bernard Spilsbury was called in and the question arose of whether the overdose had been an accident or if the unhappy young women had taken their own lives. The doctors considered that they had been taking the drug for a long time. In those days veronal could be obtained from any chemist without a prescription.

At the inquest a verdict was returned of death under circumstances that could not be explained. Nevertheless many people assumed that it was a case of suicide.

This assumption shocked the family profoundly. Olive, to Ivy's fury, even considered dropping the name "Compton" in order to disassociate herself from this family disgrace, but was dissuaded from this move. Although Ivy talked little about this tragedy within her family, it affected her deeply.

As soon as Tertia was well enough she decided to live in a cottage in the country. Before long she found what she wanted and Eva Fox moved in with her. Dorothy and Ivy then decided to set up house together and found a flat, still in Bayswater, at 59 Leinster Square. Here they continued their verbal sallies, which were by no means without acerbity. How could they be, with a woman of Dorothy's fiery temperament? Ivy was always proud of her academic and classical education, but Dorothy could not bear to lose a game and was determined that Ivy should not "come the bluestocking over her". Ivy, it is said, was not permitted to "show off"—a thing it is difficult to imagine her ever wanting to do—to pose, for instance, as an authority on Jane Austen. "You may impress others," Dorothy would say, "but you don't impress me".

Ivy does not appear to have resented Dorothy's tyranny. One must remember that she did not dislike the tyrants whom she herself created, and always asserted that they were not as bad as her readers thought. In spite of Dorothy's autocracy she loved and admired Ivy, and speaks of her to this day as remarkably "clear-headed". She also says that "seldom have two women been more devoted to one another".

They entertained a little in the small Leinster Square flat—relatives, and friends mostly acquired from their two brothers. One of their constant visitors was a gentle, scholarly and good-looking Civil Servant. Mrs Janet Beresford comments that for some time she did not know which of the two young women Mr Kidd was courting, but in fact, although he liked Ivy, his heart was always Dorothy's. He was a friend of Jack Beresford's, whom he had met a few years before at the Board of Education, and he saw Dorothy for the first time at Jack's and Janet's wedding. "If only I could marry a woman like that," he observed. But Dorothy was then engaged to another man, and with great consideration Alan Kidd waited until she was free and established with Ivy in Leinster Square before he proposed to her. Her engagement did not distress Ivy in the least. Although Ivy considered that Dorothy belonged to her—so Dorothy herself said—she did not resent the prospective marriage, any more than she had resented Noël's alliance with Tertia. "She was delighted that I should be engaged to anybody," Mrs Kidd says, "because it kept me employed while she was occupied with her writing". From this it seems clear that even in those days, seven years before the publication of *Pastors and Masters*, Ivy was practising her art. At the time of their marriage Alan Kidd gave Ivy a handsome set of books to atone for depriving her of Dorothy, and the friendship between the three of them was unbroken.

In the autumn of 1918 came the deadly epidemic of Spanish influenza, Dorothy was away and Ivy was alone in the flat when she contracted the disease. The daily maid discovered her sitting at a table with her head on her arms, scarcely conscious. As soon as they heard of her plight Vera and Minnie hastened over and nursed her, day and night, through a long and serious illness, the after-effects of which, Ivy said herself, lasted for years. It was during the period of convalescence that she first took to doing embroidery—with wool on canvas—for the seats of chairs.

In 1919 Dorothy married Alan Kidd and left Leinster Square, but it was not long before Ivy was joined by another woman who was to become even closer than Dorothy. Margaret Jourdain, who had become a friend through Elliott Felkin, joined Ivy in this same year in Leinster Square. Thus began an alliance which was to last for the rest of Margaret Jourdain's life.

On 3rd November Ivy wrote from 59 Leinster Square to Katie:

"Here I am and very well, in answer to your question how & where I am. I wish you were as fixed & at leisure. Margaret Jourdain is with me again—at least she is away at the moment . . . Vera and Judy are very well and are taking up handicrafts (weaving & spinning & dyeing & the like) with great enthusiasm. I like it better for them than theosophy. They came to tea with Minnie the other day. Dorothy is very well, but disposed to be over-whelmed by her big house. Tertia [who had moved back to London] is well & has her little sister (21 or so) with her for the time. I see her nearly every day—Tertia I mean, Jack and Janet are just settled back in London for the winter, with their brood—no longer increasing I am glad to say. Have you seen the Life of Samuel Butler by H. F. Jones? Pleasant to get from the library, too dear to buy. My maid is a very pleasant creature & I trust will remain contented. I am on the alert for any sign of dissatisfaction, so that at any cost to myself it may be soothed. She calls me M [Ma'am], not Miss. I suppose she thinks I have reached that time of life when it is suitable. I have no real news.

"Much love to all of you. Don't overwork dearest. Neglect your duty sooner. It's best in the end."

Jessie, the maid referred to in this letter in fact stayed with Miss Compton-Burnett and Miss Jourdain for nearly twenty years.

CHAPTER IV

The New Life

MARGARET JOURDAIN CAME from a gifted family. Her mother, who used to dress like Queen Victoria, her small mantle hung with bugles, was the widow of a clergyman of Huguenot descent. She had many children, most of whom were to distinguish themselves in literary and artistic fields. The eldest daughter, Eleanor, became famous as co-author with Miss Moberly of *An Adventure*, the book describing the vision they believed they had had at Versailles. It was first published anonymously in 1911, the year always remembered for the *Titanic* disaster, and ten years after the adventure occurred, but in later editions the pseudonyms Elizabeth Morison and Frances Lamont were used, and finally the authors' real names were revealed—C. A. E. Moberly and E. F. Jourdain. The two women were at this time respectively Principal and Vice-Principal of St Hugh's College, Oxford, Eleanor Jourdain being Miss Moberly's senior by twenty years. They did much research to throw light on their experience, while declaring their horror of all forms of occultism and refusing to let the adventure dominate their thoughts or time.

Many other members of Eleanor's family had psychic gifts, and the Versailles adventure was not her only experience in this field. Margaret Jourdain knew that her sister had what she called "second sight". She had visited a house in Paris—probably Molière's—and seen stage scenery which was not there. Later she exactly foretold the date on which one of her brothers was to be killed in the first world war.

J. W. Dunne, author of that famous book *An Experiment with*

Time,* contributed a note to the fourth edition of *An Adventure*, considering the possibility of the writers' "mental time-travelling" aided perhaps by telepathic communication with the mind of the young "cottage girl" whom they had encountered in the Trianon. The mystery has now, it is generally believed, been explained rationally by the discovery that what the authors thought to be a vision of Marie Antoinette's Versailles was simply an encounter with Robert de Montesquiou and a group of other people wearing eighteenth-century costume for a masque or some such activity, on the day of the two ladies' visit to Versailles. There is, however, not the least doubt that both authors of the book were sincere, and they always declared that it was not their business to explain or even to understand their experience, but simply to record it.

Margaret's brother Philip and her younger sister Millie were cripples, their limbs twisted by a terrible affliction which from time to time occurred in the family. In later years Margaret told her friend Hester Pinney† that she had never in her life experienced the slightest sexual feeling, and said that she wondered if this was due to subconscious fear of the disease which haunted her family. In spite of this asexuality, however, she had a fondness for young men, particularly for young men of unusual quality, and they reciprocated her liking. Philip and Millie were both brilliant; Philip distinguished himself in mathematics at Cambridge and Millie was a gifted artist—he wrote charming fairy stories which she illustrated, and in spite of his disabilities he eventually married. Millie also, under the name of Joan Arden, wrote a rather odd little book of early memories called *A Childhood*. A clergyman brother was a gifted ornithologist, while another, who became Colonel Henry Jourdain, was a writer in a different vein. His three-volume history of his regiment, the Connaught Rangers, and others of his books are well known to military historians.

Margaret herself went to Lady Margaret Hall, Oxford, and in 1909 she published *An Outdoor Breviary*,‡ a poetic essay extolling

---

* Faber, 1927.   † Later Mrs Basil Marsden-Smedley.
‡ The Academy Press.

nature and influenced by Thomas Traherne. This was followed
two years later by *Poems by M. Jourdain*,* an erudite volume
dedicated to her great friend Janette Ranken. It contains not only
her own poems but many quotations and translations from Greek,
Latin and French.

For some years before and during the first world war the
Jourdain family lived in the Manor House at Broadwindsor, in
Dorset. In 1908 Colonel (later General Sir Reginald) and Mrs
Pinney came to live temporarily at Broadwindsor to be near
their family home, Racedown, where they were later to settle.
It had been built by his forebears in 1753 and was lent by later
Pinneys to William Wordsworth. Margaret Jourdain, who was
then spending much of her time at home with her younger
brothers and sisters, and who became an intimate friend of Mrs
Pinney and her first intellectual companion, took a lively interest
in helping with the furnishing and decorating of Racedown. She
was active, too, in instituting research into the days—from
September, 1795, to June, 1797—when Wordsworth lived there,
a piece of history which was greatly to interest Ivy Compton-
Burnett in later years.

It was here, when William was twenty-six, that he and Dorothy
first realised their dream of sharing a home, and both of them
loved the place.

"Racedown is a square-built house lying beside the road from
Crewkerne to Lyme, just where it begins to descend into a
hollow before rising again to the hamlet of Birdsmoorgate.
It stands high, with a long view westward; to the south beyond
the hollow is a ridge of hill. . . This hill, which is over nine
hundred feet high, covered as it still is with furze and heath,
must be very much as it was when William and Dorothy
Wordsworth roamed over it."†

Mrs Pinney, who came of Quaker stock and was the sister
of Henry Head, the distinguished neurologist, was a remarkable

* Truslove and Hanson.
† *William Wordsworth: A Biography*, by Mary Moorman, Oxford University
Press, 1957.

woman; she was a fine amateur artist—brilliant at lightning sketches—and she also had strong literary interests. When she and Margaret Jourdain became friends, Margaret was making frequent excursions to London in pursuit of the treasures of knowledge she was to acquire of furniture, tapestry and interior decoration, and Mrs Pinney much enjoyed sharing these interests. While in Dorset the two enlivened the neighbourhood by organising Shakespeare readings in many villages. Later, when Colonel Pinney was posted to Cairo, Margaret promised to keep an eye on the young Pinneys when their mother joined her husband in the winter. The children were headed by Hester, named after her mother and at that time eight years old, and her small brother Bernard.

Margaret Jourdain was not the kind of young woman usually given to child care; indeed, she was unusual in every way for a young spinster in a small country village early in this century. The Vicar's daughter, a gay, pretty girl, was also asked by Mrs Pinney to keep an eye on the children, and there was some conflict between her and Margaret Jourdain, who was not at all pretty but could be gay, as to how the young should behave. There was conflict too with Miss Partridge, the governess, who was intensely religious, while Miss Jourdain scorned orthodox beliefs. To the young Hester's shocked amazement Margaret even told her that she and her brother Philip were atheists, and, while encouraging the Pinney children to read the tombstones, at the same time permitted them to jump on the graves. Her professed atheism, however, did not prevent her from going to church at Broadwindsor to sit with the rest of her family in the Manor pew, somewhat to the annoyance of Colonel Pinney when he was on leave, as he was the actual Lord of the Manor, and it was by pure chance that the Jourdains had rented the Manor House and were therefore accorded this privilege. This story, and other accounts of village feuds in the early years of the century, were later to delight Ivy Compton-Burnett.

Margaret Jourdain went to church as a concession to convention, and although in her characteristic way she poked fun at social observances, she none the less impressed on the children that manners and etiquette had made many people the useful members of society that they were and the fabric of this country what it is. Hester has never forgotten her words and still in this swiftly changing world breathes an echo of Margaret Jourdain's teaching to the younger generations. "Ask Margaret Jourdain" was the Marsden-Smedley motto when any advice was needed.

Irreligious as she was, Margaret Jourdain nevertheless had a leaning towards the supernatural, an attraction towards the "unknown". She found the idea of "Marjery Jourdain, the cunning witch", in *Henry VI* intriguing, and used often in childhood's theatricals to dress up and play the witch. To the fascination of the young Hester she used to practise automatic writing and table turning, her brother Philip often joining in these psychic activities. Hester witnessed a table moving, but to her disappointment, as she too was fascinated by the unknown, she did not hear any startling revelations. Miss Jourdain told her that she was one of the few people who attended seances without having any wish to get in touch with a relative or friend who had "passed over"—Hester can remember to this day the irony with which Margaret pronounced these words. What interested her was the possibility of some other existence in a different measure of time, and Hester remembers her saying: "Time may go on even when the clock has ticked away the hours in which we are living."

During the first world war Margaret Jourdain was living in Chelsea and making her way with poetry, translations and articles in many periodicals, besides working for Lenygon, a firm specialising in furniture and decoration. By the end of the war she was also connected with the Victoria and Albert Museum. Her constant companion at this time was Janette Ranken, with whom she had been at Lady Margaret Hall. After being briefly on the stage herself, in 1917 Janette married the actor Ernest Thesiger, and both of them were soon to become members of Ivy's and Margaret's circle.

It was in 1918 that Hester Pinney remembers first seeing Ivy as a friend of Margaret Jourdain's. As a girl she was fascinated to watch the growth of this relationship between two women who were to become "best friends" for the rest of their life together, and thought how wonderful it must be to have a best friend. Ivy was the more emotional of the two, and in the beginning Margaret was the more dominant, although in a less dramatic way than Dorothy Beresford. Visitors to Leinster Square, and later to their flat in Linden Gardens—the first of their homes to have large rooms and to be beautifully furnished through Margaret's knowledge and taste—remember that in those early days, although Ivy Compton-Burnett was their hostess, she stayed in the background, sitting very still with her small delicate hands folded or working at some piece of embroidery, while she listened attentively to the scintillating conversation of Margaret and her friends, observing everything and occasionally contributing a terse, sometimes witty and sometimes oddly flat remark. She does not appear at this time to have had the exuberant conversations in Margaret Jourdain's presence that she had with Dorothy Beresford.

In 1920 Tertia married Horace Mann, a Civil Servant who, like Noël, had been a friend of Jack Beresford's at King's, and they too were regular visitors.

Hester often stayed with Margaret and Ivy, and they also went to see her in the series of odd lodgings which she inhabited in the early twenties. Margaret's friendship continued, too, with Hester's uncle, Alban Head, begun years before in the Racedown days, when they used to play together the then fashionable game of diabolo. He sometimes took Hester sight-seeing in France—he gave as a reason for his conversion from Anglican to Roman Catholic the better understanding that the latter faith gave him of mediaeval art. Margaret thought that this was the best reason she had ever heard for a change of faith, and this may be why she always retained a certain interest in Roman Catholicism herself, although she continued to consider his attitude to the arts that of a dilettante compared with her own professional approach. Alban Head was not considered by other members of Hester's family to be a suitable chaperone for a young girl—she was now entering her twenties, and her uncle had, she says, "a rather riotous reputation"—but Margaret brought her influence to bear and the happy

Ivy, aged about eighteen, with her family. *Back row left:* her sister Stephanie (Baby); *middle row, left:* sister Topsy; *middle row, centre:* Ivy; *foreground right:* Noël Compton-Burnett. All others are cousins

Minnie Smith

Royal Holloway
College, autumn
1902 (Ivy is among
the group top left)

trips continued. On their return Alban Head would give a party at his hotel, the Burlington in Cork Street, to which Margaret and Ivy always went. They also used to visit Racedown and Ivy soon became on warm terms with the Pinneys, while in London there were the "near-Salon" tea-parties in the elegant drawing-room of the Henry Heads' house in Montague Square. These were attended by many writers and connoisseurs of art. It was here that they met May Sinclair, then in her heyday, who became one of their regular visitors.

Ivy saw little of her sisters now. They had become followers of Rudolf Steiner, and she could share their interest in anthroposophy as little as their love of music. It was, however, Margaret Jourdain who suggested to Vera and Judy that they should buy the charming cottage in Hertfordshire where they have lived ever since. The Beresfords were frequent visitors, and so naturally were Janette and Ernest Thesiger, both to become life-long friends of Ivy's, while Margaret remained always the closest of Janette's circle. Ernest was expert at embroidery, and this was a pleasant bond between him and Ivy. Sometimes he would bring his work with him to the flat and they would enjoy this pursuit together, and he would help her too in choosing a pretty design for a chair cover. Janette was also one of their constant companions for visits to the theatre. Lady Waechter (Mollie) was another friend who took a great interest in embroidery. She was a large, rather untidy Irish woman, a contrast with the neatness of her hostesses and the dandyism of Ernest Thesiger.

Another friend of Margaret's who was always to remain of importance to Ivy was Helen Rolleston, an anthropologist of New Zealand origin, niece of the distinguished surgeon, Humphrey Rolleston. She was herself in every way a woman of stature and was later an active member of the Women's Corona Society. She was an ardent Christian Scientist, and stands out among Ivy's friends as one of the few to whom the latter listened when they talked about international affairs. And there was Willy King, a great authority on English porcelain, particularly Chelsea, and presently also his wife, Viva.

"Anyone who wants to be a writer writes," Ivy used to say

when asked for her advice by aspiring authors, and as she made it quite clear that she herself never lost this desire we may assume that in these years since the publication of *Dolores* she had been writing. We have Eva Fox's impression of Ivy at Easton Grey involved in some private activity, and Dorothy Kidd's assertion that at the time of her engagement Ivy was writing. Now she was helping Margaret Jourdain with her numerous articles for *Country Life* and other periodicals, which the latter signed simply with the initial "J". It was at this time, in the early twenties, that Margaret began to publish her series of distinguished books on English furniture and decoration, the first under the pseudonym Francis Lenygon, the name of the well-known firm for which she was working.

Margaret Jourdain had the gift of taking an interest in whatever interested her companions—an ability which Ivy Compton-Burnett did not share. If a conversation took a turn alien to her, Ivy would bring it to heel. For example, one day at a friend's tea-party a number of people began discussing a Russian icon hanging on the wall. Ivy listened for a few moments abstractedly, then observed decisively, "I do like a laburnum." So close, however, was her friendship with Margaret Jourdain that in a slightly indirect way Ivy did come to share her interests. She had an inborn feeling for quality and was delighted with the beautiful home that Margaret created for them both, and even contributed a little by painting some of the woodwork herself. She visited museums, galleries and innumerable houses, known and unknown of architectural or domestic importance in passive support of Margaret Jourdain's indefatigable research. Ivy appreciated craftsmanship, and Margaret's work embraced every corner of this field, including cabinet-making, plaster-work, English secular embroidery and old lace. (Paintings interested her only in their decorative function.) Her scholarship was noted for its wide knowledge, strict accuracy, authority and wealth of detail. She did a great deal to bring to light and to distinguish many of the craftsmen of the eighteenth century, whose work, of the highest quality, had been for years loosely labelled "Chippendale", "Hepplewhite" or "Sheraton". She found Ivy's embroidery so

exquisite and skilful that she even allowed her to repair some
early fragile embroideries on the beautiful old chairs.

Margaret made her notes on the backs of old envelopes,
invitation cards, torn bits of paper, anything that was at hand, and,
usually sitting on the edge of her bed, produced scripts written
not very legibly on thin foolscap paper, which she sent out to be
typed. She was a somewhat divided character; on one side she
resembled an eighteenth-century connoisseur and sceptic, and
she liked to put on an eighteenth-century act—her quizzing glass
hanging round her neck on a fine gold chain was useful here.
On the other hand she was a poet, the author not only of several
volumes of verse but also of *belles lettres*, besides her fine classical
and other translations. She was as little interested as Ivy in music,
but they both enjoyed the theatre and went to it frequently,
sometimes several times a week. Ivy greatly appreciated the
economy of dramatic dialogue. The starkness of Greek writing
had always appealed to her and now she enjoyed modern drama,
particularly Tchekov, and liked to read plays and to study
dramatic technique. She decided to make fuller use of this in her
future work than she had done in *Dolores*, in which her gift for
dialogue had already been acclaimed by the critics. Margaret and
Ivy read a great deal of fiction, both old and new. Indeed, after
the Holloway College days, Ivy read little other than novels and
plays. She and Margaret had the lending library habit and the
Hon. Andrew Shirley, head first of Harrods and then of the Times
Library, became a valued friend.

They made many trips abroad together, to France for the
cathedrals, to Vienna for the buildings and museums, where on
occasion they met Lady Pinney and her small son John. Sometimes
in London Margaret and Ivy used to take John to the circus and
enjoy it as much as he did. Their visits to Switzerland and the
Tyrol were to enjoy the scenery and have the pleasure of picking
wild flowers. Ivy may have lagged behind Margaret in appreciation of monuments, but they completely shared their love of
flowers.

By the mid-twenties Margaret Jourdain was earning good
money. The successive flats that she shared with Ivy were taken

in the latter's name, but Margaret paid rent and a share of expenses, and meticulous accounts were kept. The ladies, particularly Miss Jourdain, did themselves well in the matter of clothes, and a "Paris model" occurs from time to time in a receipt; furs go to Bradleys to be remodelled or an old fur coat is given in part exchange for a new one. Goods, as Cameo Corner, Mosheh Ohved's famous jewellery shop, then in New Oxford Street, was called, repaired and reset Ivy's jewels. Dr Compton Burnett had bought a good deal of jewellery for Katharine, who had a fondness for it, and on her death it had been divided between her daughters, who kept what they wanted and sold the rest. All her life Ivy had a taste for elegant, delicate pieces, particularly those set with diamonds, and she wore her jewellery, usually small earrings inset with diamonds, a brooch and a ring, with equal elegance. Many of her mother's jewels were exchanged at Goods, on Margaret Jourdain's advice, for pieces of Georgian jewellery.

By this time Ivy, settled and happy at last, felt that the strength of which she had been robbed by Noël's death and her long illness had "come back by itself" and brought with it new creative energy. From childhood she had assumed that she and her brothers would be writers, a belief encouraged by her parents. So now, always regretting that neither brother was there to share its fruition, she set to work on *Pastors and Masters*, the first of the astonishing sequence of novels which would only cease with her death.

CHAPTER V

Oh the Family!

"THERE'S NOT MUCH to say," Ivy would observe when asked about her life. "I haven't been at all deedy," she explained to her friend Kay Dick.* Her books on the other hand are full of deeds, although these are not always openly performed.

I. Compton-Burnett never kept a notebook and never "jotted things down". She felt that when you had "got a thing" this would be too valuable for you to forget it, and she could scarcely believe that some writers actually record dialogue in order to use it in their books.

"People always seem to me to talk so flatly," she said.

Ivy thought about each of her novels for a considerable time before writing anything down, finding that if she had the book clearly mapped out in her mind she could write with more assurance than if she started off hoping that it would develop of its own accord. The plots, on the other hand, did seem to her to take shape in some way on their own, for she had no knowledge whence they came and so supposed that she must plan them sub-consciously. It is a little surprising to find her saying: "I think people work at very different levels of consciousness: I think I must work rather low down," because she gave one the im-pression of hyper-conscious rather than sub-conscious mental processes.

When at last she was ready to begin a book because one "seemed to be trying to come out", she made such full notes that these amounted to a first draft. They were written, as the final

* Interview, *The Times*, 30th August, 1969.

text would be, in what were in those days penny exercise books—
in pencil, so that anything could be rubbed out. A great deal of
rubbing and crossing out went on, for Ivy, again in her own
words, had "nothing against making corrections", although she
did sometimes express pity for her typist. Corrections were for
her, on her own telling, subtraction rather than addition. That
first draft, however, was never typed but completely scrapped,
after which she started on the real manuscript. She went straight
ahead once the book had been mapped out, although on occasion
when she had got some way she found it necessary to modify
the opening. She wrote quickly, often several hundred words in
a day, without ever setting herself a time-table, and she and
Margaret used to laugh at one another's methods—the latter
still sitting on the edge of her bed, scribbling notes with a pen
on the backs of envelopes, and Ivy in an armchair in the drawing-
room with an exercise book on her knee, busy with her pencil
and indiarubber.

The short book which was now filling a few of these small
exercise books does not have, like most of the later novels, a
title connected with the family relations; it is called *Pastors and
Masters*, and its setting is not the usual Victorian or Edwardian
household, but a private school for boys. Schools, of which she
knew little personally, always interested Ivy, and she followed
with close attention the education of Hester's brothers and the
children of other friends. She also enjoyed hearing from Joyce
Felkin, Elliott's wife, of her brother's experiences as a schoolmaster, and she had memories of her own brother, Guy, wanting
to be "a great headmaster".

The Herricks' establishment, however, in *Pastors and Masters*
was a pure figment of Ivy's imagination, with which she had a
great deal of fun.

All her other novels are set between 1885 and 1910, for as she
put it:

"I do not feel that I have any real or organic knowledge of life
later than about 1910. I should not write of later times with
enough grasp or confidence. I think this is why many writers

tend to write of the past. When an age is ended, you see it as it is."*

Pastors and Masters, however, takes place at a slightly later date as there is a reference to women having gained the vote.

The plot, which concerns a purloined manuscript, unfolds within the daily round of school life with telling portraits of masters, a pastor, and the proprietor's middle-aged half sister, Emily Herrick, the predominant figure in the book. She "sees through" Herrick, yet admits that he is necessary to her, a characteristic illustration of I. Compton-Burnett's own view of life. This necessity of the exploited for the exploiter, and vice versa, constantly recurs. Emily is described by another character as "a woman with a good deal of the man in her", and when she is asked by a friend if a certain elderly don does not wish to marry her replies: "As much as he can want to marry anyone. Anyone who is a woman. And that is not very much." On which her friend exclaims: "Oh dear! These dons and people!" and Emily observes: "Yes, it is something of that way, I knew you knew all the time." The author thus reveals in a subtle manner the nature of these characters. She also allows Emily to say in an Ivyish tone: ". . . I find I only like wickedness and penetration."

One thing in this new work that must have struck readers of *Dolores* (which had been as quickly forgotten as it had been acclaimed) was the author's complete change of attitude to duty. Instead of her former morbid concentration on this theme, Ivy gives Emily Herrick the first of her witty exponents of irony, as her opening speech:

"The sight of duty does make one shiver. The actual doing of it would kill one, I think."

Pastors and Masters was published in the spring of 1925. Decades later Ivy told Lettice Cooper that she was glad she had not produced a novel for so long. "People cannot write for the whole of

* *The Novels of I. Compton-Burnett* by Robert Liddell. Victor Gollancz, 1955.

their lives," she said, "so it was a good thing I had that gap."

There could be no better description of the setting for the book's debut than that by Pamela Hansford Johnson in her pamphlet on I. Compton-Burnett.* On the fly leaf there is this quotation from *Tristram Shandy*:

"Writing, when properly managed (as you may be sure I think mine is) is but a different name for conversation."

And speaking of *Pastors and Masters* Miss Hansford Johnson says:

"This was the age of Mrs. Meyrick the night-club queen, Tallulah Bankhead, *Vile Bodies*; of *The Waste Land*, Aldous Huxley, Lawrence and Joyce; of Russian boots, bottle parties, pogo-sticks, and the epicene silhouette. It was the hopeful year of the first Labour Ministry, the return to the Gold Standard, the Locarno Conference. It saw the publication of *Mrs. Dalloway*, Wells's *Christina Alberta's Father* and Huxley's *These Barren Leaves*. Into this year, into this world, and unrelated in any way to its realities, fantasies, hopes, and fears, came this small, quiet, blistering book. . . ."

Pastors and Masters did not receive such striking notices as those of *Dolores* acclaiming I. Compton-Burnett as a new writer, but prominent among them were the perceptive review in *Vogue*† by Raymond Mortimer, a gifted young journalist lately down from Cambridge, and also one in the *New Statesman* proclaiming the author a genius.‡ To quote Raymond Mortimer:

"*Pastors and Masters* is a very short novel whose praises, were it but a little different, I should like to trumpet in every direction. As it stands I suppose I can only recommend it to those whom imperfections do not daunt, and who are prepared to strain for nuggets. . . . To read it is like listening to a poor record of a very fine voice. But to anyone who reads contemporary fiction

* The British Council and the National Book League, 1951.
† April, 1925.   ‡ June, 1925.

Ivy in 1912

Noël
Compton-
Burnett
in 1914

College
days

it is a blessed relief to find for once expression unequal to conception. Usually novelists have nothing to say, and say it so
successfully. I do not know how better to describe the quality
of Miss Compton-Burnett's talent than by saying that Jane
Austen might have written this book, if she had lived to be
seventy and lost all her accomplishment. The wit of it often,
the acidity and quiet cynicism always, are a delight. With a
little revision it would have been an astonishing book: as it
stands, it is rare and remarkable."

The *New Statesman* review runs:

"As for *Pastors and Masters*, it is astonishing, alarming. It is like
nothing else in the world. It is a work of genius. How to describe
it—since there is nothing of which to take hold? There is
practically no story. A horrible schoolmaster; the proprietor
of the school, a don (incidentally, but quite incidentally, a liar
and a cheat); the don's colleagues; the schoolmaster's sub-
ordinates; some clergymen and their families—these are the
characters; and the plot, so far as there is a plot at all, turns
mainly on the attempt of the old dons to deceive one another
about the authorship of a book. There is also a prize-giving.
But what happens does not matter. The canvas is crowded; the
conversation is close-packed; the unconscious self-revelation
of the characters extraordinary. No quotation could do this
book justice; the flavour is in the whole; and it is worth
discovering there."

It came as a shock to Ivy's and Margaret's circle of friends to
find that the former had written a novel. "You must mean
Margaret Jourdain," people would say when the book was
mentioned, for she alone of the two was known to be a writer.
Hester Pinney, although she was so often at Linden Gardens,
was also taken completely by surprise. One day, when she was
about to go to Racedown, Ivy handed her two books, saying
simply, "One of these is by me." When she got home Hester,
who had not had time to look at them, handed her mother the

wrong book—a volume borrowed from Harrods—whereupon Lady Pinney told her how foolish she was to imagine that Ivy could write a book.

Before long Ivy had begun to plan a longer, more ambitious work with an elaborate plot, the first true example of her series of astonishing family novels. Robert Liddell aptly starts one chapter of his book about Ivy's work, called *The Tyrant*, with a quotation from Amiel's *Journal*:

"Oh, the Family! If the superstition with which loyalty and religion have surrounded that institution would allow the truth to be told, to what account would it not be called!"

After which the Journal continues with a terrifying list of atrocities perpetrated by the family, many of which dire deeds might have been committed by Compton-Burnett characters, but always politely, quietly, clandestinely. Appropriately, *Brothers and Sisters* is the first of the many Compton-Burnett novels to bear a family title, the first in which a family living in what Elizabeth Bowen calls "sinister cosiness" and whose address, as R. Glynn Grylls says, might be Huis Close,★ is explored and the skeleton in the cupboard revealed, and the first to portray one of the authors monstrous domestic tyrants. Ivy herself did not consider these characters such monsters as her readers. She confessed to a fondness for the people she created, good or bad, and thought the badness exaggerated by the readers.

This recalls a surprising passage in her interview with Kay Dick, published after her death.†

K. D.: That reminds me. You said once you were a woman of blameless character.
I. C.-B.: So I am.
K. D.: What do you mean by blameless?
I. C.-B.: I mean quite perfect morally.

★ *Ivy Compton-Burnett*, published for the British Council by Longman Group Ltd.
† *Ivy and Stevie*. Duckworth, 1971.

K. D.: What do you call perfect morally?
I. C.-B.: Well, I mean without sin.

After which they discussed sin, and the need both in life and literature for moral laws, which for Ivy had nothing whatsoever to do with religion.

Brothers and Sissters does not open with dialogue, has a number of descriptive passages and also, unusual in Compton-Burnett, gives a name, Moreton Edge, to the village of the Manor House, where the scene is set. The incest theme, the title ironically giving the clue to it, is unmistakably Greek, and Ivy conceded that it would be odd if, having had a classical education, nothing of this should appear in her work. One character is drawn from her own childhood: the Compton-Burnetts' beloved Minnie is a prototype for "Patty", Miss Patmore, Sophia's housekeeper-companion, to whom the children turn for comfort.

"Miss Patmore had been their nurse and nearly their mother in childhood, and they had for her much of the feeling that might have been Sophia's. She was . . . a spare little, middle-aged woman, with large kind eyes and questioning nose much as they had been in her youth."

Something of Katharine Compton-Burnett too crept into the drawing of Sophia. Ivy's memory of her mother's beauty, her leisured attention to her toilet and her recognised way of putting anyone else present into the shade certainly colours this portrait.

An entertaining piece of literary history comes into Ivy's story here. Richard Kennedy, then a very young man, had joined the Hogarth Press in 1928. To quote from his diary *A Boy at the Hogarth Press:**

"L.W. [Leonard Woolf] has given me two MSS to read and report on. One is called *Sligo* by Jack Yeats and the other *Brothers and Sisters* by I. Compton-Burnett.

"*Sligo* is very meandering with no story, but is very poetic.

* Whittington Press, 1972.

Brothers and Sisters has no atmosphere at all. I think I will ask Uncle George's* opinion of it as I would like to say something intelligent.

"*Brothers and Sisters* back from Uncle George. He handed it to me and said, 'It's a work of genius. I can't say more.' This is rather exciting. I made out a very professional reader's report on a sheet of foolscap. I wrote a few lines about *Sligo*, saying I did not think it had enough general appeal, although it had poetic qualities and plenty of atmosphere. Against *Brothers and Sisters* I just put A WORK OF GENIUS.

"L.W. took my report and glanced at it. His lip curled when he read the words, but he did not say anything.

"Perhaps I have discovered a genius and he will be eternally grateful to me.

"L.W. gave me back the two MSS and told me to return them to their authors with the usual letter of rejection.

"Evidently he doesn't think *Brothers and Sisters* 'a work of genius.'

" 'She can't even write,' he said, handing the manuscript to me. 'At least this man Yeats knows how to write. . . .'

"As I was going home this evening I had a great surprise. I bought my *Evening Standard* from the newspaper seller who looks as if he is suffering from an incurable disease, I turned to the book page, which is written by Arnold Bennett, to see if he was reviewing any of our books. The first thing I saw was a headline: A WORK OF GENIUS after which was written 'Miss Ivy Compton-Burnett's new novel is a work of genius'. So Uncle George was right."

Brothers and Sisters was therefore published in the spring of 1929 by Heath Cranton, who before long advertised its "second large printing" with extracts from the reviews, as their "Novel of the Year". The Book Society placed it on their recommended list, "because", as Hugh Walpole put it, "it is so unusual a book that it would be a thousand pities if those who would like it failed to hear of it." What Arnold Bennett said was:

---

* George Kennedy, the eminent architect.

"I am not sure but I think it is quite possible that a novel lying at the moment here will one day be the cause of research, envy, covetousness and other vices. I have never heard of the author, who I am informed is a woman. . . . She may be a new star, low on the eastern horizon . . . but I do not propose to pontificate concerning her. I might guess wrong."

Leonard and Virginia Woolf, apparently unaware of their rejection of the novel, invited the author to tea. Ralph Strauss was "startled into a very real admiration", while admitting that *Brothers and Sisters* would not be to all tastes, and Raymond Mortimer was there again, this time in the *Nation*, telling readers that the author "makes one laugh aloud", while V. Sackville-West in a radio talk on new novels observed that this was "a very queer book indeed. . . . But this novel is, I think a genuine work of art."

Miss Sackville-West continued with a fascinating proposition, illustrating her theory that enjoyment of certain works may be greatly increased by keeping an eye on the author's design and intention.

"If you read *Brothers and Sisters* in the ordinary way you will very quickly find yourselves exclaiming, 'What an absurd book! it isn't like life at all'. But if you will think of it as a chessboard, on which the author has invented a purely artificial game—as chess is—and if you will think of the characters as chessmen, being moved about by the hand of their creator in queer, stilted, conventional moves, like the Knight's sudden leap-frog, the Bishop's obliquity, or the Pawn's strict limitations—then you will see, I think, that the characters in this book have an existence and a significance entirely their own, living and moving in a world entirely their own, false, invented, make believe, but true to their own rules and their own conventions. And you must think of Sophia, the central character, as the Queen, able to make startling and devastating moves in any direction, swooping down on some unlucky little piece from the opposite end of the board; a really tremendous and alarming figure, a real creation in the world of fiction."

This was the first of the Compton-Burnett novels to be published in America.*

Although such notices drew the attention of the literary world to their new colleague and Ivy began to meet other writers, the guests at the small luncheon and dinner parties in Linden Gardens still came chiefly from Margaret's circle. There was always good food: Jessie had a gift for preparing creamed mushrooms, and boiled bacon was a favourite dish. They liked fish, too, and junket, and that old favourite among puddings, stone cream. Margaret collected recipes and had envelopes stuffed with them. She never cooked herself, but she did sometimes induce the housekeeper to try new dishes. It was Margaret who chose the wine with great care; she knew about it and liked it, while Ivy scarcely drank at all. Among these guests were Herman Schrijver, the Dutch interior decorator, who was to become for the rest of her life one of Ivy's closest friends, Ernest and Janette Thesiger, and of course the Elliott Felkins, all of whom she shared with Margaret. Then there were her own old friends —the Jack Beresfords, the Alan Kidds, Arthur Waley, Raisley Moorsom—so many of Noël Compton-Burnett's Cambridge côterie.

Hester was constantly there and received sympathetic council from both her hostesses about her recurrent heartbreaks. Margaret, in spite of a rather gruff manner, was in fact very tender-hearted, and Hester had been accustomed to ask for her advice ever since she was a child. She found Ivy too not only keenly interested in her love affairs but also very understanding.

One of the young men Hester used to talk about to Margaret and Ivy was Basil Marsden-Smedley. Her uncle, Alban Head, took greatly to this charming and gifted young man, with whom he could discuss their mutual interests in the realm of art. Basil, who was born in the same year as Hester, 1901, had contracted polio while he was at Harrow. Although through his own deter-

* Harcourt, Brace, New York, 1929.

mination and his mother's loving care his general paralysis was overcome, his right arm never regained its power. Instead, therefore, of training as an architect he went to Trinity College, Cambridge, took an Honours Degree in History and then read for the Bar. He met Margaret and Ivy for the first time at one of Alban Head's parties at the Burlington Hotel. He and Margaret, having so much in common, liked one another at once, while Ivy, as usual in these days, was a rather silent figure in the background, although later she developed a great affection for Basil, which was wholeheartedly returned. After this first encounter he was warmly welcomed to Linden Gardens. He was deeply impressed with Margaret's prowess and fame, and referred to Ivy as "Margaret Jourdain's Boswell".

After years of friendship Hester and Basil decided to marry. His family was very much against the match, thinking him too young to marry, particularly as he had not yet been called to the Bar, and disapproving of the jolly, unworldly, country Pinneys. The Marsden-Smedleys were keen on sport, but not on riding or hunting, in which the Pinneys delighted. Then there was the question of money, of which the Marsden-Smedleys had plenty and the Pinneys little. Mr Marsden-Smedley refused to settle money on the young couple unless General Pinney did likewise, and wrote to the latter saying, "You must be rich as you hunt", to which General Pinney replied, "We would be nearer so if we did not."

Shortly before she and Basil were married in 1927, Hester helped Margaret, who that year was one of the advisers at the Daily Telegraph Furniture Exhibition, and to show Hester's future in-laws her ability to earn money Margaret added a considerable sum to her small fee. This did not work at all as she intended for, while the Marsden-Smedleys would have welcomed a daughter-in-law with a dowry, they were not impressed by one who had nothing but brains.

Mr Marsden-Smedley did suddenly offer his son a job in Derbyshire in the family mills, but Hester, who was abroad at the time, wrote saying that if he accepted this she flatly refused to marry him. And Margaret backed her up, saying: "London is a healthier life for people such as you, and Ivy and I would love to have you near us."

As a result of this situation there was no marriage settlement and Hester and Basil married on a very small income. They lived in Chelsea in what was known in those days as a "Bohemian" way, not approved of in conventional circles, and were often visited by Margaret and Ivy.

A propos these friendships which were never to break, somewhere in Ivy's novels there is a reference to a broken friendship to which comes the swift retort: "Then it cannot have been a friendship." And indeed Margaret and Ivy never lost their friends except through their deeply mourned deaths.

Presently admirers of Ivy's books began to appear at Linden Gardens. Rose Macaulay, May Sinclair, Francis Birrell, David Garnett and Victoria (Vita) Sackville-West were among the first. It was Vita Sackville-West who brought Ivy and Virginia Woolf together again, although they never became intimate. Ivy admired Virginia Woolf's art, but was doubtful if she should properly be called a novelist. The Bloomsbury domain was unknown territory to Ivy. Edward Sackville-West was also an early acquaintance who, years later, wrote: "The effect of her art recalls the aims of the Cubist Movement in painting, at its inception,"* which must have seemed to her pure nonsense. As these literary figures came to pay homage to Ivy, Margaret found, somewhat to her surprise, even slightly to her chagrin, that she was no longer the only star at Linden Gardens.

"It's odd," she observed to Hester, "when someone you know very well suddenly becomes famous."

Nobody remembers her talking about Ivy's books, although there is an impression that in the earliest days she thought they were nonsense, and in spite of them she remained the dominating character.

Hospitality was widely returned by the visitors to Linden Gardens and was much enjoyed by the friends. Although they were hearty eaters, Ivy could not tolerate anything rich—bread and butter for her had to be bread and scrape. On the other hand

---

* "An Appraisal". *Horizon*, June, 1946.

she doted on sweets. "Holland is best for chocolate," she affirmed, "England for Harrogate toffee and America for marshmallows." Failing Dutch chocolate, however, she was very happy with a box from Charbonnel et Walker or some other first class firm, and her friends, as years went on, were happy to provide her with such tokens of their regard.

One thing, however, which perturbed them both was their plumpness. Presently they visited a specialist in Harley Street to find out how, as one friend unkindly put it, to lose weight while remaining greedy. He prescribed injections, which they duly had, at the cost of many hundreds of pounds. The treatments were on the whole swiftly successful, although Margaret remained on the stocky side, while by the late thirties Ivy had become very slim.

These were happy days, only upset by the great slump in 1930, when Ivy, in common with so many others, lost a fair amount of money. "I am ashamed to be so poor," she complained to Basil.

Her happiness did not prevent her from writing one of her most profound and alarming novels, *Men and Wives*. After the publication of *Brothers and Sisters* Rose Macaulay had suggested to Ivy that she should go to her, Rose's, agents, Curtis Brown, and let them arrange for the publication of her next novel, and in 1929 Curtis Brown made a contract for her next three novels with Heinemann. Consequently, in 1931, *Men and Wives* came out under their imprint.

This book contains very many characters and needs the reader's close attention in order to realise the skill of the diverse portraiture. It is the first of the novels to demand such concentration in the earlier part, which led Ivy herself to say later, "Anyone who picks up a Compton-Burnett finds it very hard not to put it down." But it is a "deedy" book and in the later chapters it becomes sheer melodrama; the characters—a bevy of egocentrics —have all materialised, and the reader is held in shocked suspense as in the most skilful of thrillers, besides having his breath taken away by the author's outrageous irony. The leading figure in the large cast is Harriet, wife and mother, whom Charles Burkhart

perceptively calls "a love tyrant", and whose loving tyranny
brings about her own death at the hands of her eldest son.

Servants, seldom absent in late novels and always given a highly
individual treatment, appear for the first time in *Men and Wives*.
Buttermere, the butler, raises the curtain and is a useful "Extra",
although more slightly sketched than many of the later "below-
stairs" characters. Of Compton-Burnett servants Mary McCarthy
says:*

"Their voices, coming from near at hand, strike the ear with
surprise, like talking animals in a fairy tale."

Men and Wives, although essentially different, bears a general
resemblance to its predecessor, for the setting and period are
standard. To quote Mary McCarthy further:

"One of the mischievous originalities of Compton-Burnett is
to have pursued this insular tendency to the extreme, making
it her trademark. She produces Compton-Burnetts, as someone
might produce ball-bearings. . . . Hence the uniformity of
labelling in her titles and the open-stock patterns of her incidents
and dialogue. The author, like all reliable old firms, is stressing
the *sameness* of the formula; senior service. She has no imitators.
The formula is a trade secret."

Gerald Gould, reviewing *Men and Wives* in the *Observer*,†
found its author's outlook on life "little short of desperate", and
the effect of her style "startling, but . . . also wearing". Consequently, while already acknowledging I. Compton-Burnett as
"one of the most powerful and original of living writers", he
ended his review "it is a pity her book should seem too long".
In fact he was one of the readers who found it difficult "not to put
it down".

More Women than Men, the only other novel to be written in

* *The Inventions of I. Compton-Burnett. The Writing on the Wall and other
Literary Essays*. Harcourt, Brace & World, New York, 1970.
† 29th March 1931.

Linden Gardens, is easier going. Like *Pastors and Masters* it is set not in a home but in a school—this time a girls' school with the headmistress as tyrant.

The scene is painted in brighter colours than that of *Men and Wives*, the book opening with a lively description of the terrible Josephine Napier's staff. Although later passages are macabre, including a subtle murder, the novel sparkles with fun, much of which is provided by Felix, a preposterous, sprightly homosexual, who constantly moves with "a dancing step" and whose usual seat, when he is in his home with Josephine's brother, is on the latter's knees. And his words are often as mirthful as his actions, as for instance when he excuses a speech, saying: "I had no time to make it spontaneous". If one is a reader of the same calibre as Raymond Mortimer, Felix makes one "laugh aloud".

Many of the relationships in this book are mutely homosexual. This form of emotion was a subject which Ivy liked to discuss freely and academically with some of her intimate friends, to whom she described herself and Margaret as "neuters". The love affairs of her acquaintances, of whichever nature, never ceased to fascinate her, and her judgment of such alliances was penetrating, tolerant and wise. She also enjoyed hearing about transvestites, and was disappointed when a friend who knew one well did not bring him to see her. Margaret did not share these interests but she enjoyed a "naughty story", while Ivy detested such things. Nevertheless, when she heard that a reader considered Felix sitting on an older man's knee rather shocking, Ivy announced with satisfaction that she had intended this to be shocking. Rather surprisingly, considering her own brand of prudishness, Ivy was entertained rather than shocked when an occasional improper telephone call reached her ears. She did not slam down the receiver, but listened with amusement to endearments and indecent suggestions and even with some satisfaction to the first four-letter word that she had ever heard.

Ivy was also interested in so many other aspects of her friends' lives, such as their appearance, finances, failings, and of course their relations with their relatives. What Graham Greene says in his autobiography* comes to mind: "I suppose too that every novelist has something in common with a spy: he watches, he overhears, he seeks motives and analyses character. . . ."

This description could not be more true of any novelist than of I. Compton-Burnett.

* *A Sort of Life.* Bodley Head, 1971.

CHAPTER VI

Cornwall Gardens

BY THE TIME *More Women than Men* was published in 1933 Ivy and Margaret, knowing that the Linden Gardens lease would shortly come to an end, had been spending much time house-hunting. They did this assiduously, consulting many agents and gradually widening their field of search for a flat with very large rooms from North Kensington to the more fashionable Kensington, south of the park. A number of their friends helped in this hunt, which was finally rewarded by finding 5 Braemar Mansions, a spacious flat on the high first floor of a late Victorian mansion block which Margaret described as looking like Balmoral, at the end of Cornwall Gardens. The long flat was L-shaped, fronting other houses. It had enormous windows opening on to a balcony, while the view from the back which was only seen from the dining-room, was on to a flight of fire-escape steps and a sheer drop to the back yard—like some stark American film-set.

Once Ivy and Margaret had seen this flat, they did not look further. In 1934 they moved into what was to be their home for the rest of their lives.

More Women than Men had its quota of respectful and scathing reviews. It is illuminating to recall the impressions of the poet Humbert Wolfe:*

"Miss Burnett does her utmost to conceal her genuine insight into human character under a style where George Meredith ruefully collides with Henry James. No human beings ever

* *Observer*, 13th August, 1933.

spoke or even thought like these strange puppets of Miss Burnett's creation. But gradually it appears that the style disinfects and makes almost tolerable the squalid ugliness which has engaged the writer's attention. Curious relations between the sexes, strange cruelty and even murder do not confront the mind with their native brutality but, like characters in a Restoration Comedy, by virtue of their style acquire a curious, if not pleasant, artistic significance."

Ivy did not in fact enjoy Henry James; he offended what Christine Brooke-Rose calls her "classic economy", as did Proust and Meredith. But Humbert Wolfe was none the less right: Henry James and I. Compton-Burnett have certain affinities. Reviewing her books at a later date, the writer Julian Mitchell★ found in these two novelists a similarity of plot though not of style, but, in fact, sometimes a few lines of Henry James do surprisingly resemble a passage of Compton-Burnett.

Jessie, the housekeeper, had moved with her two ladies into the new flat, and this was soon looking very elegant with pale oyster walls and superb period furniture gradually collected by Margaret Jourdain, who used to say that no chair worth sitting on had been made since the Reform Bill. There were no pictures except one nineteenth-century print of Kensington Palace in the hall and one Chinese glass picture which hung above the bureau in the drawing-room. This is surprising considering Margaret's knowledge of, for instance, Japanese and Chinese prints. But neither of them liked pictures in the home.

In the dining-room were two corner cupboards which Ivy particularly liked, the larger one of mahogany and the other of stripped pine. In these Margaret displayed her collection of coloured glass and some decorative pieces of china. In the centre of the room was the large oval oak dinner table over which hung from the very high ceiling one small electric bulb with blue and white dangles hanging round it, which gave out very little light and lent a slightly oriental air to the otherwise completely English scene. Beside the window stood a handsome mahogany

★ *New Statesman*, 12th December, 1965.

sideboard on which were glass dishes piled with fresh fruit and wooden boxes of preserved fruits. Also an open box of treasured knives with ornamental handles, in onyx, shagreen, cornelian and, rarest of all, Wedgwood blue china. The back wall of the dining-room was taken up by big white built-in cupboards in which linen was kept and which also served as a box-room. The floor, as everywhere in the flat, was covered in linoleum.

In the drawing-room, oriental mats lay on the linoleum and on the walls were five large ornamental gilt-framed mirrors, both Regency and of later date, which had been given to or purchased by Margaret. There were two glass-fronted bookcases, one Chippendale and the other Sheraton, the latter being also a writing table, although never used as such. These housed Margaret's extensive library connected with her profession and many treasured books from Ivy's earlier days, including *The Anatomy of Melancholy*, *Religio Medici* and volumes by Addison, Steele and Samuel Butler, including *The Notebooks*, Butler being one of Ivy's most esteemed authors. There was also the beautiful leather-bound *Spectator*, Volume 1, of 1766, given to her by her brother Guy, and *The Life and Entertaining Adventures of Mr. Cleveland, Natural Son of Oliver Cromwell, written by HIMSELF*. Close by was a small bookshelf and a table on which books were laid. Ivy's own books were mainly kept in her bedroom, stored away in drawers, and the latest books presented by her writer friends were usually kept on the drawing-room floor—under the sofa when there came to be one.

For a long time there were only two armchairs and several beautiful upright ones. Ivy sat in her own armchair beside the fireplace with her back to the light—the handsome windows always had their blinds half-drawn—while Margaret sat on an upright chair. The other smaller armchair was reserved for a woman guest, and when some young man stole this privilege in the presence of such a guest this was not smiled upon. "Nothing goes deeper than manners," Ivy was to write in her last book, and indeed in her life they mattered profoundly.

The size of the windows and the loftiness of the ceiling made the room chilly in winter-time, and Ivy was often occupied in piling on coal, poking very carefully to achieve the maximum amount of heat and flame—she loved the flames of a fire—perhaps remarking with that small quizzical smile: "You can't get a good fire without smoke" or else characteristically deploring the cost of using so much coal.

For a long time the friends resisted the idea of getting any form of settee, although Ivy would tell people that she knew Margaret wanted a chesterfield and Margaret would strongly deny the imputation, but allow that it would be more comfortable for the guests. Eventually a straight-backed settee was purchased, and like the armchairs covered in black velvet. Although it had beautiful legs, even with cushions it was difficult to sit comfortably on it, and while ostensibly there was room for three people, as Ivy kept papers, magazines, chocolate boxes and her current exercise books in the corner of it nearest her chair, it was seldom that more than two visitors could sit there.

Behind Ivy's chair—between it and the windows—stood her small walnut writing-table, chosen by Margaret, of which Ivy was very fond. On this were two opaline vases and sometimes one of a pair of handsome Sheffield plate candlesticks, wired as lamps, with almost opaque white shades. Although Ivy was several times photographed sitting at this bureau, she seldom used it for writing anything other than letters and her innumerable postcards. For her scripts she preferred to sit in her armchair and write on her knee.

Also in the drawing-room were four pedestals of interesting design, all supporting alabaster and other bowls as very shaky lamps. There were two tall Sheraton fire screens and dotted about on little tables many ornaments in which the friends delighted, such as two blue-john urns and a small stone box from China. Many of Ivy's friends remember this strange box with a frog squatting on its lid, for in it Ivy kept special chocolates which had been brought as gifts and which were handed round to guests. She particularly liked chocolates which came from the best stores in bags because they tended to be fresher than those in boxes. She liked soft centres, coffee or truffle, or best of all, but rare, plain white centres.

Ivy during the early twenties

Margaret Jourdain, 1910

Ivy at Bettiscombe, 1942

Ivy's bedroom was large. She seldom had any form of heating in it, whatever the weather, declaring that she liked a cold bedroom. In these ways she showed the influence of a normally spartan turn-of-the-century upbringing, although she was by nature rather more self-indulgent than Margaret. The latter's bedroom was the smallest in the flat, smaller even than the housekeeper's, containing little beside her narrow bed, a wardrobe and the dressing-table at which she would write, with papers and reference books strewn on the bed. Ivy's room, on the other hand, was well-furnished and meticulously tidy. She could not bear any untidiness except in that one corner of the sofa. She liked women guests to leave their coats neatly folded on her bed and the men to dispose of theirs neatly on chairs in the hall. The way people carelessly flung down their wraps never ceased to annoy her.

Here were more fine old mirrors, these ones framed in wood. In the centre of the room stood her good, rather hard mahogany bedstead. On the wall opposite the window was the wardrobe, a gentleman's wardrobe with suitably masculine coat-hangers on which to hang her black Bradley suits. Underneath was a row of neat black shoes, each pair on their trees. In the far corner was a pretty, not very big, glass-fronted corner cupboard, in the top part of which Ivy stored an assortment of such things as scarves, and in the lower part kept her hats. "Hat-fitting" is an appointment which from time to time appears in Margaret's engagement book.

There was also a bridal chest with books ranged on its lid and a plain dressing-table with a small mirror, prettily topped by a carved shell, in which it was not easy to see a reflection. On the table lay an old toilet set of ivory, bearing very worn initials, and there was also a large flask of lavender water from Floris, with which Herman Schrijver kept her amply supplied. She liked this very much, although she only used it in small quantities. There were also pots of face cream, for Ivy took fond care of her delicate skin and her beautiful hands were always perfectly manicured.

On the chest-of-drawers, supported by book-ends, was ranged

a row of favourite volumes, including works by Charlotte Yonge, Charlotte Brontë, Somerville and Ross and Thomas Love Peacock—the work of the last being more to Margaret's taste than to her own. The only contemporary author included in this special selection was Elizabeth Bowen, and for a while Ivy also kept here a foreign translation of one of her own novels.

The bathroom was old-fashioned and completely cheerless and the kitchen was neither well-equipped nor attractive. When, however, a refrigerator was acquired, the kitchen gained some charm for Ivy. She played with the new possession like a little girl with a doll's house, delighted that each time she opened it a light came on. From the kitchen one stepped on to the small square terrace at the end of the long narrow balcony, trimming both sides of the house with flower boxes all along the stone balustrade. (The great drawing-room windows on to it were never opened.) As the years passed these boxes became more and more Ivy's garden. To tend them she would put on brogues, a country coat and a garden hat. She grew little fuchsias, little old-fashioned pinks, small roses and even a tiny hydrangea, besides great mounds of flowering thrift, thyme and other herbs. (Those five rose trees have now been planted by Arthur Waley's widow on his grave.) Ivy loved to have flowers around her indoors too: not so much the large bouquets that admirers sometimes sent— although their cellophane wrappings, when these came into fashion, amused her—as informal posies. "Floppy but fresh," she would say with approval on being given such a bunch. The only flowers she disliked were chrysanthemums. What she detested was flowers being wired. She would always sniff even the ones which have no scent at all. In her late years she used to arrange small vases on the floor on the far side of the room from the windows where she could look at them from her chair. She said the flowers preferred to be low down.

One reflection of her young days in Hove was the way in which she, like her mother, was the one to carve the joint. This she did standing up and wielding the utensils skilfully. The knife had to be in proper condition for the task. If it were not she would send it out to the kitchen to be sharpened. She did not like this to be done in the dining-room; it reminded her of some childhood's episode when the grating noise had upset one of her small sisters. Just once, in some domestic crisis, she allowed Basil Marsden-Smedley to do this service in the dining-room and greatly admired the way he stuck the steel between his paralysed arm and his ribs, and with the help of his knee sharpened the knife perfectly without making a disagreeable noise.

The dinner service was Wedgwood, the *Liverpool Bird*, and for tea there was an unusual and pretty Coalport set, decorated with black and white stripes and tiny flowers.

The circle continued to expand. How the ladies found time to write is hard to fathom. It was about now that Soame Jenyns the orientalist, newly back from Hong Kong with a post at the British Museum, met Margaret through Willy King and was brought by her to Cornwall Gardens where he became an habitué. He dedicated his *Background to Chinese Painting*★ "to Margaret Jourdain without whose encouragement and criticism this book could not have been written." There was also James Lees Milne, who had a high regard for Margaret's erudition in his field of architecture and its allied subjects. In the preface to his *Tudor Reconnaissance*† he thanked her for "her wise advice which led me to recast my whole thesis".

Shopping in the excellent provisioners in the near-by Gloucester Road, done with great attention both to quality and to cost, was a daily pleasure which also took time. Ivy once told a young man who was enquiring how and when inspiration came to her that she never allowed thoughts of the book she was writing to interfere with her shopping.

Besides this busy home life, there were the expeditions to great houses, museums, galleries and sale rooms, and frequent sorties to see a play—"theatre at night" is a recurrent phrase in Margaret's tiny engagement books of those years. Visits to friends abroad and at home, among the latter now being weekends at Bottisham Hall, the splendid Regency house near Cambridge belonging to

★ Sidgwick and Jackson Ltd., 1935.
† Batsford, 1951.

Soame Jenyns' mother, and at Ramdean, Raisley Moorsom's house near Petersfield. On at least one occasion he drove his guests to the sea, and they both donned long, old-fashioned bathing dresses and voluminous caps and paddled about in the shallows. Margaret used also to wear an old-fashioned boudoir cap, frilled and ribboned, when in night attire.

Although they did not venture out to sea on this occasion both ladies could swim—Ivy well from her young days at Hove. Margaret, though not a good swimmer, was a keen bather, and her enthusiasm for this activity was shared by Basil Marsden-Smedley. They constantly visited baths and pools together, and went to the Ace of Spades on the Kingston By-pass the day it opened in the mid-thirties, to sample the new pool. These outings, in which Ivy did not join, were very gay, as were Margaret's and Basil's expeditions to various golf clubs, not to play, but to wander about the links and enjoy eating at the club houses, particularly those which had orginally been beautiful old private dwellings. Margaret often visited friends without Ivy, an arrangement well understood by the Marsden-Smedleys, who also liked a measure of social separation. Devoted as Margaret and Ivy were, as the years passed there was naturally at times some friction between them, but this was never allowed to get out of hand. "One must," Margaret explained to a friend, "cultivate a blind spot about anybody one lives with."

A second Basil—the architect and decorator Ionides—was also a frequent visitor at Cornwall Gardens. Lord Bearsted's daughter, Nellie Levy, was one of Margaret Jourdain's oldest friends, the closest perhaps after Janette Ranken (Thesiger) until Ivy came on the scene. She had a fine collection of pictures, furniture and porcelain at Buxted Park in Sussex, and after a long widowhood had in 1930 married Basil Ionides. On account of their interests they were naturally closer to Margaret than to Ivy, but the latter used to refer affectionately to "my two Basils", although Marsden-Smedley remained the dearer friend. Another acquaintance of this period was Dame Una Pope-Hennessy, herself an authoress. She was introduced to Ivy by Rose Macaulay and brought her two sons into the circle. Sir John, through his publications as a historian and his appointment at the Victoria and Albert Museum, naturally became a friend of Margaret's, while James later, when the end of the war released him to become a writer and the literary editor of the *Spectator*, was more drawn to Ivy.

In spite of all these distractions composition continued and *A House and its Head* came out in 1935, once more under the imprint of Heinemann. Here we have another large cast of fully painted portraits, and a change of sex for the tyrant. Those holding the theory that women writers cannot create male figures would do well to study Duncan Edgeworth. He is undoubtedly a man, rather larger than life, with power-mania, strong sexual needs and an abnormal affection for his nephew which survives even the latter's seduction of his second wife. Yet, although a tyrant, Duncan is not a villain—he even has a certain nobility.

Other characters in *A House and its Head* are also brilliantly drawn, including the ridiculous Dulcia who, to quote Charles Burkhart, "is the most broadly comic personage in the novels". She is extraneous to the plot but steals the scene whenever she appears. It is not easy at first to hold all the characters in mind, but they reward study. The plot too is ingenious but complicated, and as in *Men and Wives* develops slowly until the melodrama reaches its pitch and then the book races and becomes a sophisticated thriller, laced as ever with wit.

This was the first of the Compton-Burnett books read by Robert Liddell, who was to become such an admirable exponent of her work. For the first few pages he thought she could not write at all, and then discovered her to be one of the most original and brilliant novelists of the day. And the poet, William Plomer, without knowing of her skill at embroidery, wrote in the *Spectator:**

"Miss Ivy Compton-Burnett, a very peculiar and talented writer whose novels are well known to connoisseurs, again opens a family cupboard full of skeletons, with which she proceeds to

* 19th July, 1935.

play spillikins, a game that calls for a very delicate touch. . . .

"She works at it as an intricate embroidery, and every stitch tells: a crisis, a passion, a crime may be hinted at in a few words. For most readers her approach is likely to be too subtle, her irony too dry, her 'peculiar outlook' too bitter, and her manner too stilted. . . .

"But those who have tired of superficial and sentimental family sagas will be ready to give this author her due, which is considerable."

So life continued unchanging through the thirties, except that Jessie left and was succeeded by a more formidable housekeeper who was anxious to impress upon everyone that her work was as important as that of her employers. Nobody denied this. Ivy used to say that she thought she would have been rather good below-stairs herself.

Visits abroad were made each year. When they went to Geneva Margaret stayed with the Felkins—this was in Elliott's League of Nations days—and because of lack of space Ivy slept at an hotel near by. She would arrive at the Felkins directly after breakfast, hatted and gloved and expecting to be taken out. Other hosts and hostesses, such as Raisley Moorsom, have similar memories, and the nanny who looked after Hester's children remembers Ivy as "the lady who always wore gloves in the garden".

In 1937 Dorothy Kidd's son Roger went to Westminster School and in 1942 up to Cambridge, to the college which had played such an important part in his family and Ivy's—King's. He records his boyhood's memories.

"During my time at Westminster and King's we saw Ivy Compton-Burnett and Margaret Jourdain constantly, more than any of my mother's other friends. Ivy was like a favourite aunt. She showed interest and never patronised. She would often, rather surprisingly, level a direct question about one's life with a searching glance.

"She took evident pleasure in things: relish in eating something in a restaurant, glowing fires, sunlight, flowers; I remember her bending over wild flowers in a Dorset wood and saying, 'Oh, you darlings!' She delighted in gossip, but not maliciously and always tempered with honesty. Looking back one is aware of a classical integrity—a dispassionate examination—and not of intellect so much as of perception. Sometimes she would laugh so much while recounting some absurdity that she wept.

"My mother and Ivy spoke together intimately. My mother had a direct unpremeditated approach to things which Ivy responded to: they were able to relax in each other's company. They appreciated each other's value for truth and spontaneity. Ivy was amused by mother's remarks and my mother laid store by Ivy's observations—one was never quite sure whether they were talking about relations, friends or characters from a novel. When they met there was often conversation about my cousins, uncles and aunts. Ivy felt closely connected. There was never mention of Jim* or of her sisters. She would occasionally refer to childhood incidents, but they were incidents—no more was said about them; they never led to reminiscence.

"We made constant visits to places, museums, galleries, these were always a delight to my mother and me. I remember no difficulties, only a sense of ease and pleasure. These expeditions were always planned by Margaret quietly and efficiently to give amusement to us all. Her consideration for Ivy was remarkable; tender, self-denying and dignified. When Ivy was demanding, Margaret would say, 'She's like a child.' She encouraged Ivy to meet new people and introduced her to many of her museum friends.

"Their love and intellectual generosity, particularly Margaret's, was a great influence, but it was effected undogmatically, as naturally as the leaves on trees."

The fact that in spite of a growing number of fans and golden tributes from many critics her books did not sell as well as those of some of her contemporaries annoyed Ivy considerably. Mr Curtis Brown now suggested, with Rose Macaulay's approval,

* Noël Compton-Burnett.

that as Ivy's contract with Heinemann was fulfilled and she was still dissatisfied with her sales she should try that enterprising publisher Victor Gollancz. *Daughters and Sons* was consequently published by Gollancz in 1937.

"For years the cognoscenti have considered Miss Compton-Burnett one of the finest of living novelists," one of the big advertisements of the new novel declared, "but 'the public' has appeared to prefer — and —. Will 'the public' now show that it is not without taste and discrimination?

"Probably not."

Daughters and Sons, although its tyrant, Sabine—a very old woman this time—is one of the most extreme examples of this species, with almost as terrible a daughter, is not a dark book. "This author," as Charles Burkhart says, "is here viewing human foibles with what seems an amused and bemused detachment", and the result, in spite of dire events, is brilliant comedy.

Ivy had not yet reached that gallery of wonderful, devastating children, but there is a forerunner here in Muriel, the laughing eleven-year-old, who induces laughter along with her first governess, Miss Bunyan. In the days when most upper class families employed a governess, having a "governess's appetite" was a description often given of somebody in light disparagement. Ivy made the most of this with Miss Bunyan.

The critics were lyrical. "Not a boring page, not a banal phrase, not one damp squib, not a joke below sample," Rosamond Lehmann wrote in *The Spectator*, and Desmond Shawe-Taylor declared in the *New Statesman*, "Her strange books have about them the golden touch of perfection: in their own sphere they are flawless works of art."

"The public" acted up to expectation and did not show anything. Ivy was extremely disappointed. Mr Spencer Curtis Brown well remembers her complaining that other people's novels sold many thousands. Why didn't hers? They had good plots, interesting characters and plenty of sex. She did not actually add that they had incest thrown in.

On a later occasion she wrote him a postcard, enclosed in an envelope, saying: "Why does Mr Gollancz stop people from reading my books?"

His one claim to fame, Mr Curtis Brown says, is that he made a successful editorial amendment to one of Ivy Compton-Burnett's books. Having read a long passage of single-line dialogue he found himself having to turn back and work out which characters were speaking. He wrote:

"Dear Miss Compton-Burnett,
"You have forgotten the telephone. If your reader must answer this, when he returns to your book he has to look back to find out which person is speaking. . . ."

Ivy replied that she *had* forgotten the telephone and added to the dialogue in one place the words "he said".

Regularly every two years now Ivy had a new book ready, and Mr Curtis Brown determined to do all he could to keep the old ones in print.

"Power and money and death," Phyllis Bentley lists as Ivy's usual subjects, and *A Family and a Fortune*,★ the last novel to come out before the war, has money as one of its main themes and is also concerned with illness and death, subjects which often stimulated the author's brilliance. The cover of the Penguin edition describes *A Family and a Fortune* as the "kindliest" of Ivy Compton-Burnett's works. This comparative mildness of climate is due to the absence of power in action. There is a frustrated invalid aunt who craves for it and a maddeningly officious niece who attempts it, but there is no tyrant. One portrait drawn with great delicacy and kindly humour is of a retarded boy of fifteen. His allusive remark "Aubrey saw his family as they were," and his grins of mirth or near tears, nicely point the general dialogue. There is a sympathetic portrait too of poor Miss Griffin, Aunt Matty's ill-used companion, and the theme of money is underlined by a young man being unexpectedly disturbed as he fingers a stream of golden coins.

★ Gollancz, 1939.

D

At the end of this book Ivy herself sums up the plot. The two middle-aged brothers, whose love for one another has always transcended all other affection, are talking together.

" 'How much has happened in the last fourteen months,' [Edgar says, and Dudley replies:]

" 'Yes, Matty came to live here. I inherited a fortune. I was engaged to Maria. Blanche fell ill and died. You became engaged in my place. You and Maria were married. Matty's father died. Matty drove her old friends out into the snow. I ran away from my home . . . I was sick almost to death, and was given back to you all. . . . Oh and Clement was gradually becoming a miser all the time.' "

This was the first of I. Compton-Burnett's novels to be translated into a foreign language—German—soon after the war.

Years later Christopher Sykes produced adaptations of this novel and of *Men and Wives* on the air.* These successful productions led him to consider particularly what the works were *not*. One of the ideas he came "to consider highly erroneous is that Miss Compton-Burnett is a social satirist. *A Family and a Fortune* . . . shows the extraordinary effects on a family of a large sum of money being left to one of the members, but I cannot agree with the frequently expressed opinion that in this story the author points the finger of scorn at those who covet riches. I think rather, that she shows how almost entirely helpless are people, both good people and bad people, to live independently of quite small material accidents." And of the characters in *Men and Wives* he says, "A satirist must have shown them either defeated or futilely rescued with everything saved except honour."†

One event in the late thirties disturbed the even tenor of life in Cornwall Gardens. During a brief absence of the housekeeper and her employers, a burglar broke into the flat and took much of Ivy's jewellery. Margaret's smaller collection they did not

* 1952/1953.
† *Radio Times*, 18th September, 1953.

touch. The jewels were fully insured and replaced by further purchases from Good's. Nevertheless, the fact of the flat being broken into was a shock which Ivy took a little time to get over.

A worse shock was soon to follow—war.

CHAPTER VII

Running Away from the Bombs

DURING THE SUMMER holidays of 1939 Basil Marsden-Smedley was at the Watch House near Chideock in Dorset, with his three children—Luke, now ten (who was Margaret Jourdain's godson), Christopher, eight, and Henrietta, four—in the care of their nanny and a maid. Late in August Hester went to Belgium as correspondent of the *Sunday Express*.

Margaret and Ivy were also in Dorset having their normal summer holiday in lodgings at nearby Lyme Regis. On Sunday, 3rd September, Basil wrote in his diary:

"Spent morning finishing off correspondence, etc. Margaret Jourdain and Ivy called, just in time for the Sunday Watch House hymn-singing and bible-reading. 11-15 Prime Minister broadcast announcing declaration of war.

"Sea very rough, but we bathed, lunched and with last words were off."

Hester, meanwhile, was hearing the Declaration of War on Antwerp station, surrounded by weeping but neutral Belgians.

Basil went back to London that afternoon but returned to the Watch House for the following weekend. This was a delightful holiday home, rented for several years by the Marsden-Smedleys, consisting of coastguards' cottages painted black, with little gardens full of flowers. Margaret and Ivy always loved visiting this place, and on 10th September Basil once more recorded them as being present for Sunday reading and hymn-singing, held on the little lawn in front of the house, sheltered by a very high hedge, tilted against sea-winds. Both friends, although unbelievers, much enjoyed these occasions and took a great interest in the children—Ivy was always specially kind to Henrietta, who became very fond of her.

"Afterwards," Basil wrote, "we bathed. Luke and Christopher swam like fishes . . . Ivy a good sound swimmer. Margaret and the others were water's edge bathers.

"After bathing I walked some of the way back with Margaret and Ivy."

Soon Ivy was to say: "When war casts its shadow I find that I recoil," and indeed on both occasions on which this shadow fell across her life she as far as possible kept its menace at bay. This second war, however, started far more calmly for her than that of 1914, when Noël joined the army and their home was breaking up for ever. Now she had Margaret at her side, and after those first pleasant days in Dorset on 24th September they went to stay with Mrs Jenyns at Bottisham Hall near Cambridge.

Mrs Jenyns was a somewhat formidable lady, of Quaker stock and very religious. Although Ivy maintained that her characters had nothing to do with living people, and although she did not have any actual tyrants among her acquaintances, she did know a number of domineering women, among whom were Elliott's mother, Mrs Felkin, Mrs Jenyns and Lady Pinney. Some shade of these ladies, as also of her own mother, surely lent colour to her portraits, nor can she have been unaware of that streak of despotism in her own nature, so clearly revealed when she became mistress of 20 The Drive.

Mrs Jenyns considered that Margaret had a bad influence on Ivy and did her best to counteract it. Both her guests obeyed her injunctions to accompany her to church and had their lives arranged by her. Soame, still at his post in the British Museum, came down for weekends and was eagerly welcomed by them all, for the weeks were long although they were living in great beauty and luxury. One social event they greatly enjoyed was being taken to see the lawyer Michael Browne, his wife Anna and their two young daughters at their nearby country home. Michael and Anna were to become close friends and Ivy took a lasting interest in the girls. When she visited Bottisham Hall at the right season, Ivy spent delicious hours among the raspberry canes, picking and eating large quantities of fruit—"fruiting", in fact. This expression, used in childhood at Hove, remained in her vocabulary and was added to that of several of her friends.

Not counting *Dolores*, Ivy was now finishing her eighth novel. This one, *Parents and Children*, is a much longer, more complex work than its predecessor. The huge cast includes a family of nine, ranging from young adults to small children, their parents, grandparents, nurses and governesses. The star is the three-year-old Nevill, a lovely creation, tenderly described. He always speaks of himself in the third person, as did Mrs Molesworth's *Him*, surely a favourite character in Ivy's childhood. Mary McCarthy's comment on Ivy's children and servants cannot be bettered:

> "Their treble contributions make you jump, like a sound coming from an impossible quarter. . . . Children who are not heard are not seen, just as a servant, waiting at table, usually remains invisible until his voice is raised. . . .
>
> "It is the unexpectedness of the voices that creates an effect bordering on the supernatural. . . . Children and servants are astral bodies."

The nurse, once more like the Compton-Burnetts' Minnie, is more loved than the mother, and the under-nurse and the governesses are drawn with humour. Again there are full portraits in which this time hands—"sensitive" or "gentle" or "large"—play a prominent part. And the book is full of acute psychological studies which repay patient concentration. Reading would be aided by a list of characters.

There is no tyrant in *Parents and Children* and the plot is strange indeed. Late in the book the father of the nine sons and daughters is believed to have died in South America, and the mother is just about to marry a neighbour when the husband and father returns, a deeply felt and beautifully realised scene.

After a short time back in Cornwall Gardens, the ladies repaired once more to lodgings in Lyme Regis. They remained in Dorset throughout the dramatic events of 1940—the capitulation of France, Dunkirk and the Battle of Britain.

Hester came back to England in May, 1940, and in October of this year her uncle Harry, Henry Head, the neurologist, died and left her the lease and contents of his great house, Hartley Court near Reading. There she moved her three children. Basil (now in the Ministry of Economic Warfare and sleeping at his office, as the Tedworth Square house was occupied by Czechs) went down at weekends. There was a constant influx of family and friends and service people billeted on them.

At the turn of the year, after the great destruction in London by incendiary bombs, Hester invited Margaret and Ivy to join the household. Fond as she was of these two friends, who had now left middle-age behind them—Margaret was in her mid-sixties and Ivy some years younger—it was not without mis-givings that Hester asked them to come to Hartley Court. For one thing the place swarmed with children, and although Margaret was so good with children and Ivy so much interested in them Hester wondered how, used as they were to the even pattern of life in Cornwall Gardens, they would adapt to this heterogeneous community. It was particularly Ivy she had doubts about, for while Margaret had strong likes and dislikes she was in general the more adaptable of the two.

They accepted the invitation gladly—in later days Ivy seldom mentioned these years without a whimsical smile and the com-ment "when we were running away from the bombs"—and in February 1941 moved from Lyme Regis, which was shortly to be a "regulated" area out of bounds to visitors, to Hartley Court. On the whole the plan worked smoothly. The place was well-stocked with poultry, vegetables and fruit. It was also well-serviced, for Hester had kept on some of her uncle's staff and added Alice Read, who stayed with her for twenty-five years, and waited on the ladies like a lady's maid.

Rationing was in force by the time they joined the household and oranges were in short supply. Ivy had a passion for oranges—

normally she would eat two or three after a meal, attacking them with skilful avidity. Hester's nanny still remembers with surprise how, when many adults renounced their right to such luxuries as sweets and fruit in favour of children, "the lady who wore gloves in the garden" insisted on having her exact share of oranges. "My need is greater than theirs," she affirmed. "They have that nasty yellow bottled stuff at school." When points rationing came in the friends found this system practical and amusing.

Hester was right in assuming that Margaret and Ivy would not mix well with all her other guests, and their chief companion, whenever he was free, was her first cousin Michael Pinney, who was serving as a gunner nearby and billeted at Hartley Court. Margaret had known him for years and he had become a valued friend of Ivy's at his home, Bettiscombe, the other stronghold of the Pinneys in Dorset. His family used to go over to the sandy beach at Lyme Regis during Ivy's visits and build sand-castles, not to amuse the children but to amuse Ivy. Basil's company too was of course eagerly sought at weekends, but besides walks and talks Hartley Court had a magnificent library in which Ivy spent much time. In her usual way on most days she devoted several hours to her writing.

Parents and Children came out in May, 1941, while she was at Hartley Court, and Elizabeth Bowen wrote: "To read in these days a page of Compton-Burnett dialogue is to think of the sound of glass being swept up, one of these mornings after a blitz." Another of Miss Bowen's war-time parallels was that I. Compton-Burnett's characters "advance on each other's houses in groups, like bomber formations".

By now she was at work on *Elders and Betters*. Meanwhile she continued as far as possible to ignore the war, but she naturally could not ignore the death in action of Hester's brother, Bernard Pinney, news of which came on Boxing Day 1941. His death was a great grief not only to his family but to Margaret Jourdain, who had known and loved him since childhood, and for Ivy it awoke heartbreaking memories of the loss of her own beloved brother, Noël, in the first war.

During the last weeks of their sojourn at Hartley Court Margaret and Ivy were much occupied in bus rides to neighbouring parts of Berkshire to find a home of their own. They moved in the autumn of 1942 first to a cottage at Thatcham near Newbury, and after some months to a small house in the town itself, called Zealand Cottage. They had a few friends in the neighbourhood whom they regularly visited,* by bus whenever possible and otherwise in a hired car.

They did not stay away from London altogether at this time. They were, for instance, present in April 1943 at a reading of contemporary poetry in the presence of the Queen and the young Princesses, organised by Osbert Sitwell in aid of the French in Great Britain Fund. During this visit they went to the Lowndes Square flat of the American poet Hilda Doolittle ("H.D."), with whom her friend, the well-known literary figure, Bryher, was staying, and here met the three Sitwells. Bryher and "H.D." also went to tea with Ivy and Margaret in Cornwall Gardens.

Elders and Betters was published in 1944 when the friends were back in Lyme Regis for the final months of the war. It had been the most absorbing book to write, tight in texture and full in characterisation. As Charles Burkhart says: "What distinguishes this novel from the earlier novels is a more complex view of personality, and what is essentially a less literary conception of character." An extremely interesting development as Ivy embarked on her middle novels.

Miss Hansford Johnson declares that the novels "have an extraordinarily good effect upon the critic, because they enforce his entire attention. It is absolutely essential to read every line of a Compton-Burnett novel, because to miss a single one turns the whole book gibberish."† This is putting it perhaps too strongly, but Ivy agreed that her books required to be read "word for word".

"I do think my books need that. It does not seem to be an unreasonable demand. If someone reads every other page or

* Including the author's stepmother and aunts.
† *I. Compton-Burnett*, The British Council and National Book League, 1951.

a sentence here and there, he writes the sort of criticism that shows that the book has eluded him, or rather that he has eluded the book. I think my books are rather condensed, but I don't think they are obscure."*

Ivy spoke of "seeing" the people whom she created, and she helps her readers to do likewise by giving exact descriptions of them. Such descriptions tend to be forgotten. Thus Jocelyn Brooke, comparing Elizabeth Bowen's work with that of Ivy Compton-Burnett, writes:

"The latter is almost entirely an auditory writer—the visible world is indicated, in her book, in the most perfunctory manner, the story is welded together entirely by means of dialogue, one has a sense of perpetually eavesdropping on her characters."†

Indeed one does this eavesdropping, but the speakers are visible. Adults, servants, children—each one of the eighteen characters in *Elders and Betters* is vividly portrayed. For example, the heroine-villain of the piece is thus described on the first page:

"Anna Donne was a short, high-shouldered woman of thirty, with a large head that seemed to dwarf her height; round, open hazel eyes set under a receding forehead and close to an irregular nose; and an unusual reddish tinge in her hair and brows, that contributed to an odd appearance."

An odd appearance and also an odd character—the fact that she is not wholly bad adding to the value of her role.

The mutually devoted housemaid, Ethel, and Cook are among the characters who most surely make one laugh aloud.

"Cook was short and thin and pale, with yellowish hair and lashes, no discernible brows, prominent, pale blue eyes, a

* *Review of English Literature*, October, 1962.
† *Elizabeth Bowen*, The British Council and National Book League, 1952.

violently receding mouth and chin, and a large, bare oval forehead. Ethel was tall and dark and upright, and had an imposing presence in her professional garb.

"No one knew Ethel's surname, or knew for certain that Cook had any names."

In one of the two families that people the stage there is a young boy who, like Aubrey in *A Family and a Fortune*, is a weakling. Reuben again is portrayed with sympathy and given a special perception, a kind of fool's wisdom.

The young children, the eleven-year-old Julius and his sister Dora, a year younger, are remarkable inventions, showing the author's knowledge of childhood's half-play-acting, half-believing religious rites, which Julius and Dora themselves describe as "hidden and sacred orgies".

The plot chiefly concerns death and tampering with wills, which lawyers say happens more often than one would expect. The dialogue continues in its accustomed form and there is a great deal of it. One is struck by the great number of "Oh"s and "Well"s with which speeches begin, not only in this novel, and with the infrequency of abbreviations such as "can't" and "didn't". These idiosyncrasies contribute to the tune, to the fugal quality of Ivy's dialogue.

"Oh, it was only words, words, words," Anna justifiably exclaims at one point, but Ivy could when she wished write dramatically without using dialogue. Take the passage describing the exchange of wills. Anna's dying Aunt Sukey has just asked her to destroy the scroll of the second will she has made, she now believes mistakenly, in her niece's favour. After this she has requested Anna to read her to sleep.

"Anna read until the sleep was sound, and then closed the book and rose to go, taking the scroll from the table. It seemed as if Sukey knew what she did, for her face settled into youth and calm. Anna looked at her and looked again; stood as if she hardly knew where she was; approached her and touched her hand and face; made a movement to the desk, and drew back and glanced round the room, as if to make sure she was alone. Then she went to the desk and sat down, with her hands lightly playing on its board; and without breaking the movement, unlocked the drawer and exchanged the scrolls and closed it; and sat with the older scroll in her hands and her eyes gazing before her, as it might be in the vacancy of shock. Then she locked the drawer and left the room, carrying the scroll openly in her hand, and with her rapid hurrying step sounding as usual. She seemed prepared to encounter anyone and give an account of what she did. She walked to the gate in the same manner, glancing about in readiness to exchange a greeting, but when she was out of sight, quickened her pace and walked swiftly to her home.

"The drawing-room at that hour was deserted, and she took the will to the fire and burned it, showing neither furtiveness nor haste. Her aunt had given her directions, and she was fulfilling them. Her word was ready for anyone who asked for it. When it was done and she found herself still alone, she disposed of the ashes and sat down with a book. She still maintained her natural air; she might have been acting to herself; Anna remembered that walls have ears and eyes."

A page from a highbrow thriller.

CHAPTER VIII

A Conversation

IN THE LATTER months of 1944 Rosamond Lehmann, Edwin
Muir, Denys Kilham Roberts and Cecil Day Lewis completed
their plan to produce *Orion, A Miscellany*, a literary periodical,
their aim being:

"To publish good writing, creative and critical, in prose and
verse. It is attached to no group or movement. If it has a bias,
it is towards the 'written' and away from the improvised,
towards the imaginative and away from the reportage."

They invited a distinguished list of writers to contribute to
the first number, including Walter de la Mare, Rose Macaulay,
Edith Sitwell, Stephen Spender, William Plomer, John Lehmann
and John Piper. There were also passages from the diaries and
notebooks of Franz Kafka. It was Rosamond Lehmann who
thought that it would be a "scoop" to have something by I.
Compton-Burnett in the first issue of *Orion*, and with the warm
agreement of her colleagues wrote to ask Ivy for a contribution.
She replied that she did not think that she could manage this
herself, but that she would try to work out something with
Margaret Jourdain. Before long a manuscript arrived from
Dorset, and in 1945 appeared in *Orion*. In *A Conversation*, some
of which follows (by kind permission of Denys Kilham Roberts,
Rosamund Lehmann and the late Cecil Day Lewis), Ivy for the
first time briefly expressed her attitude towards her writing and
its critics.*

* *A Conversation* appears in full in *The Art of Ivy Compton-Burnett* by Charles
Burkhart. Gollancz, 1972.

A CONVERSATION

M. J.: We are both what our country landladies call "great readers", and have often talked over other people's books during this long quarter of a century between two wars, but never *your* books

I. C-B.: It seems an omission, as I am sure we have talked of yours. So let us remedy it.

M. J.: I see that yours are a novel thing in fiction, and unlike the work of other novelists. I see that they are conversation pieces, stepping into the bounds of drama, that narrative and exposition are drastically reduced, that there is less scenery than in the early days of the English drama, when a placard informed the audience that the scene was "a wood near Athens", and less description than in many stage directions. There is nothing to catch the eye in this "country of the blind". All your books, from *Pastors and Masters* to the present-day *Elders and Betters*, are quite unlike what Virginia Woolf called the "heavy upholstered novel".

I. C-B.: I do not see why exposition and description are a necessary part of a novel. They are not of a play, and both deal with imaginary human beings and their lives. I have been told that I ought to write plays, but cannot see myself making the transition. I read plays with especial pleasure, and in reading novels I am disappointed if a scene is carried through in the voice of the author rather than the voices of the characters. I think that I simply follow my natural bent. But I hardly think that "country of the blind" is quite the right description of my scene.

M. J.: I should like to ask you one or two questions; partly my own and partly what several friends have asked. There is time enough and to spare in Lyme Regis, which is a town well-known to novelists. Jane Austen was here, and Miss Mitford.

I. C-B.: And now we are here, though our presence does not seem to be equally felt. No notice marks our lodging. And we also differ from Jane Austen and Miss Mitford in being birds of passage, fleeing from the bombs. I have a feeling that they would both have fled, and felt it proper to do so, and wish that we could feel it equally proper.

M. J.: I have heard your dialogue criticised as "highly artificial" or stylised. One reviewer, I remember, said that it was impossible to "conceive of any human being giving tongue to every emotion, foible and reason with the precision, clarity and wit possessed by all Miss Compton-Burnett's characters, be they parlourmaids, children, parents or spinster aunts". It seems odd to object to precision, clarity and wit, and the same objection would lie against the dialogue of Congreve and Sheridan.

I. C-B.: I think that my writing does not seem to me as "stylised" as it apparently is, though I do not attempt to make my characters use the words of actual life. I cannot tell you why I write as I do as I do not know. I have even tried not to do it, but find myself falling back into my own way. It seems to me that the servants in my books talk quite differently from the educated people, and the children from the adults, but the difference may remain in my own mind and not be conveyed to the reader. I think people's style, like the way they speak and move, comes from themselves, and cannot be explained. . . .

M. J.: The word "stylised", which according to the *New English Dictionary* means "conforming to the rules of a conventional style", has been used in reviewing your books, but the dialogue is often very close to real speech, and not "artificial" or "stylised". It is, however, sometimes interrupted by formal speech. . . .

I. C-B.: I cannot tell why my people talk sometimes according to conventional style, and sometimes in the manner of real speech, if this is the case. It is simply the result of an effort to give the impression I want to give . . .

M. J.: Reviewers lean to comparisons. Some have suggested a likeness between your work and Jane Austen's. Mr Edwin Muir, however, thinks it is "much nearer the Elizabethan drama of horror"—I can't think why.

I. C-B.: I should not have thought that authors often recognised influences . . . But I have read Jane Austen so much, and with such enjoyment and admiration, that I may have absorbed things from her unconsciously. I do not think myself that my books have any real likeness to hers. I think that there is possibly some likeness between our minds. . . .

M. J.: Mr Muir in an earlier review says that you remind him of Congreve—a formidable list, Congreve, Jane Austen, Henry James and the Elizabethan dramatists—and the odd thing is that they are all disparate.

I. C-B.: The only explanation I can give, is that people who practise the same art are likely to have some characteristics in common. . . .

M. J.: I see one point of contact between your novels and Jane Austen's. She keeps her eye fixed upon the small circle of country gentlefolk who seem to have little to do but pay calls, take walks, talk, and dine, in fact—the comfortable classes. . . .

I. C-B.: I feel that I do not know the people outside my own world well enough to deal with them. I have no idea that my characters did nothing but call, walk, talk and dine, though I am glad you do not say that they only talk. Their professions and occupations are indicated, but I am concerned with their personal lives; and following them into their professional world would lead to the alternations between two spheres, that I think is a mistake in books. . . .

M. J.: I don't see any influence of the "Elizabethan drama of horror", nor much of Jane Austen. I think there is something of Henry James. What about the suggestion that the Russian novelists affected you—not Tolstoy of course, but Tchekov or Dostoievsky? Dostoievsky's method, "a mad jumble that flings things down in a heap", isn't yours. And how about the Greek dramatists?

I. C-B.: I am not a great reader of Henry James, though I have seen it suggested that I am his disciple. . . . I enjoy him less than many other writers. He does not reveal as much as I should like of the relations of his characters with each other. And I am surprised if my style is as intricate as his. I should have thought it was only rather condensed. If it is, I sympathise with the people who cannot read my books. The Russian novels I read with a sense of being in a daze, of seeing their action take place in a sort of half-light, as though there was an obscurity between my mind and theirs, and only part of the meaning conveyed to a Russian came through to me. I always wonder if people, who think they see the whole meaning, have any conception of it. So I am probably hardly influenced by the Russians. . . . The Greek dramatists I read as a girl, as I was classically educated, and read them with the attention to each line necessitated by the state of my scholarship; and it is difficult to say how much soaked in, but I should think very likely something. I have not read them for many years—another result of the state of my scholarship.

[Some readers have found Ivy's use of στιχομυθια, dialogue on alternate lines answering back, proof of the Greek influence.]

M. J.: There is little attention given to external things and almost no descriptive writing in your novels, and that is a breach with tradition. Even Jane Austen has an aside about the "worth" of Lyme, Charmouth and Pinhay, "with its green chasms between romantic rocks". And there is much more description in later novels, such as Thomas Hardy's. In *The Return of the Native* the great Egdon Heath has to be reckoned with as a protagonist. Now you cut out all this. . . .

I. C-B.: I should have thought that my actual characters were described enough to help people to imagine them. However detailed such description is, I am sure that everyone forms his own conceptions, that are different from everyone else's, including the author's. As regards such things as landscape and scenery, I never feel inclined to describe them; indeed I tend to miss such writing out, when I am reading, which may be a sign that I am not fitted for it. I make an exception of Thomas Hardy, but surely his presentation of natural features almost as characters puts him on a plane of his own, and almost carries the thing described into the human world. In the case of Jane Austen, I hurry through her words about Lyme and its surroundings in order to return to her people. . . .

M. J.: I see a reviewer says that *Elders and Betters*—which has the destruction of a will by one character [Anna Donne] who afterwards drives another to suicide—"has a milder and less criminal flavour than most of its predecessors". There is a high incidence of murder in some of your novels, which is really not common among the "comfortable classes". I remember, however, talking of the rarity of murders with a lawyer's daughter, who said that her father asserted that murders within their class were not so rare. He used to call them "Mayfair Murders".

I. C-B.: I never see why murder and perversion of justice are not normal subjects for a plot, or why they are particularly Elizabethan or Victorian, as some reviewers seem to think. But I think it is better for a novel to have a plot. Otherwise it has no shape, and incidents that have no part in a formal whole seem to have less significance. I always wish that Katherine Mansfield's *At the Bay* was cast in a formal mould. . . . A plot is like the bones of a person, not interesting like expression or signs of experience, but the support of the whole.

M. J.: *At the Bay* breaks off rather than comes to a full stop. A novel without a plot sags like a tent with a broken pole. Your last book had a very generous amount of review space. . . . How do you think reviews have affected you and your work?

I. C-B.: It is said that writers never read reviews, but in this case it is hard to see how the press-cutting agencies can flourish and increase their charges. I think that writers not only read reviews, but are subject to an urge to do so. George Henry Lewes is supposed to have hidden George Eliot's disparaging reviews, in case she should see them; and if he wished to prevent her doing so, I think it was a wise precaution. I think that reviews have a considerable effect upon writers. . . . I remember my first encouraging notices with gratitude to their authors. Much of the pleasure of making a book would go, if it held nothing to be shared by other people. I would write for a few dozen people; and it sometimes seems that I do so; but I would not write for no one. . . .

Letters from readers must come under the head of reviews, and have the advantage that their writers are under no compulsion to mention what they do not admire. I have only had one correspondent who broke this rule, and what he did not admire was the whole book. . . . Someone said that I must have liked this letter the most of all I had had, but I believe I liked it the least.

Some writers have so many letters that they find them a burden. They make me feel ashamed of having so few, and inclined to think that people should write to me more.

M. J.: In all your work you go back to the period between the South African war and the "Great" War, when time stood still. One novel [*A Family and a Fortune*] is dated 1901, and the others are all round the same date. England is still on the gold standard; the miser Clement Gaveston has a pile of sovereigns in his desk—carriages are horse-drawn, and there is an ample supply of servants.

I. C-B.: I do not feel that I have any real or organic knowledge of life later than about 1910. I should not write of later times with enough grasp or confidence. I think this is why many writers tend to write of the past. When an age is ended you see it as it is. And I have a dislike, which I cannot explain, of dealing with modern machinery and inventions. When war casts its shadow, I find that I recoil.

M. J.: Did you take any suggestions for the characters or plots in your novels from actual life; I mean from our own friends and acquaintances?

I. C-B.: I think that actual life supplies a writer with characters much less than is thought. Of course there must be a beginning to every conception, but so much change seems to take place in it at once, that almost anything comes to serve the purpose—a face of a stranger, a face in a portrait, almost a face in the fire. And people in life hardly seem to be definite enough to appear in print. They are not good or bad enough, or clever or stupid enough or comic or pitiful enough. . . .

As regards plots I find real life no help at all. Real life seems to have no plots. And as I think a plot desirable and almost necessary, I have this extra grudge against life. But I think there are signs that strange things happen, though they do not emerge. I believe it would go ill with many of us, if we were faced by a strong temptation, and I suspect that with some of us it does go ill.

M. J.: . . . Isolation and leisure seem necessary for the rearing of strange family growths.

I. C-B.: Isolation and leisure put nothing into people. But they give what is there full play. They allow it to grow according to itself, and this may be strongly in certain directions.

I am sure that the people who were middle-aged and elderly when I was young were more individualised than are now my own contemporaries. The effect of wider intercourse and self-adaptation seems to go below the surface, and the result is that the essence of people is controlled and modified. . . .

M. J.: I don't think you have the note-book habit, I mean the collection of unrelated notes of things seen and heard. Katherine Mansfield filled note-books with memoranda and worked these up into what she called vignettes, or into her stories. She also made notes of phrases and sentences for as she said, "one never knows when a little tag like that may come in useful to round off a paragraph". I like to know how people work.

I. C-B.: I daresay you do, but the people themselves are not always quite sure. I have not the note-book habit; that is, I do not watch or listen to strangers with a view to using the results. They do not do or say things that are any good. They are too indefinite and too much alike and are seldom living in anything but the surface of their lives. Think how rarely we should ourselves say or do anything that would throw light on our characters or experience. . . .

I cannot understand her [Katherine Mansfield] noting phrases and sentences for future use, and find it hard to believe that they served any purpose. Rounding off a paragraph, occurring in the normal course of writing by a tag overheard and stored up, seems to me too unnatural to be possible. She said that she never knew when such things would come in useful, and I suspect that she never found out.

M. J.: What is odd, but of course it isn't serious criticism, is the recoil of some reviewers from what they call "the sorry spectacle of adult human nature" presented in your novels, as if they were a board examining the degrees of moral turpitude among a group of immigrants. . . .

I. C-B.: I should have said that there were a good many good people in my books, and this may mean that I hardly see eye-to-eye with the reviewers. But I think that life makes great demand on people's characters, and gives them great opportunity to serve their own ends by the sacrifice of other people. Such ill-doing may meet with little retribution, may indeed be hardly recognised, and I cannot feel so surprised if people yield to it. I have been told that I treat evil-doing as if it were normal, and am not normally repelled by it, and this may be putting my own words in another form . . .

M. J.: Going back to the reviews . . ., it is only *adult* human nature that is criticised. This reminds me that in *Parents and Children* children play as large a part as parents. Is that not a change?

I. C-B.: Yes, it is a change, though one or two children have appeared in my other books. I think it may be the result of an instinct to do something different.

It is difficult to avoid apparent repetition, if books remain too much on the same line. The words "apparent repetition" are my own, and it may in effect be real repetition. However differently characters are conceived—and I have never conceived two in the same way—they tend to give a similar impression, if they are people of the same kind, produced by the same mind, and carried out by the same hand, and possibly one that is acquiring a habit.

And I do not think children have less interest than older people. I think their experience tends to be deeper and sharper, and even if more transitory—and I am not sure of this after very early years—to leave a deeper impression and memory. This seems to be borne out by the current phrases about the despair and ecstasy and observation of childhood.

But I do not claim that the children in my books, any more than their elders, resemble the actual creatures of real life. When I meet them, they are open to the same objection, and fail to afford me assistance.

And now I feel I know nothing more about myself, and hope the inquisition is at an end. And in spite of what I said about Katherine Mansfield, I am sorry that I have no tag stored up to round off the last paragraph.

*   *   *

A Conversation was broadcast in June 1950 while Ivy and Margaret were on holiday in the north in a "most pleasant hotel, though too expensive". Ivy wrote to Mrs Watson-Gandy:

"The bangs and bursts caused by the disturbance from the hills in Yorkshire rendered our hopes of hearing our own voices null and void. . . . One critic, favourable otherwise, complained that mine was too high and light, as though I had purposely ordered the wrong one."

Many friends, including Rose Macaulay, heard the broadcast clearly in London and commented on the great contrast between the two voices.

CHAPTER IX

Four o'Clock Tea

So, THE WAR over, Ivy's and Margaret's life at Cornwall Gardens began again with the gayest years that they were to have together. Margaret had a little more money now, in addition to what she earned, for she had recently been left an annuity with the unusual proviso that she should not try to discover the donor—and she never did.

The Saturday tea-parties, which were to become so famous, started now with gatherings of old friends and new. The successive house-keepers were starched and formal, and announced the guests by name at the drawing-room door. Woe to those who arrived even three minutes late for four o'clock tea. "They have gone in," such guests would be sternly informed and would creep shyly in to take their places under the blue dangles.

There was only space at the table for six guests, and these might include any of the old habitués such as Arthur Waley, the Thesigers, Soame Jenyns, Herman Schrijver, Basil Marsden-Smedley, usually without Hester (who saw Margaret and Ivy at other times), Cecil Gould of the National Gallery and Willy and Viva King. Ivo Pakenham remembers seeing Ivy and Margaret for the first time sitting stiffly side by side on a sofa in Mrs King's drawing-room in Thurloe Square, and he too soon became an habitué of Cornwall Gardens. Vere Pilkington of Sotheby's and his wife Honor were also frequent visitors—Ivy used to enjoy going to sales at Sotheby's with Margaret—and it was at a party of the Pilkingtons' that Lady Ashton (Madge Garland), who was to become one of Ivy's inner circle, first met her, as did the Vaughan-Morgans, now Lord and Lady Reigate.

Others of the new, in many cases younger, visitors to Cornwall Gardens also owed their introductions to the côterie to the Pilkingtons, and Theodora Benson, the novelist, was one of those brought by Madge Ashton. Herman Schrijver also brought Charles Burkhart, the Philadelphian scholar, to see Ivy. He had done a thesis on her when at Cornell and had also had an article about her published in the *Western Review*. Ivy was, he says, always very kind to him, but he "knew under the kindliness was the terrifying mind that produced the novels, and was frightened of her. Anyone should have been. She knew too much about us." Later he was to write an important book about her work.★

Ivy and Margaret now went to many parties, enjoying themselves greatly. They still dressed in those unchanging coats and skirts, and long dresses (Ivy's never anything but black). The practice that had come in with clothes-rationing of having their coats and skirts "turned" and made into dresses continued. They went on wearing their delicate Georgian and Victorian jewellery, and in winter they were both wrapped in Persian lamb coats from Bradley's.

And still they wrote. Margaret had not produced much during the war years, but she was now writing *Scottish Enterprise*, a new book about furniture, and also revising *Regency Furniture* (published earlier by Batsford) for an American publisher. Ivy, meanwhile, was at work on the brilliant *Manservant and Maidservant*, which is grim, poignant and deeply serious, and at the same time, as Charles Burkhart says, "has an élan that borders on hilarity". The American edition† is called *Bullivant and the Lambs*, and the book reaches its height in the portrait of Bullivant, the butler, and the unrealistic below-stairs conversation (the servants even comment on this themselves) which creates a preposterous reality of its own. The other characters, too, are superbly drawn. Once more there is a deep attraction between two men—the middle-aged Lamb cousins—and an intricate plot to be acted by the large cast, which includes servants and gentry, the fantastic woman who keeps a shop and guards the secret of

★ *I. Compton-Burnett*. Gollancz, 1965.
† Knopf, 1948.

her inability to read, and a whole string of children, once more ending with a tenderly conceived seven-year-old, beautifully exploiting his innocent wisdom.

It is often said that Compton-Burnett characters have no bodies and no physical contacts, just as it is widely assumed that there are no descriptions in her books. Both these observations are inaccurate, although caresses are more often between children and parents than between adults. They may not kiss, but mothers constantly fold their arms about their daughters, daughters bury their heads on their mothers' shoulders, and small children have an endearing way of leaning against their parents' knees or of taking their hands for affection or protection.

Manservant and Maidservant is studded with gems:

"'I wonder who began this greeting of people as fellow creatures,' said Charlotte. 'It is never a success'."

Or:

"'Is there something in Horace that twines itself about the heart? Perhaps it is being his own worst enemy. That seems to be thought an appealing attribute'."

It is also frequently said that the Compton-Burnett novels are all alike, but this too is a fallacy. It is true that her admirers often choose a volume at random to re-read, but this is rather in the same way that a listener chooses at random a record by a favourite composer. Unlike as the works may be, the unmistakable signature of their creator is on them. It is interesting to analyse the idiosyncracies that point her style, but each work is a new creation.

Many English writers contributed to the publisher's blurb for the American edition of *Manservant and Maidservant*. Among other tributes Elizabeth Taylor wrote that "her books are for ever and ever", Storm Jameson said: "Take her to your heart or hurry her out of the house . . . she is not to be ignored", Rosamond Lehmann opined that she was "probably the purest . . . of contemporary English artists" and Robert Liddell declared: "It does not seem too much, or nearly enough, to claim for her that of all English novelists now writing she is the greatest and most original artist."

In England *Manservant and Maidservant* sold best of all her novels, and it had an excellent reception in the States. The *New York Herald Tribune*★ declared that: "Miss Compton-Burnett is immensely unfair to most other contemporary British novelists.... Her apparently effortless skill shows them up. They seem to be breathing too hard by comparison."

And the *New Yorker*† added:

"Our English cousins across the sea have every reason to be proud of the writing talents of Ivy Compton-Burnett. Certainly the publication of her novel here will give cause for endless chuckles to those of us somewhat starved for original wit in our reading today. And to an even greater number Miss Compton-Burnett's conversation pieces will come as a refresher in an era of stale and laboured prose."

These American reviews gave great pleasure both to Ivy and to Margaret.

While Ivy was still at work on *Manservant and Maidservant*, Cicely Greig, a well-read young woman who taught English at an evening institute, wrote love stories and did a certain amount of typing—of, for instance, students' theses—wrote to Gollancz and asked if there were any chance of her being allowed to type the next book by I. Compton-Burnett. About ten years earlier she had read David Garnett's review of *A House and Its Head* in the *New Statesman*, in which he declared that for ages there had not been such a good English novel. Miss Greig had wondered at the time who *he*, the author, could be, and then had started to borrow all the Compton-Burnett books from Boots Library in Notting Hill and read them with growing admiration.

It was some time before Miss Greig had a reply to her enquiry, but on 27th March, 1947, to her great delight, she received a postcard saying:

★ Charles Poore, 13th June 1948.
† Richard McLaughlin, 19th June 1948.

"Can you type a novel for me without much delay? If so, I will leave the MS at your address in a few days."

So Ivy brought the package of exercise books to Cicely Greig in Holland Park.

"The script wasn't difficult to read,' Miss Greig says. "Although a lot was rubbed out and written over it was very clear. It took me about three weeks to type it with one carbon copy and then Ivy came to fetch it."

Ivy was delighted with Miss Greig's work and particularly by having the little manuscript books returned intact instead of "pulled to pieces by an agency".

The following summer she and Margaret went to Saint-Cast in Brittany, their first trip abroad since the war, to celebrate each of them having published a book.

Miss Greig was herself, during these and later years, trying her hand at writing novels, and Ivy warmly encouraged her. "I am glad you are *writing and not working*, as I find people put it!" she wrote to her on one occasion. Ivy was always loyal to the cause of novelists, and regretted that people wrote so many biographies instead. She thought one of the reasons for this was that novels were more difficult to read because they didn't just go straight on and didn't provide titbits of gossip. They needed more effort, but she found that unfortunately in these days it was seldom worth the making. She was sorry when novelists set their books in foreign countries or discussed public affairs, for she was unashamedly insular, and she liked novelists "to write about people not things".

"There is hardly a novel today that is a novel at all," she said. "I am tired of being disappointed."

Ivy enjoyed Graham Greene's books and he hers, and he was anxious that she should come to Eyre & Spottiswoode, of which firm he was at this time a director, and give them a chance to improve her sales. This led to crises and confusion, but Eyre & Spottiswoode did republish four of the earlier novels.

The next few years passed happily with the Cornwall Gardens circle becoming more closely knit, but while a number of its habitués made close friends with one another, there were some who never met at all. Ivy enjoyed discussing with her intimates which of her friends disliked each other; in fact she enjoyed slightly malicious gossip and a little unkind fun about her friends' religious beliefs. But when any of them were ill or in trouble she was kindness itself, sending them delicacies and telephoning to them constantly, although this was an instrument she disliked. Among these treasured post-war friends were Carol Rygate, who met Ivy through John Bordewich of The Central Chancery of Knighthood, who shared Margaret's interest in furniture, and James Brandreth, the son of their old friend Mrs Watson-Gandy, who lived at Buckland Newton, a fine old house in North Dorset which Margaret and Ivy both admired.

They also paid frequent visits to friends in other parts of the country, and now and then took a journey to France. Margaret went away from time to time by herself, usually to pursue some piece of work. Ivy used to complain of her constant flittings and of being left too much alone.

Changes of housekeeper happened frequently and always disturbed Ivy, who very much disliked having to adjust to a new personality in the house. One or two of the housekeepers in these days were by way of being "superior", and there was an end of aprons and of the names of guests announced at the drawing-room door. One of them came from the corset department of Barkers and left because she was offered a pensioner's residence, one returned to her native Ireland and used to send Ivy a five-shilling book of stamps every Christmas, and yet another gave notice because the ceilings were too high.

"Frightfulness has fallen on us," Ivy wrote to Mrs Watson-Gandy, "in the shape of the loss of our valuable Jayne, who is taking a long-wished-for chance of leaving 'sleeping-in service' and going out to work from a home of her own. She has found good quarters in a horrid coal-mining place called Pontefract, in Yorkshire, and I expect will be miserable . . .

"We have engaged an elderly superior woman for the simple reason that we could get her, as 'her lady' had died, and hope for the best."

Christmas was a time for festivity each year. A small tree was purchased and decorated by the ladies with much pleasure and care, one or two extra ornaments being bought each year in Kensington High Street. Ivy was delicate-fingered, whether engaged in such pursuits as this or bandaging somebody's cut finger. It was Margaret, however, who spent much time wrapping up little presents, for Ivy was not by nature such a giver as her friend. Before the war the Marsden-Smedleys had always dined with them on Christmas Eve, and on the day itself Margaret and Ivy supped in Tedworth Square, and greatly enjoyed eating cold plum pudding. Now this custom was occasionally revived.

Shopping in the Gloucester Road became again for Ivy a daily adventure, although for a while she lost Ernest Thesiger, her favourite shopping companion, who went to play Jaques in *As You Like It*. When he returned "successful and in funds", Ivy commented that he looked "absolutely worn out. What a bad thing work is!"

Ivy and Margaret used also to make shopping and other expeditions together. A friend remembers how on one occasion they were met leaving Kensington Gardens with their arms full of twigs and small branches. When asked what they were doing, Ivy replied: "We often go faggotting".

The fare at Braemar Mansions was good, but a careful economy was maintained both in the market and in the kitchen. "It's wrong to waste," Ivy observed, adding with a twinkle, "but what's worse it's vulgar." She may have had a snobbish side, but she was caustic about any such trait in other people. She despised ostentation. She referred to seeing one woman of their acquaintance "outspread in all her magnificence".

During 1948 Ivy wrote another novel about schools which differs greatly from the two earlier ones—*Pastors and Masters* and *More Women than Men*—although the settings are similar. *Two Worlds and their Ways* has no melodramatic plot and no tyrant worthy of the name—Lesbia Firebrace being "more irritating than awful". Nor is the plot melodramatic; there are no crimes beyond veiled bastardy, the theft of an earring and children's peccadillos, but the book is full of complex relationships and packed with small surprises. It is a remarkable work, compassionate and funny, the result of wonderfully concentrated perception. How the commonplaces of speech are ventilated!

"'There is only one thing for us to say, and so, of course, it goes without saying,' said Lesbia.

'It is fortunate that things that go without saying are such harmless things,' said Juliet. 'If they were not, we should live in danger, as they always seem to be said.'"

"'. . . But I have the grace to feel ashamed.'

'Why do you call it grace?' said Oliver. 'Things that are mixed up with shame ought to have some other name, and really have it.'"

"'. . . And I shall soon have a change of work, and that is known to be a rest.'

'It is a good thing it is known,' said Juliet. 'Or how should we find it out?'"

"'Something normal is going to happen to me today,' said Oliver.

'Do not normal things usually happen?' said Maria.

'Surely you have noticed they do not.'"

The two worlds of the novel are those of home and of school, and there are two schools, a large establishment for girls and a small one for little boys. At each of these schools a small sister and brother cheat, in order to do well and fulfil their parents' ambitions. The differences in the nature of the schools and of their staffs and pupils are clearly shown, and one wonders how the author can have come by so much knowledge. There is also once again one of those whimsical young men, who might well be described by that otherwise tiresome epithet "queer", for whom their creator had a special sympathy and affection.

The book was duly typed by Miss Greig and brought out by

Gollancz in 1949. The reviews were respectful, although it was clear that the book was found difficult. Both Elizabeth Jenkins and C. P. Snow* spoke of the great demands made by the author on her reader, and this is certainly one of the novels needing extreme concentration, but amply rewarding it. After a short respite Ivy started on her twelfth novel, *Darkness and Day*. In 1950, to her great satisfaction, she was made a Fellow of the Royal Society of Literature.

In the late forties Margaret developed a persistent bronchial cough. "A smoker's cough without smoking", she used to complain, and not only did she find this ailment very trying but it was an annoyance too to Ivy, and she did not always succeed in hiding her irritation. Margaret paid frequent visits to doctors, but none of the remedies they prescribed had any effect. It was a bitterly cold winter, fuel was short and there were frequent power cuts. Hester brought one of the oil stoves which had been at Hartley Court to the flat, and Margaret would sit huddled over this. By the end of 1950 her breathing had become difficult and she had X-rays taken of her heart and throat.

Margaret's ill-health did not prevent her from working or continuing to share a social life with Ivy, whose circle of admiring young writers continued to grow. At the end of February 1951 Pamela Hansford Johnson, then preparing her Ivy Compton-Burnett pamphlet, went to tea at Cornwall Gardens, arriving late and therefore having, in her own words, "a rather terrifying time". The following day the friends went to an hotel in Worthing in the hope that the sea air would do Margaret good. This experiment failed, and early in March they returned to London.

On 13th March Margaret went into a nursing home in Knaresborough Place. Ivy found visiting her rather difficult, as there were many stairs and she did not like the long narrow lift, designed, she opined, for coffins. After five days Margaret returned to Cornwall Gardens, and on Easter Tuesday noted in her diary "end of fortnight bedridden". She was, however, only to be briefly on her feet again, for on 3rd April she became desperately ill and was moved to Charing Cross Hospital. Ivy, who had only realised

* Lord Snow.

the seriousness of Margaret's condition during the last weeks, was now in an agony of anxiety. Fortunately their close friend, Helen Rolleston, was staying in the flat and was with Ivy when, on 5th April 1951, news came of the death of Margaret Jourdain.

CHAPTER X

Audacity of Analysis

HELEN ROLLESTON STAYED on for a while at Cornwall Gardens, but although Ivy was glad to have her, for, as she put it, "Helen knew what to do," she also said that she was "horrible" to her, because she could not forgive her for not being Margaret. Nor could she forgive herself for ever having been impatient with the latter—she really suffered from remorse—but most of all she could not forgive Margaret for having left her. This was a recurrent theme over the years.

During the first days after Margaret's death her godson Luke Marsden-Smedley drove his father Basil and his sister Henrietta, to Cornwall Gardens to see Ivy. They found her very quiet, and the young ones sat with her in silence while Basil went alone into Margaret's bedroom, which Ivy refused to enter, and after a long time emerged with the will. A day or two later the Marsden-Smedleys went to the well-attended cremation service at Golders Green, but Ivy stayed at home. By the terms of her will, except for a family legacy, Margaret Jourdain left her estate and royalties to Ivy for her lifetime and after her death to Luke Marsden-Smedley, Basil being appointed both executor and trustee.

Ten days after Margaret died *Darkness and Day* was published, there now being more darkness than day in the author's life and also in this book. It contains no tyrant and no crime, but there are tortuous mysteries of parentage—"Was it strange", as one character remarks, "if confusion arose?" There is also a brilliant sketch of two outrageously wilful little girls. Ivy admired rebellious children. Once when shown a drawing of

E

an obviously naughty little girl she observed with approval, "*She* didn't put her pudding down the lavatory. *She* said, 'I won't!'." Ivy told a friend how she herself as a small child, in the brief absence from table of the governess, had flown to the lavatory and disposed of a plateful of "spotted dog" which she had been ordered to finish up. On the governess's return she found Ivy sitting with a demure expression in front of a pudding-smeared plate.

Darkness and Day was welcomed by Ivy's growing army of fans. Raymond Mortimer wrote in the *Sunday Times*:*

"I can boast that I was one of Miss Compton-Burnett's earliest admirers. Though almost all my friends who are writers came quickly to share my enthusiasm, her reputation has taken a long while to expand. It seems somehow characteristic that *Darkness and Day* should be got up to look more like a school text-book than the thirteenth novel of a pre-eminent author. Yet a great many readers have now acquired a taste for her peculiar flavour, and four of her previous works have been reissued in pleasing attire by Eyre & Spottiswoode.

"She is in the first place 'a writer's writer', because she is fascinated by words and phrases as such, juggling with them like a logician; and because no novelist has been less concerned to seem plausible. What we usually look for in novels, and what the great novelists have usually given us, is a picture of human beings talking and acting in a way we recognise as 'like life'. We are ready to accept fantasy and caricature, but Miss Compton-Burnett challenges us with creatures that might inhabit another, colder and more intellectual planet. . . .

"Indeed, the writers of whom she most reminds me are not novelists: they are Sophocles and Plato. Though often she makes me laugh aloud, she must be read with the same un-hurrying vigilance as those pithy, formidable Ancients. . . .

"To prophesy that these novels will resist the tooth of Time would be foolish, because our civilisation seems to be drifting helplessly, like the Roman West fifteen hundred years

* 15th April 1951.

ago, into dark ages of unlettered rudeness. I maintain only that no living writer has produced works more conspicuously endowed with the quality that has hitherto made literature immortal."

The weeks passed and Ivy was desolate. Writing to Miss Greig, she spoke of "my great trouble—the greatest I could have had". And in a letter a few weeks later to Dr Pasmore, who had written to congratulate her on the C.B.E. which she had received in the Birthday Honours that year, and to tell her that he had seen some-body reading one of her books in a public vehicle, she wrote:

"Thank you very much for your letter and congratulation. I don't wonder that you missed the name in the papers. I never wade through the lists myself.

"I am glad you saw an authentic reader. I never have too many. Thank you again, I am trying to get over the shock and strain of Margaret Jourdain's death. It is the loss itself that I cannot get over, and I find it hard to look forward."

Even in girlhood days Ivy never wanted to live by herself, and the time after the break-up of the Hove home, until she joined with Dorothy Beresford, had been miserable. Ivy was not practical about such things as arriving at some destination at a given time, and apart from her grief she was panic-stricken at the thought of living alone in the big Braemar Mansions flat. Nor did she want to move out of it, so the solution seemed to be to find a companion. As a result of advice from friends she launched a number of enquiries, besides writing to Dame Janet Vaughan, then Principal of Somerville College.

"June 11th, 1951.

"Dear Madam,

"I hope you will forgive my broaching a personal matter.

"I have lately lost a friend who had lived with me for many years, and I now have accommodation in my flat for another woman, and should like to meet one who would like to live at a moderate cost in London, and who would up to a point share my life and interests.

"I am myself in the sixties, and am a novelist, in so far as I have a profession; and I thought the arrangement might perhaps suit some don who is retiring, and does not want living expenses on a large scale. I would make the expense about £3. 10. 0. a week, for anyone who would like to take the life in my flat as it is.

"Yours sincerely,
"Ivy Compton-Burnett.

"My own friends are settled in homes of their own."

On June 20th she wrote again:

"Dear Dr. Vaughan,

"I feel I must write a word to thank you for the kindness of your letter.

"I am afraid I have made the mistake of solving my problem along too many lines, and have become rather involved at the moment. But I hope I may write . . . later, if my way is clear.

"And thank you so very much.

"Yours sincerely and gratefully,
"Ivy Compton-Burnett."

The plan of sharing her flat did not succeed, although she had one candidate to stay for a few weeks. Ivo Pakenham, who lived at Braemar Mansions for a fortnight about this time, while he was moving, recalls Ivy saying to him: "After so long it is difficult to settle with a lesser companion".

So now, in her solitude, Ivy became ever more dependent on the visits of her friends. The old ones were there, of course, among them the Kidds, Arthur Waley, the Marsden-Smedleys, Herman Schrijver, but a group of younger writers also gathered about her now, among whom were Kay Dick, Kathleen Farrell and Olivia Manning. Ivy enjoyed their company and admired Olivia Manning's craftsmanship as a novelist.

After receiving an honorary degree at the University of Leeds, 19th May 1960. With the Princess Royal, Chancellor of the University (*Photo Yorkshire Post*)

Tea in the sixties (*Photo The Guardian*)

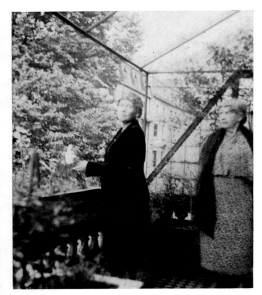

Ivy Compton-Burnett with
Margaret Jourdain on the balcony
at Cornwall Gardens

"I first saw Ivy at a party given by Rose Macaulay in the base-ment of a Soho restaurant," Olivia Manning recalls. "The place was packed to the doors. I was very young, nervous and unimportant. Everyone else seemed a celebrity. Ivy was there with Margaret—they stood together, observing and, it seemed to me, talking to no one. They looked severe and unapproachable. As a pair they gave me the impression of close self-sufficiency."

But when a few years later, after Margaret Jourdain's death, Kay Dick, in spite of Olivia Manning's diffidence, introduced her to Ivy, she found her charming.

"She seemed to be totally different from the Ivy I had seen at Rose's party. Our friendship began that afternoon and per-sisted until her death.

"I once asked Ivy if she still missed Margaret and she said 'I miss her more with every day that passes.'"

Another admirer to become a close friend, who first met Ivy at Rose Macaulay's, was R. Glynn Grylls (Lady Mander).

At about this time, too, Madge Ashton brought two new-comers into the circle, Dr George Furlong of the Dublin and London National Galleries and his friend Rex Britcher. They both used to bring plants for the balcony boxes and Rex Britcher regularly baked cakes for Ivy, which delighted her. Another welcome addition was Francis King, introduced by Olivia Man-ning and her husband R. D. Smith. Ivy appreciated Francis King's writing too, and was much entertained by his con-versation.

After Margaret Jourdain's death there were no more Christmas trees, and Ivy gave the ornaments to the children of the Hayward Hills, in whom she had always taken a great interest. He, the bookseller, had long been a friend of hers and Margaret's, and for some years now had helped Ivy to sell the manuscripts of her novels.

Changes of housekeeper continued to bother Ivy, but she was

teaching herself not to expect too much. "One mustn't mind," she used to say of some domestic short-coming. "One must take things as they are."

In 1952 came the first performance by the B.B.C. of a Compton-Burnett play. It had earlier been suggested to Christopher Sykes by Harman Grisewood, under whom Sykes was working in 1948 as Deputy Controller of the Third Programme, that he should choose one of her works for broadcasting. "I had read into some of her books but had never finished one," Christopher Sykes says, "nor did I succeed in doing so on this occasion. I found her obscure, wearisome, and utterly unlifelike, and could not imagine such material having any success on the air."

So the project was dropped, but a few years later, when Christopher Sykes was working in the Features Department of the B.B.C., Peter Mellors, who had already written about Ivy in 1961 in his little publication *Essays*, brought Sykes a draft he had made for a radio version of *A Family and a Fortune*.

"Mellors was then very young but I was impressed by his intelligence and his mastery of radio technique. I promised to put aside prejudice and study his draft. As soon as I did so, I saw how wrong and blind I had been. I hastened to read the original book, and any others by this author that I could get hold of. It was a Damascus Road conversion. In turn I converted the Third Programme which was now under John Morris.

"Peter Mellors was without any professional training and inevitably his draft had to be submitted to editing. Ivy was attached to Mellors and readily agreed to write additional narration for him. I thought a conference with her would be a wise move. So thus it was that I went to her flat and met the great lady for the first time. As was usual with her she had asked me to tea, the sort of substantial tea that was common in my Yorkshire childhood.

"Rather to my surprise I found her easy to get on with. All her friends will agree that she was a delightful conversationalist.

[In fact many visitors were disappointed by Ivy's conversation, which could be flat and banal. Some admirers of her books even refused to meet her for fear of being disillusioned by her talk.] There were, however, things she would not talk about. At our first meeting I all innocently made a gaffe. I could not resist saying how very much I admired *A Family and A Fortune* as a book. A look of almost panic, rather than embarrassment, passed across her face, and she could not help me out with her accustomed 'Yes, yes, yes'. . . .

"*A Family and a Fortune* on radio proved a great success, and we followed it quickly with an adaptation, also by Peter Mellors, of *Men and Wives*. Shortly after this he went to Canada, and I took over from him and adapted as many of Ivy's books as were amenable to radio treatment. Not all of them were. I remember saying once to her: 'I can make good radio out of any of your books provided that not more than two major characters are under the age of five'. She enjoyed this facetious criticism. She liked talking about writing provided that the talk was strictly confined to technicalities, and did not attempt to plumb the depths. In this she was very like T. S. Eliot. My wife and I brought them together and they got on very well, but anyone unaware of who the great poet and the great novelist were would never have guessed from their talk that either of them were remotely interested in literature.

"The more I knew Ivy the more I liked her. I found, again to my surprise, that she was without shyness, and was as easy with people she had never met before as with old acquaintances. She was not moody, and seemed to enjoy a serene temper. She was very conventional, though I was always surprised at the way she kept her handkerchief in the garter of her stocking and would pull up her skirt when she wanted to get at it. She had beautiful manners and expected them from others. Once I asked her to come to my studio during rehearsal so that I could introduce her to the actors and actresses. She came like a queen with Rosamond Lehmann as her lady in waiting. She had a gracious word for everyone except a leading actor who was coatless and had his sleeves rolled up. I could see that she did not like this, and with deadly politeness she showed it in her manner. . . ."

All these radio adaptations of Ivy's novels—the last was *Manservant and Maidservant* in 1957—were well received. Many people who found the books difficult to read greatly enjoyed the broadcasts.

In the autumn of 1952 Ivy received a long tribute from Sybille Bedford, who was then living in Rome. Ivy admired Mrs Bedford's writing and was pleased by her wide knowledge and acute perception of her own books.

To quote briefly from Mrs Bedford's letter:

"Throughout these years, reading and re-reading, I have been enchanted by their pruned and polished surfaces, astounded by their workmanship; the perfect, the beautiful joinery, the wit and precision of the talk that is at once conversation and communication, those multilogue compositions that unfold the characters and betray them all while they shape, carry and convey the action, and of which every stroke, every line is always the missing piece, always in character and always itself."

Mrs Bedford clearly saw Ivy's fundamental regard for truth and the way in which she constructed her plots to have the satisfaction of laying truth bare.

"Whenever truth is out, it rights a balance, removes spokes from wheels, restores a pattern and leaves a basis to go forward on. The point is that it should be out, no matter for how long or to how many, and this is the beauty and the subtlety of it. . . .

"I have talked of your audacity of analysis of human conduct under pressure. It has led to a feature in the novels, unique in modern literature, the treatment of murder with frankness."

Not surprisingly, after she received this letter Ivy Compton-Burnett and Sybille Bedford became friends. They continued to read one another's books with great appreciation, and whenever Mrs Bedford was in London she visited Cornwall Gardens.

CHAPTER XI

The Fifties

In 1953, at Dr Pasmore's instigation, Ivy, who was greatly interested in the history of Kensington, became a founder member of the Kensington Society. Another event early in this year which she enjoyed was the marriage of Luke Marsden-Smedley to Marygold Lansdell. Ivy, in a sprightly mood, attended the engagement party in Tedworth Square, reminding Basil and Hester that she was representing Luke's godmother, Margaret Jourdain. Marygold being a Quaker, the couple were married at the Friends' Meeting House at Jordans in Buckinghamshire. Hester described the service minutely to Ivy, who was much interested, and reminisced a little about her mother's chapel-going in the old days at Hove.

In the spring of 1954 Ivy went with Madge Ashton to a festive party given by Mr and Mrs Ralph Edwards for the Oxford and Cambridge Boat Race in their beautiful house on Chiswick Mall. Ralph Edwards had been curator of the Woodwork Department at the Victoria and Albert Museum and co-author with Margaret Jourdain of *Georgian Cabinet-Makers*,* so Ivy knew him well, and many other friends were there too. Anthony and Lady Violet Powell remember seeing Ivy then for the first time. Shortly after her death he wrote:

"The setting was appropriate, because this fixture always peculiarly evokes in the mind a sense of the late nineteenth century, and the varsity men of that era, rather than the undergraduates and sporting events of today.

* Country Life, 1944.

"Miss Compton-Burnett herself was wearing a black tricorne for the Boat-Race. She was looking formidably severe. I think she was severe. She saw life in the relentless terms of Greek tragedy, its cruelties, ironies—above all its passions—played out against a background of triviality and ennui. Later we met on two or three occasions, but I never knew her well. . . . This was absurd in a way, because we shared a lot of literary likes and dislikes (she wrote to me of Emily Brontë: 'Posterity has paid its debt to her too generously, and with too little understanding'), and we might be said to have 'got on' together very well."

(Anthony Powell might also have mentioned that another of their shared opinions was the unusual one that E. M. Forster too is an overrated novelist.)

"No writer was ever so completely of her books, and her books of her," he went on, and spoke of "death being a subject never very far away in her books or, one may guess, in her imagination too. Nevertheless death, like everything else, is treated by her with a sense of proportion, an awareness that its threat is only for those who fear it. . . ." Ivy may not have "feared" death, but there is no doubt that she dreaded it for others and for herself. Anthony Powell then compared her with Harold Pinter:

"Mr Pinter certainly allows himself more down-to-earth language, but conveys much of the same ironic despair set against drearily humdrum circumstances."

"A final word I think she would like said. When, a long time ago, I spoke of some novel by 'I. Compton-Burnétt' to the late Roger Hinks—no less astringent as a wit and mimic than in the famed region of his Elgin Marbles spring-cleaning—he replied, in a tone of quiet reduction to ponder that, although still unmet, I knew must be Miss Compton-Burnett's own: 'Búrnett, we call it'."*

* Obituary in the *Spectator*, 6th September 1969.

As a matter of fact Ivy was not feeling severe on this occasion in 1954; she was enjoying not so much the boat race as the company and the swans, and she was fascinated by the unusually high tide which washed right across the road. Her hosts remember with amusement how she peered inside the sandwiches to see what each kind contained.

The following year Helen Rolleston suggested that she and Ivy should spend Christmas together at Broome Park near Canterbury, where Christmas was always a time of discreet festivity. This seventeenth-century house, one of the most beautiful examples of Carolingian brick-work, set in peaceful acres of garden and parkland, had been bought by Lord Kitchener in 1908. He lived in one of the pretty lodges in the grounds while carrying out extensive and somewhat portentous alterations to the house, which he intended as a family home. When in 1914 he became Earl Kitchener of Khartoum, he took Viscount Broome as a secondary title. The present Earl Kitchener of Khartoum and Broome is his great-nephew.

In the late thirties the property was bought by Mr and Mrs Dennis Jell, who re-opened it after the war as a residential hotel. It houses a fine collection of furniture and pictures, and contrives to retain the atmosphere of a great country house. The place at once appealed to Ivy; Pauline Jell is a painter and a great reader, and she and Ivy quickly became friends. Ivy and Helen Rolleston both took an interest in the Jells' young son, Jimmy, who was also a painter. They had a great deal of amusement together, the first hilarity Ivy had shared in since Margaret's death. When a few years later Jimmy Jell tragically died, Ivy's sorrow and compassion with his parents was sincere. Once again memories were wakened of her own brother's early death.

The first book Ivy wrote after Margaret Jourdain died was *The Present and the Past*. This is a slighter novel than its predecessor, although the cast is very large. As Charles Burkhart says, "Always the most economical of writers, Miss Compton-Burnett has become parsimonious."

The irony is very sharp: the master of the house has two wives—one divorced—who become bosom friends, and his own pretence of suicide as a lesson to his family is followed quickly by his real death. One of Ivy's loved "queers" appears again, living with his sister: "It was clear that their relation went deep and would last for their lives." This recalls one of Ivy's characteristic observations, lightly thrown out: "I suppose incest went out when buses came in."

The brother and sister indulge in a pretty wit.

"'I do enjoy this personal talk,' said Elton. 'I know I ought to be ashamed, but creditable pleasure is so hard.'"

The highlight of *The Present and the Past*, however, is once more provided by its children. How amazing Ivy's perception of them is, and how compassionate her understanding of the young. She had always taken a great interest in the children she knew, and was concerned about their welfare. Her cousin Katie remembers how in the old Hove days, when a little guest sat hunched over her books at her studies, Ivy made her sit up and told her to "get rid of that hump".

And of some lines about a little girl in the earlier novel *Parents and Children* Robert Liddell says:

"This is one of the many passages in Miss Compton-Burnett's books that anyone who is about to become a parent, a grand-parent, a step-parent, an uncle or aunt, a tutor or governess, ought to read and take humbly to heart. And no diploma in education ought to be given except after a course in which she is a compulsory set author."

The Present and the Past opens with Henry, "a tall, solid boy of eight, with . . . something vulnerable about him", making his usual sad remark: "'Oh dear, oh dear!'" This time it was about the persecution of a sick hen, but it might as well have been about some human misfortune. His three-year-old brother, Toby, arouses tender mirth with every line. And the scene of the burial service for a mole conducted by Toby and his brother and sister, with the gardener and the nursemaid as congregation, is inimitable.

"'O dear people, we are gathered together. Dearly beloved brethren. Let us pray. Ashes and Ashes. Dust and Dust. This our brother. Poor little mole! Until he rise again. Prayers of the congregation. Amen.'"

This is in the same delightful vein as the Calderon children's worship of their gods Chung and Sung-Li in *Elders and Betters*, with rites depicting the strange superstitious beliefs of childhood.

On 15th February 1955 Mr Victor Gollancz, answering a letter from Ivy suggesting that her novels could be better advertised, wrote:

"Dear Miss Compton-Burnett,

"I need not say that I want to obtain the last possible sale: and our whole campaign (including the publication of Robert Liddell's book* on the same day as *Mother and Son*) is planned to this end. Press advertising takes its proper place in that plan. I really do understand advertising, as I am sure any literary agent or any other publisher would confirm.

"In the case of a book like yours, 'splash' advertising is not only useless (in the sense that it would not sell a single extra copy), but actually—in my experience—damaging, at the stage when there cannot be a single person who reads books at all who doesn't know that *Mother and Son* has been published, or what its quality is—it has had enormous splash reviewing, that no one could possibly miss, in the *Sunday Times*, the *Observer* and *The Times Literary Supplement*, as well as very prominent notices in such papers as *The Times*, the *News Chronicle*, etc., and many provincial papers.

"At that stage the very most that is wanted is a line reminder. It is later on that headline type is required.

"I take the opportunity of enclosing the script that has

* *The Novels of I. Compton-Burnett.*

just come in of Arthur Calder Marshall's broadcast last
Sunday.

"Yours very sincerely,
"V. Gollancz."

This broadcast by Arthur Calder Marshall* concerned Robert
Liddell's book and *Mother and Son*, and began:

"This afternoon I am going to talk about the strangest, the most
bewildering, the wittiest and in the opinion of Robert Liddell
the greatest living English novelist. Her name is Ivy Compton-
Burnett and her photograph by Cecil Beaton is to be seen as
the frontispiece of Robert Liddell's study of her novels. Her
hair, dark streaked with grey, is bound with a black riband in
an old-fashioned, not to say almost prim, way: and her face,
especially the forehead and the area surrounding the mouth, is
almost as wrinkled as that strange and curiously lovely face of
the late Algernon Blackwood; and like Blackwood's her eyes
are the most haunting feature; the eyes, I have heard it said, of
one who has looked through a keyhole and seen terror."

Mr Calder Marshall then quoted many passages from *Mother
and Son*, analysing the novel according to Liddell's categories,
"deliberately those of Greek tragedy, because, as he points out,
the great tragic themes of the Greeks are family tragedies".
He admitted that "once you are in the Ivy Compton-Burnett
world, you can detect the differences between her characters,"
but observed that the fact that every Compton-Burnett character
"is so much more like every other one than he is like anyone in
the world around us" made this detection difficult. However, he
assured his listeners that it was "worth a little trouble" to get
into the Compton-Burnett world.
The titles of Ivy's books do not help the reader to remember
which is which, and it is often a help to have a list of the characters
before one as one reads. *Mother and Son*, however, has a smaller
cast than many of its fellows, and its clear plot carries the reader

* *Talking of Books*, B.B.C. Home Service, 13th February 1955.

along with growing curiosity and suspense. "Nothing is wanting to the drama," as one of the characters so aptly says.

Margaret Jourdain had disliked dogs and Ivy disliked cats— she had been observed at Broome Park pushing a cat firmly away with the toe of her neat laced shoe (the only animals she really liked were horses). In *Mother and Son* there are, however, no less than two cats, and much space is devoted to them. Plautus is a dominating character, and the way he is treated demonstrates that his creator's extraordinary perceptiveness was not reserved for human beings, but was used too on the beasts for which she had no liking but which she permitted her characters to adore. And Plautus provides much fun. Asked by the new companion why he was thus named, his owners reply:

"'Oh, because he *is* Plautus. Because the essence of Plautus is in him . . .'
"'Who was Plautus in real life? . . .'
"'He was a Latin writer . . . I think he wrote plays; not very good ones.'
"'Why did you call the cat after him?'
"'Well he has not written any good plays either. . . .'"

Miranda, the old woman of this book, is one of the most wholly tyrannical of Ivy's creations, and although she dies half-way through the story her influence lives after her.

Mother and Son, to its author's great satisfaction, won a James Tait Black Memorial Prize. These prizes had been inaugurated in 1919 by the widow of Mr James Tait Black, a partner in the publishing firm of A. & C. Black Ltd. The prizes are awarded to the year's best biography or book of that nature and to the best work of fiction, the winners being chosen by the Regius Professor of Literature at Edinburgh University.

Ivy was in good company. Several of her friends had won the award in the past, including Arthur Waley for his translation of the Chinese novel *Monkey*, L. P. Hartley for *Eustace and Hilda* and Graham Greene for *The Heart of the Matter*. And to Ivy's special pleasure Rose Macaulay gained the prize the following year with *The Towers of Trebizond*. How generous Ivy always was about her friends' successes, and how truly she grieved for their misfortunes.

In 1956 Hester Marsden-Smedley went to the Congo. With her intimate knowledge of Belgium, she particularly wanted to study conditions there. Ivy was not in the least interested; Helen Rolleston remained almost the only friend who was permitted to talk about international affairs or foreign parts. Ivy really could not understand why anyone should want to make long journeys, and she deplored people going to live abroad.

In August of this year she received the following letter from the novelist Joyce Cary, which pleased her although she disapproved of his mode of address.

"Dear Ivy Compton-Burnett,

"I don't know if you saw some thoroughly comic letters in the paper about the literary giants in literature.

"My friend Miss Helen Gardner, probably the finest English scholar at Oxford, and one of the most brilliant women I know, was here yesterday and we were making our own list; we agreed warmly that you were among the three or four supreme women novelists of the country. Helen suggested that you were the best since Jane Austen. I put in a word for Emily Brontë and a slightly less confident one for George Eliot, but I perfectly agreed with Helen that you were among the real giants.

"I am writing this because I think it is so scandalous that you have not had the kind of appreciation you deserve."*

Two years later, in his book *Art and Reality*,† Joyce Cary wrote:

"I was once sitting at tea with that great artist and brilliant technician, Miss Compton-Burnett, and she said, 'Mr Cary, I

---

* Permission to quote this letter and the extract from *Art and Reality* kindly given by Mrs W. K. Davin.

† Cambridge University Press, 1958.

have been wondering when your novel is to be published, I saw it advertised at least a year ago, but it doesn't seem to be out yet.' I said that I had run into difficulties; the novel had indeed taken nearly three years. But I thought it was nearly finished because when I changed it for the better in one place, I found I had damaged it in some other. Miss Compton-Burnett answered me at once, 'I know exactly what you mean. It happens to me too. At a certain point my novels set. They set just as hard as that jam jar. And then I know they are finished.'"

Robert Liddell, whose *The Novels of I. Compton-Burnett* so admirably brought her work to a wider public, had been an admirer of her books ever since reading David Garnett's review of *A House and Its Head*;* he did not meet her, however, until 1940, when he had written an article about her books and went to call at Cornwall Gardens. Ivy was growing slender then, and she struck Liddell as small and retiring, compared with Margaret Jourdain, surrounded by her entourage of young men of the fine arts. He also had a slight impression of Miss Jourdain, who had for so long been the better known of the two, being a trifle jealous of her friend's growing fame.

He saw Ivy again a few years later when an article about her which he had written some years earlier, entitled "A brief Bibliography", appeared as an appendix to his book *A Treatise on the Novel.*†

In this article he pointed out what he was to stress in the later book, that: "Intensely humorous though she often is . . . her ironic view of family life is also serious, and even tragic." And he drew this interesting parallel:

"It is not surprising that the only successful, living writer of English verse tragedy should show signs of Miss Compton-Burnett's influence both on the situation and the dialogue of *The Family Reunion*—though its action is more diffuse and less tragic than the greater moments in her novels. Perhaps it is not entirely fanciful to see Mr. Eliot acknowledging this

---

* *New Statesman*, November, 1935.   † Jonathan Cape, 1947.

influence when he names one of his characters Ivy, and gives another an invitation to stay at 'Compton-Smith's place in Dorset.'"

In his next book, *Some Principles of Fiction*,* Robert Liddell continues to analyse Compton-Burnett and explains why she set her novels in the past.

"She is thus enabled to depict a world unshaken by modern warfare, a community rooted in a single place, and lives still ruled, and even laid waste, by family tyranny. She can do this, because she need only take a period fifty years ago, when she was herself already alive—therefore she can recreate this age without the artificiality and falsity of the historical novelist.

"Already this device causes some readers to make the mistake of dismissing her novels as 'Quaint'—but in time their date of publication may cease to be relevant, and they may come to seem novels of English life between 1888 and 1910, which might have been written at any time."

Mr Liddell has a most interesting view of characters by Henry James and Miss Compton-Burnett who "do not", he says "talk like other people".

"In their speeches, often long, and usually unrealistic, they show a subtlety quite foreign to the stage—for which Henry James proved unfit, and for which Miss Compton-Burnett has said she has no inclination."

He also says most truly that Ivy Compton-Burnett's novels:

"Abound in stage directions: if she makes her characters speak more than any other writer's, no other writer tells us more precisely how the people speak, or how they move when they speak."

And he gives the reader a fine list of such directions, "picked, more or less at random, from one only, of her novels".

* Jonathan Cape, 1953.

None the less, the Compton-Burnett novels that have been dramatised for radio or stage have been metamorphosised with little added to her dialogue. And Henry James's books are equally successful when made into dramas, operas or television plays.

When Liddell began *The Novels of I. Compton-Burnett* she urged him to stress the goodness of her characters. Even the tyrants must, she felt, have something good in them, because they were so intelligent. Stupidity was the one thing Ivy could not tolerate.

In 1956 she gained as a new adherent the brilliant French writer, Nathalie Sarraute, the exploiter if not the creator of *Tropisms*. In her article* Madame Sarraute congratulated "the English critics and a certain portion of the English reading-public" for according this writer, still little known in France, "her proper place: that is, of one of the greatest novelists that England has ever had".

This esteem of Madame Sarraute for the work of Ivy Compton-Burnett stemmed chiefly from finding that her dialogues lie "somewhere on the fluctuating frontier that separates conversation from subconversation"—the same frontier on which the French author had chosen to pioneer. Her concern had always been less with conversation than with subconversation, the things left unsaid while somebody is speaking.

By this time several of Ivy's novels had been translated into French, and Maurice Cranston enhanced her reputation in France with a comprehensive article in which he illuminatingly compares her work with that of Racine and Cézanne.†

There was a crescendo now in what Roger Hinks of the British Museum called the Braemar Gatherings. In 1957 Ivy gave a special tea-party for Lucille Iremonger, whose book, *The Ghosts of Versailles*,‡ about the Moberly/Jourdain adventure, had recently been published. It was an animated occasion. Mrs Iremonger was there with her husband Tom, the M.P., and the other guests

---

* *Conversation et sous-conversation*, Nouvelle Revue Française, January-February, 1956. This essay also appears in *Tropisms and the Age of Suspicion*, translated from the French by Maria Jolas, John Calder, 1963.

† *Les Lettres Nouvelles*, October, 1958.

‡ Faber & Faber, 1957.

were Rose Macaulay, Basil Marsden-Smedley, Cecil Gould, James Brandreth and Carol Rygate. Rose Macaulay at once asked Mrs Iremonger why she had "such an animus against the poor women", and the author denied, as she had already done in the preface to her book, having any personal feeling about the writers of *An Adventure*.

Ivy's name is in the long list of people to whom in her preface Lucille Iremonger expressed acknowledgements and thanks. None the less, although she had been sceptical about *An Adventure*, Ivy disapproved of Mrs Iremonger's book, which, although it does not mention Margaret by name, gives a disparaging impression of the Jourdain family in general.

There had recently been another strange happening in connection with *An Adventure*. In the second volume of his autobiography, *The Flowers of the Forest*,* David Garnett told the story of his close friend "Frankie" Birrell having fallen fast asleep, as was his habit when tired or bored, while dining with "two elderly spinsters". One of these ladies was, the author correctly stated, Margaret Jourdain, but he confused her with her elder sister Eleanor and thought that she was one of the authors of *An Adventure*, and that Ivy, the other hostess, was her collaborator Miss C. A. E. Moberly.

Elliott Felkin told David Garnett of his "appalling blunder" and Garnett wrote Ivy a letter of profound apology in which he also acknowledged her kindness in having forgiven Frankie, and took the opportunity of telling her that he, Garnett, was one of her "ardent admirers".

In 1957 Basil Marsden-Smedley became Mayor of Chelsea, an appointment which gave great pleasure to Basil himself, Hester, their children and their friends, especially Ivy. She loved the pomp and circumstance (the last words to be applied to the Marsden-Smedleys), and attended the Inauguration, the "Mayor-making", as she called it, in her perennial tricorne hat. She did not go to the evening parties as she said that she had not got "a real evening dress", but she liked the small tea-parties in the Mayor's Parlour. To one of these gatherings Basil invited

* Chatto and Windus, 1955.

Wordsworth's biographer, Mrs Mary Moorman, daughter of Dr G. M. Trevelyan, the historian, and the wife of the future Bishop of Ripon, and Ivy particularly enjoyed her conversation. She also liked hearing more about Hester's old home, Racedown. Mrs Moorman had stayed there several times while doing research for her book on the Wordsworths, and Lady Pinney had lent her the family papers.*

While he was Mayor—he was elected again the following year—Basil drove Ivy down to Royal Holloway College, her only visit since those student days half a century earlier, to meet his friend the Principal, Miss Edith Batho. To Miss Batho Ivy Compton-Burnett had been "a legendary student", until she had suddenly come to life by responding generously to an appeal for a College cause. On this occasion Ivy had observed that her student days "seemed to belong to another existence", although she always remained proud of her university education.

Miss Batho now met Miss Compton-Burnett for the first and only time, the encounter leaving her with "a clear impression of a shy, odd and likeable character". All three enjoyed this occasion, during which they walked round the College and the grounds and had tea, although, according to Miss Batho, "there was nothing more memorable about it than her [Ivy's] comment on a casual remark—'that is a very interesting statement'—which made the speaker wonder what sinister light had been thrown on her subconscious".

Ivy was in fact not shy—anyone so much interested in other people seldom is—but her reserve sometimes gave this impression.

This year Helen Rolleston and Ivy went to Broome Park together once more for Christmas, and Ivy continued to go there quite often, sometimes with Madge Ashton or with Carol Rygate but also alone, usually staying for about two weeks. When there by herself she seldom appeared in the public rooms except for meals, but spent her time in her own room or walking in the grounds. With friends she also enjoyed going for drives in the countryside or even to the sea by bus, and occasionally paying a visit. When, Mr Jell says, he had any conversation with her, it

* Mrs Moorman's description of Racedown appears on p. 61.

was always concerned with the running of the estate. She ques-
tioned him minutely about the cost of every aspect of Broome
Park. Pauline Jell's memories of Ivy's visits are very vivid.

"Sometimes," she writes, "one would find oneself walking
behind her along the main corridor, and would overhear a
lively dialogue as she was on her way to the bathroom, which
one could hear continuing in full spate through the closed
door. Occasionally this oral trying out would break into
ordinary conversation between us; she would slip in a sentence
that had nothing to do with what she was saying, but was
obviously something that had come to her in connection with
her current book—this without any change of voice or
expression. She would then resume the conversation as though
nothing had happened.

"She had a staggering power of concentration. She would
go on writing, without any feeling of irritation, while the
chambermaid made her bed and tidied up her room. She told
me that noise and interruptions didn't worry her at all.

"She invariably came back from her walks with a little posy
of wild flowers. One spring, just before a visit, the men who
cut the lawns got to work on the bank outside her bedroom
window. The cowslips which had just begun to appear were
ruthlessly mown down. Ivy cried out in real distress: 'What
have they done to Broome? They've shaved Broome! Where
are all my cowslips?'"

Ivy also used still to stay in Dorset with Mrs Watson-Gandy,
and another pleasure at this period was going to see Lady Ashton,
now living just north of Holland Park Avenue. I had also moved
to the same district. Ivy was very scathing with those who
deprecated these moves. "W.11 is just as nice as W.8," she would
announce, "and far less expensive". Madge Ashton's elegant house
had a beautiful garden, richly beflowered in spring and summer
time, and here Ivy loved to have tea and to do a plant-to-plant
inspection with her hostess. She visited Sissinghurst with Madge
Ashton too and sometimes with other friends, not only to enjoy

the gardens at every season of the year but also to see her friend
Vita Sackville West.

In spite of this full and enjoyable life, Ivy continued to miss
Margaret every hour of the day, and to include her in her living.
Once Lettice Cooper took a fellow novelist to tea with Ivy.
"They talked," she says, "not about novel writing—that was not
likely to be Ivy's way with anyone at a first meeting. I remember
a detailed discussion of their favourite wild flowers." Which *was*
likely.

"Then, as sympathy grew between them, they came to discuss
bereavement. The visitor, like Ivy, had lost some years ago her
greatest friend, a woman with whom she had probably had
the deepest and most valuable relationship of her life.

"'You know,' she said, 'when I am puzzled or in doubt
about something I often ask myself what my friend would
have thought about it.'

"'Oh,' Ivy said, 'I *talk* to mine still. I say "What do you
think? Do you like it? Would you advise me? What shall I
do?"'"

The novel which, in spite of Ivy's busy life, followed the
prize-winning *Mother and Son* only a year later is a harsh book.
Into it she put a great deal of her own knowledge of human
nature, which had grown steadily with the years as she continued
to sharpen her perceptions and intensify her observation. Sometimes she put some thought of her own, almost at random, it
seems, into the mouth of one of her characters, and they often
murmur to themselves as Ivy did. Sometimes she talked to herself
aloud when other people were present, even on occasion about
them. In these later novels characters do not so often listen at
doors as suddenly arrive at them either silently or with a remark
showing that they have overheard what was not meant for their
ears. This could never have happened at Cornwall Gardens, for
Ivy did not allow the large heavy doors to be left ajar.

There are some preposterous characters in *A Father and His
Fate*. Miles, the said father, round whom the plot revolves, with a

good deal of suspense to relieve a certain heaviness, is an intoler-
able creature.

"'I wonder if there is anyone in the world who cares for me'."
is typical of his utterances. "'I often ask myself that question....
Always some excuse to leave me high and dry, a forgotten hulk
on the strand! Well, I am learning to suffer it. I expect nothing.
I ask for nothing. I would accept nothing. I go my way alone.'"

Which does not prevent him, a man in his sixties, from stealing
his nephew's fiancée and attempting to marry her even when he
had discovered that his wife had not been, as was presumed,
drowned at sea.

This nephew's mother is another shocking character.

"'I grant her superhuman qualities,'" says a niece. "'Her self-
esteem and insistence on support for it are above the human
scale.'"

There is plenty of irony in this book, but little to make one
laugh aloud. When one opens the next novel it is, as *The Times
Literary Supplement* reviewer said, "like resuming a conversation
that had temporarily ceased but not ended", for here once more
are the same fundamental subjects and the same characteristic
manner of presenting them. *A Heritage and its History*, the last of
I. Compton-Burnett's books to appear in the fifties and the first
to take the stage a few years later as a play, has many of the
well-known ingredients—brothers who appear to live as a
devoted married couple, a man "whose look of complete resigna-
tion was the key to his character", and a couple of very small
children, once more tenderly and drolly drawn.

The tyrant this time is not a human being but the old house,
whose heritage dominates the characters. The building is never
described, although we learn of its largeness and of the creeper
"encroaching as old things do" and impregnating the house with
darkness, just as death permeates the thought and often the
speech of its inmates and lends darkness to the book itself.

Although Julian Mitchell made of it an excellent play, structur-
ally *A Heritage and Its History* is not one of the best Compton-
Burnett novels. It is short and crowded with a great many
characters, some insufficiently realised, and the considerable melodrama is condensed into the final chapters. To add to the difficulties of holding the plot in mind, there are large gaps in time—a
couple of decades between two chapters and at least five years
between two more, robbing the work of continuity, but needless
to say it is full of treasure for the discerning seeker.

The Times Literary Supplement, while commenting on the
"what seems deliberate obscurantism in her writing", goes on to
praise the author's increasing mastery both of speech and of
situation, and comments on her "realism, startling and almost
ruthless in its perception of the transience of individuality as well
as of life. Is it for that reason," the reviewer asks, "that Miss
Compton-Burnett always seems to be advocating that places are
more rewarding task-masters than people?"★

In October, 1958, Rose Macaulay suddenly died, which was a
great grief to Ivy. Over the years a strong friendship had grown
between them—they were both expert in friendships. They much
enjoyed one another's company and conversation, and Ivy was
the recipient of Rose Macaulay's private confidences. Their
intimacy continued and deepened, although Ivy could not
understand Rose's return to the Church, nor was Dame Rose one
of Ivy's most fervent admirers as a novelist.

"Ivy Compton-Burnett is a writer I don't think you would
care for," she had written to Father Hamilton Johnson in 1955.
"I find her entertaining and sometimes brilliant; but her novels
are certainly odd and often awkwardly written."†

Without any doubt Ivy missed Rose Macaulay sorely.

Before the end of the fifties a new worry beset her—the threat
of the Rent Act. Although staunchly Tory, she now complained
that the Conservatives (under Mr Macmillan) were treating

★ 18th September 1959.
† *Last Letters to a Friend*, Collins, 1962.

people with private means very unfairly. The rents of the Braemar Mansions flats were going up enormously, she told her friends, and her co-tenants seemed prepared to pay the increase. At one time she even believed that she would be turned out of Braemar Mansions and lamented "the dreadful scarcity of flats above two rooms". The misfortune did not occur, but the fear of it caused great anxiety. Always underestimating the amount of her private income, and shocked by the idea of touching her capital, she began to envisage an old age—she was now seventy-three, although this was admitted to no one—of growing hardship.

On 19th May 1960 Ivy was granted an Honorary Doctorate of Letters by the University of Leeds. This, as she had such a high regard for academic distinction, gave her special pleasure. She travelled up with Madge Ashton and enjoyed staying with her in a comfortable hotel. She received her degree from the Princess Royal, who was Chancellor of the University, and in the evening attended a grand dinner-party—one of the rare occasions on which she wore evening dress.

In September of this year John Preston of Bristol University sent her an article which he had written as "a sort of tribute". In his letter he said, "I hope you will acknowledge that you have permanently altered the skyline; you cannot be ignored and cannot avoid being praised".

Thus Ivy, although by no means all readers shared John Preston's view, entered the last decade of her life.

CHAPTER XII

The World is getting Empty

1961 OPENED WITH a further sorrow—the death in January of Ernest Thesiger. He had been a favourite companion of Ivy's ever since those days in the twenties when they began working at their embroidery together. In recent years, living as he did nearby with his wife, Margaret Jourdain's old friend Janette, he had spent much time in Cornwall Gardens, besides joining Ivy to enjoy their local shopping. For the last five years Janette had been gradually growing blind; until it was impossible for her to pay visits she had continued to go regularly to see Ivy, and later Ivy, while she was still able to go out, went to tea every few weeks with Janette. The latter was delighted when one of Ivy's novels was translated into Danish, as this was a language she knew. In fact many of Ivy's books had by this time been translated into the better-known European languages, and more exotic ones, including Jugoslav, Roumanian, Polish and Serbo-Croat, were soon to follow.

Ivy angrily mourned Ernest Thesiger's loss, as was her way when people she loved deserted her to live abroad or, still more unforgiveable, to die. She still liked to go to the theatre, often with Madge Ashton, but not so frequently as during Margaret's life-time. She did not know many theatre people, although another neighbour and friend of the Thesigers', Jean Cadell, had briefly become a member of her circle, but she too soon died. Ivy liked to talk about the plays she saw and to relate the dramatists' work to her own. She went to *Look Back in Anger*, but could not make out what the young man was angry about or why someone well-bred should behave in such an odd way—selling

Ivy in her last years (*Photo John Vere Brown*)

Chapter, 2.

"Osbert, you ought to know how to cut a ham."

"Then I do know, Grannie. I only dare to do what I ought."

"Do you expect other people to eat the fat ~~that~~ you have left?"

"Is it any good to expect it? Do you ~~think~~ they ~~would~~?"

"The fat of ham is quite different from other fat."

"That hardly seems worth while, when it all has the same end."

"You should cut the fat and lean together, and leave what you can't eat."

"I knew waste was not wicked. That is what I will do."

"What good do you suppose the fat is by itself?"

"No good. Or with anything else. What good could it be?"

"A young man should ~~be able to~~ eat whatever is provided. The fat of ham is quite a wholesome food."

"How do you know? What means is there of knowing?"

"I knew from my own ~~experience~~."

"Grannie, what words are ~~these~~ Pray ~~do not go~~ any further."

"Can't we forget the ham?" said Osbert's sister, "It ~~to the table~~. It dominates the sideboard, but it need hardly do ~~the same~~ to our lives."

A page from the final novel, *The Last and the First*

sweets on a street stall. She also went to several of Samuel Beckett's plays and to Pinter's *The Caretaker*, of which she approved, and to Sean O'Casey's *Cock-a-doodle Dandy*, of which she did not. She saw several of Ernest Thesiger's last plays—he continued to act until the end of his life—including *The Edwardians*, in which the costumes particularly interested her.

One or two writers had by now considered adapting some novel or other of Ivy's for the stage, and she hoped that this plan would soon be realised. Her new book *The Mighty and Their Fall* was already out by 1961. She was writing more quickly now. Her spacious flat continued to be empty save for herself and the current housekeeper, while the enormous houses of her imagination overflowed with people. In this one the young Middletons fairly flood the stage as the curtain rises, "breaking into mirth" as Compton-Burnett children so often do, unless they are breaking into tears.

Hugo, the adopted brother of the horrible Ninian, is another of Ivy's preposterous men. How she delighted in inventing the conversation of these characters!

"'You will see me as I am, I am always seen in that way. I have had to get used to it. I am grateful to you for trying to see me differently.'"

As in the last book, there is much talk of death. It was without doubt a subject much in Ivy's mind, and she lets her characters speak with unusual freedom about their own and one another's prospective deaths.

"'Why is it thought that death is what counts?'" says Selina, the aged lady who dies in the course of the story. "'Why is the end of life the meaning of it?'"

There is also much talk of religion or lack of it. Agnosticism, which Ivy had long taken for granted in herself and in many of her friends, had now become something of an obsession. She seemed forced to comment on it, but her lack of belief did not

prevent her from having close and enduring friendships with a
number of staunch Christians. With them religion was never
discussed, although she might mock them a little with certain
intimates who roused in her a spirit of mischief.

There is a mild chorus from below stairs in this novel which
voices the title theme: "How are the mighty fallen" (although
there is little evidence of this fall), and from above another chorus
of young children, though not Ivy's most memorable ones, with
a truly redoubtable governess. In between, the usual apparently
respectable gentry pursue their ways in a network of incest and
intrigue. As Ivy herself grew gentler the texture of her books
grew even harder and their criticism of human nature more
steely.

Wills are not only once more a central theme in the plot of
The Mighty and their Fall but were also constantly discussed,
although Ninian declares:

"'The subject of wills is never mentioned by people in our
sphere of life. No word is said of them until they are revealed.
It is a principle that should be observed.'"*

As one listens to the well-known conversations of these
characters, many speeches again starting "Well" in different
revealing tones of voice, one observes that Ivy's characters,
specially in her later books, are seldom still. In order that the
enormous amount of eavesdropping shall be achieved they are
constantly "approaching" or "entering", "turning" or "returning", and "another voice" often suddenly joins in the conversation. It is seldom that anyone sits still.

The Mighty and their Fall is not a long book and the action, as
so often, speeds up towards the end, holding the reader in suspense
as it races downhill. One sometimes feels with young Egbert:

"'If anything else happens I shall not be conscious of it. I can't
be alive to any more. But I hardly think anything can.'"

* Arriving for tea one day at my house Ivy informed other guests on the door-
step that she wished two of them to witness her will immediately. This was not,
as it turned out, her last will.

On 16th May 1962 Ivy had a conversation about books and writers on B.B.C. Television with the playwright and novelist John Bowen, in a programme called *Bookstand* devised and produced by Christopher Burstall. John Bowen found Ivy gracious, quiet and wonderfully witty. One of her memorable observations on this occasion was that there was not so much incest in her books as people thought. John Bowen also appeared with Ivy and Alan Pryce-Jones in an A.T.V. Television programme. This time the interview was filmed in Cornwall Gardens, which the interviewers had difficulty in finding. However, although they were late, they were graciously received and entertained to tea, and the occasion was much enjoyed by both the hostess and her guests.

In this same year Basil Marsden-Smedley went into St Stephen's Hospital for the treatment of a heart condition and found waiting for him, as a present from Ivy, a case of his favourite burgundy. He was not only touched but surprised—Ivy was not interested in wine, and he could not imagine how she knew that this was the right choice to make for him. During the next two years Basil returned five times to the hospital for further treatment, and each time a similar gift awaited him. His health steadily deteriorated, although he continued to work—he was much occupied with the amalgamation of Kensington and Chelsea— and also to attend Ivy's tea-parties. When early in September 1964 he died, Ivy was overcome with grief and anger. He had always rated very high among her friends, and he and Herman Schrijver had been her two closest companions and advisers since Margaret's death. Although she did not approve of such ceremonies she attended Basil's memorial service at St Luke's, the parish church of Chelsea, both a civic occasion and one attended by a great gathering of people from every walk of life.

In 1963 her very old friend Helen Rolleston had also died, and other deaths of those close to her were soon to follow. "The world is getting empty," she would often sadly observe during these last years.

After Basil Marsden-Smedley's death, his younger son Christopher (Luke being in Australia) reminded Ivy that his father had been the trustee for Margaret Jourdain's estate, which after Ivy's death would pass to Luke, and asked her if she would like some young lawyer or business man to take on the responsibility. Ivy said she would prefer Christopher to do this himself, and he agreed.

Ivy and Margaret had always shared a lively interest in the stock market, and used sometimes to talk of the clever young broker who used to help them with their investments, especially, Ivy said, in difficult times. Now she continued to study the market and to correspond with Christopher about Margaret's investments. Ivy's income from these and from the latter's royalties were not negligible. She always answered Christopher Marsden-Smedley's queries by return of post, usually with a card but occasionally with a letter giving her views. As for example:

"I am sorry there was the confusion over Shell and Burmah Oil, but as you say we should now leave the matter.

"I agree that we had better accept the advice of transferring Princess Foods and Settle Speakman to New Broken Hill and Liebig's Extract of Meat."

When *A God and his Gifts*,* the last of Ivy's novels to be published during her lifetime, appeared, *The Times* Special Correspondent† visited her, expecting to find "a remote mandarin figure in some ivory tower, weaving her intricate, formal patterns of prose far away from the mundane considerations of everyday life in the modern world." He found many surprises in store for him.

"Miss Compton-Burnett was amused when I confessed to my consternation faced with an initial misconception that the book was called *God and his Gifts*. She affirmed that she could not possibly have used such a title and added: 'I doubt if any English novelist now writing could; it would inevitably have

* Gollancz, 1963.
† *Speaking of Writing* 1. 21st November 1963.

to degenerate into a tract. Of course many of the novels now written are essentially something else: tracts, or travel books, or autobiographies. I suppose it is a desire to be frugal: if you have this material or thought or experience, it seems wasteful not to put it into use, and to put it all into a story seems the easiest way to do so. I often find such books interesting in part, but I believe I should find them more interesting if they were entirely factual. I like fact to be fact and fiction to be fiction; it disturbs me not to know where one ends and the other begins!"

This interview was one of the most illuminating Ivy gave. She analysed a number of current plays and novels, deploring, for instance, "symbolism added on top, like a layer of thick, hard icing on a cake. I always want to take a knife and cut it off." She voiced her dislike of novels "where people act on unexplained impulses to further the story, as in many Russian novels, or in *Wuthering Heights*", and added as she had said many times before, "Charlotte Brontë seems to me Emily's superior as a novelist".
Of her own work she said:

"I have never started a novel that I have been unable to finish but I have written novels that have changed out of all recognition in the writing . . . I notice that my books seem more different to me than they do to other people. . . . I do not think that my view of life has mellowed, as some critics say. There is, after all, very little in life today to induce mellowness."

A God and his Gifts is short and extraordinary and has a huge cast, augmented from time to time by Hereward, the god in question, who besides a gift for writing popular fiction has a gift for fathering children on his female connections. The plot is far-fetched, but from time to time, as always, Ivy speaks thoughts of her own made whimsical in the mouth of one of her creations. When, for instance, Hereward's father Sir Michael remarks, "Money is money, capital or not", his wife, Joanna, a most satisfying character, responds:

F

"'Is capital exactly money? If it was, it could be spent. It is a large amount, that brings in small ones without getting any less. And the small ones are spent; and their being so small leads people into debt. But it seems kind and clever of capital. We should not ask more.'

"'True, my lady,' said Galleon [the butler]. 'We must not kill the thing we love.'

"'Do I love capital? I suppose I do. It is dreadful to love money. I did not know I did. But capital is so kind to us. I am sure anyone would love it. . . .'"

And a little later she observes to her daughter,

"'Some money has fallen in. . . . We could pay what we owe, if the money was not capital. Or if capital was money, as your father thinks it is.'"

Ivy also allows herself a small dig at solicitors in Sir Michael's voice. Although she was on very good terms with her own, she could be scathing about the shortcomings of other people's.

There is one of her most captivating infants in this penultimate book. The three-year-old Henry is magical and he is given the last line of the novel, voicing his wish to marry the two-year-old "dear little Maud", who is in fact, clandestinely, his half-sister. As Charles Burkhart truly said when writing about *A God and his Gifts*, the last novel Ivy was ever to complete (although Mr Burkhart did not then know this): "All the old themes are here— incest, power, secrets, and so on—and here are seen with a final clarity, a clarity which has the ultimate compassion, of those who understand and do not judge."

In May, 1964, Julian Mitchell asked Ivy if he might make a dramatised version of *A Heritage and its History*. She replied:

"Thank you very much for your suggestion. Of course I should like the book to appear on the stage. But I see that there are troubles on the way. The presence of the young child for example, which could hardly be either coped with or dispensed with. The B.B.C. find the book unsuitable for adapting for broadcast.

"I am afraid of your giving time and effort to a project that might fall through. And I might be difficult about the necessary changes in the book; all authors tend to be.

"I am just going to the country for about three weeks. Perhaps we might talk about it on my return. But I admit my misgivings. . . ."

Later in the same month Ivy wrote to Julian Mitchell:

". . . I think that the books you mention have all been adapted for broadcast by Christopher Sykes, and he could possibly let you use his versions.

"I fear it is almost impossible to make a popular or reasonably popular play out of any book of mine without in a sense destroying it. . . ."

Julian Mitchell had in fact neither read nor seen any of Christopher Sykes's adaptations, and so proceeded on his own with his dramatisation. In July Ivy wrote to him:

". . . The play seems to me to go well. I found myself carried along by it. Every now and then the dialogue is a little obscure. Either my fault or the result of the compression. But I think nothing that matters. On papers 42b and 98 should it not be a thought stronger and more definite? I have pencilled the places. But I leave it and all else in your hands. . . ."

On the 4th September Julian Mitchell received another letter:

". . . Curtis Brown rang up to say that an actor—I think called Richardson—wanted to see me with a view to having a part in the new play; and I said I would be glad to see him presently. . . . And perhaps you would like at some time to meet the actor."

As Sir Ralph Richardson had long been one of I. Compton-Burnett's ardent admirers, it is sad that she did not recognise the compliment that he was paying her. These two distinguished artists never met, nor did he ever act in a play by her.

In May, 1964, the *New Statesman* invited competitors "to provide an extract from Miss Compton-Burnett's unwritten *A Prime Minister and His People*". The results of the ensuing attempts at parody were not very successful, but the occasion was welcomed by Ivy as a pleasant proof that she had acquired more readers.

The months rolled gently on in their accustomed way. Tea-parties abounded, as did visits to friends in the country. Although she did not see them often Ivy retained a strong family affection for her sisters and her cousin Katie. "She always seemed pleased when every few months I went to see her," Vera says, "although she never took the initiative. I think she lived as far as the family was concerned completely in the past."

In the spring of 1965 she was conscious of feeling unduly tired. In April Dr Pasmore, who had been her London doctor since 1950, when Miss Cicely Greig, who was one of his patients, had suggested that Ivy should go to him, attended her for a chill and "noticed the first signs of her heart beginning to fail". He instructed her to be careful about climbing stairs and in general not to over-exert herself. She used after this to speak quite often of "a little trouble with my heart".

When therefore Julian Mitchell's dramatisation of *A Heritage and Its History* was presented at the Oxford Playhouse in April, Ivy declined to be present at the first night, giving as the reason for her absence the difficulty of climbing steps. It was only on the prompting of a friend that, unaccustomed as she was to theatre ways, she sent the company a much appreciated telegram of good wishes. As a matter of fact, although she was excited at the prospect of her novel being put on the stage, she felt some trepidation at the thought of seeing it. When, however, in the following month the play transferred to the Phoenix Theatre in London, she agreed to attend a matinee.

"We opened a side-door to let her in direct to the circle,"
Julian Mitchell remembers. "I sat next to her in the front row.
She took a very great interest in the clothes, and scrutinised
them carefully through opera-glasses and commented about
them. She said very little about the play. After it tea was
arranged in a box and she met the cast. One of them said
afterwards it was like meeting Queen Mary."

In October of this year Ivy helped Hester to arrange a memorial
reading at the Poetry Society as a tribute to Hilda Doolittle, who
had died in 1963. Bryher flew over from Switzerland for this,
and Ivy's knowledge of the Imagists came as a surprise to her and
to others of those taking part in the programme.

On 29th November, starting to walk from the drawing-room
to answer the telephone in the hall, which she seldom did, Ivy
slipped on the mat which lay on the highly polished linoleum
behind the settee and fell. Fortunately the pain was not severe,
but she was unable to move until, after a considerable length
of time, her housekeeper came in. She helped Ivy into an armchair, which she then managed to push into the bedroom. When
Dr Pasmore arrived he found Ivy sitting on the edge of her
bed, unable to move her left leg. "No shock, little pain," he
recorded.

Portable X-rays were taken that night and showed a fracture
of the neck of the femur. Ivy did not want to go into hospital,
and as no bed was available in the private wing of University
College Hospital, where Dr Pasmore wished her to be, nurses
were engaged at the flat until 2nd December, when Ivy was
admitted to the hospital and underwent an operation. From this
she quickly recovered, and remained remarkably free from pain.
Her room was a bower of flowers and a store-house of fruit,
much of which she begged her visitors to carry away. She looked
very trim in bed, with two neat plaits of grey hair, secured with
rubber bands, instead of her usual style of hair rolled over a black
velvet band low on her forehead. The prototype for this well-
known coiffure is, according to Cecil Gould, the recumbent
fifth-century B.C. statue in the Louvre, Pythia Barberini.

Hospital, although she had numerous visitors, bored Ivy, but on the whole she was philosophic about it and even took a wry interest in the daily routine until Christmas time arrived. Then, in spite of her protests, she was put in a wheel-chair and taken to a room hung with decorations and dominated by a Christmas tree. Here she had to sit among other patients, many of whom she was convinced were as reluctant as herself, while doctors disguised in unseemly levity and the nurses in foolish hilarity attempted to entertain them. It was a dour lady who was eventually pushed back to her room to enjoy her privacy and the many Christmas presents from her friends.

Early in the new year Ivy was back in Braemar Mansions, walking with a pair of elbow crutches which she found very tiresome. She was also bored by visits from a physiotherapist ordered by Dr Pasmore. Sockets were now put in so that the telephone could be plugged in close at hand, both in the drawing-room and in Ivy's bedroom, but she still used the instrument as little as possible. About one thing she was adamant; she would not leave the flat. Offers from friends to convey her in the lift to their cars waiting outside the Mansions, to take her on visits or for drives, met with courteous but firm refusals. Even the desire to see the first spring flowers could not lure her out. Her garden was restricted now to the array of bowls and vases on the drawing-room floor, and the well-filled boxes on the balcony to which she soon managed to step from the kitchen. Certainly she could have ventured out with the help of some of her strong male friends, but she chose now to have an entirely enclosed life, though not a solitary one.

The circle gathered about her, although to Ivy's disapproval Hester chose this time to go on a journey round the world. Ivy's closest friends were more precious to her now than ever; they were urged not to wait for invitations but to drop in of a morning or an afternoon. "Come again soon, I'm always here," became her usual valediction, and when asked what quality she most prized in her friends she replied "availability". More than once during these last years she said that were it not for her friends she would commit suicide. If there happened to be a couple of days without a visitor she was certainly depressed, but she never complained about her physical difficulties. What she did complain about endlessly was the heavy cost of living, now augmented for her by the expenses of her accident.

Herman Schrijver, who was with her continuously and more than anyone brought her amusement, now gave her a small sum of money to ease her mind. At about the same time a novelist friend informed the Royal Literary Fund that Miss Compton-Burnett had had a bad year. She had sold all her manuscripts, the R.L.F. was told, and was drawing on her "slender resources". Her great anxiety was retarding her recovery.

With John Lehmann's support, the R.L.F. Committee made Ivy a grant of £500. She sent a letter of thanks, and three months later, obsessed like many elderly people with the thought of growing poverty endangering her way of living, wrote to John Lehmann again, asking for "a regular grant from the R.L.F., in order to meet the continued expenses of my accident". A more exhaustive enquiry was then made into Miss Compton-Burnett's affairs, as a result of which it transpired that she was possessed of more than adequate resources.

At the end of June 1966 came another grievous loss. In February, as the result of a car crashing into the one in which he was a passenger, Arthur Waley's spine was fractured. His visits to Ivy had been constant throughout the years. Brought first to Hove by her brother Noël, whose death had deeply grieved him, he was her very oldest friend. Now they were never to meet again. In the words of his widow, Alison Grant Waley, the old friend whom he married a month before he died, "he was fantastically courageous and his mind was at its most brilliant during these last months". "Every moment matters," he said and constantly proclaimed his happiness and his urge to go on writing.

After his death Mrs Waley went to see Ivy for the first time. She became a regular visitor and used to take her home-made refections which were greatly appreciated, as were the cakes and other delicacies regularly made for her by many friends, including Maud Radcliffe and Lettice Cooper. Michael and Anna Browne and their daughter, Maria, were also constant visitors, as too were Francis King, Ivo Pakenham, Julian Mitchell, Sonia Orwell, Kay Dick and Kathleen Farrell.

There was a new housekeeper now, an Irishwoman, a Roman Catholic, who had to be allowed plenty of time off on Sundays and other holy days to go to Mass and pay visits. Ivy gave up having her coal fire lighted on Sundays to make less work and contented herself with the two electric fires, which she used in any case to keep switched on close to her. She never had any kind of central heating and still liked a cold bedroom. Certain close friends such as Madge Ashton, Hester Marsden-Smedly, Carol Rygate or I took it in turns to prepare luncheon or tea.

At first, if Ivy were alone and someone rang the bell, she came slowly to the front door and opened it just a crack to see who it was, warning the caller to open the door gently in case she were knocked down. It was soon decided that this was an unsafe plan, and a key to the front door was left with the friendly Polish landlady, herself a doctor, who lived on the ground floor. Theodora Benson, another constant and much loved visitor, gave Ivy a large vacuum flask in the shape of a jug, so that tea could be made at any time of the day and yet be drunk as always punctually at four o'clock. Ivy decided that vacuum tea tasted very good, and henceforth pot and flask tea alternated. When one poured out for Ivy one had to fill her cup to the brim, otherwise she complained that she did not like it "half-full". Besides cakes and chocolates, gifts of new-laid eggs gave her much pleasure, and Lady Bonham-Carter—Charlotte—was one of the people who used to bring her these from the country.

At the beginning of January 1967 Ivy fell again and fractured the other hip, which caused her to spend a further six weeks in University College Hospital. Once again she made a good recovery from the accident, and when she returned to Braemar Mansions the old routine was resumed. As soon as she was able to walk she was provided with a light steel frame, a safer aid than crutch or stick, within which she was to walk deftly for the rest of her life. She used to refer without any self-pity to the days "before I became a cripple". Dr Pasmore still attended Ivy regularly to treat her chronic tendency to mild bronchitis, and her "mild congestive cardiac failure" was kept well in control with drugs. Her sight remained remarkable—she never wore glasses, although she liked to be very close to the screen on the few occasions when she watched television. Her hearing was good, too, when she wished it to be.

In the Birthday Honours of 1967 Ivy became a Dame Commander of the British Empire. This honour gave her great pleasure and, although she was not in the least vain, she felt quietly certain that she deserved it. For a long time now she had been unassertively aware that she was among the best of the English novelists of her time.

She refused to be taken to Buckingham Palace for the investiture and received the emissary from the Palace alone in her flat. The beauty of the insignia delighted her. She kept it in the dining-room and exhibited it with serene satisfaction to her friends.

"The dignity of Companion of Literature" conferred on her by the Royal Society of Literature in the following summer possibly gave Ivy even more pleasure than her D.B.E. Only ten Companions are allowed at any one time. Her fellow recipients were Dame Rebecca West, Sir Compton Mackenzie and Mr (now Sir) John Betjeman. The presentations were made by Lord Butler, President of the Society, which also pleased Ivy, as "Rab" was one of the few political figures in whom she was genuinely interested.

Again Ivy refused to be taken to receive her honour in person, but requested Dr George Furlong to do this for her. Lord Butler made the presentation to "Dame Ivy Compton-Burnett in honour of her great gifts as a writer and in gratitude for her most excellent contribution to English Letters".

Another of Ivy's pleasures in 1968 was watching with Julian Mitchell the production on television of his dramatisation of *A Heritage and its History*. She had never wanted to have television, although she had occasionally enjoyed watching some specially interesting programme, such as Princess Margaret's wedding, at the house of a friend. Later, however, she had felt obliged to acquire a television set for her housekeeper. This was originally installed in the latter's room, but after Ivy's second accident she had it moved to the drawing-room.

An annoyance at this period was the addition of two floors to the house in Cornwall Gardens opposite Braemar Mansions. The building faced the bedrooms and the kitchen and did not affect the drawing-room windows, but none the less the cutting off of some of her sky made Ivy very angry.

The year ended tragically with the sudden death of the writer Theodora Benson, one of the dearest of Ivy's later friends, in whose beauty and bright wit she had delighted.

CHAPTER XIII

The Last and the First

ON 5TH JUNE 1969 I went to see Ivy, carrying a bunch of flowers. As I got out of my car Herman Schrijver greeted me. He had a parcel in his hand.

"So you knew it was her birthday," he said.

I did not know. I had come by chance, while Herman, who did know, had been specially invited on the day.

This was the last birthday of Ivy's life—neither of us knew her age—and over tea we all three giggled at Herman's jokes. As Katie says, "Ivy and Herman were always killing together".

Shortly after this occasion Ivy was confined to bed with her usual bronchial trouble following a tiresome cold, and was greatly upset by believing that sometimes in the day and always at night she heard hostile foreign voices in her room. At the time she was convinced that this was not a delusion, although the housekeeper announced to Hester, whom Ivy summoned to her aid, "the Dame is wandering". But when after some days this confusion of mind cleared Ivy said firmly to Hester:

"You know I am a writer and have imagination. Perhaps some of the voices were in my imagination, but this did not make them hurt any the less."

The tea-parties were over now; Ivy preferred to see people singly or two at a time. Charles Burkhart, calling on her with Herman Schrijver, to whom he had dedicated his book about her work, was one of her last visitors. At about this time, looking at some prolific author's list, Ivy once more commented on how few books she herself had written. There are in fact twenty, if *Dolores* is included, which by her it was not.

With the arrival of catalogues announcing summer sales Ivy suddenly became interested in replenishing the household linen, her stock of fine Victorian linen from Hove having at last given out. Among other things she ordered several pairs of cotton sheets, choosing them with great deliberation.

Since that illness Ivy's friends had noticed a slight darkening of her days. She had always been so keenly aware of the seasons and the weather. Now she seemed indifferent to the lovely summer days, and although she could once more get out on the balcony in her frame, she no longer wished to do the "dead-heading" or to put into the boxes the little plants provided by her friends. When it was suggested that she might like to go out, she answered a trifle petulantly that she had not time. She seemed suddenly to have a troubling sense of the shortness of time.

And then her mood completely changed. Unexpectedly she received a cheque for several hundred pounds from American royalties on some of Margaret Jourdain's books. She immediately decided to buy a diamond brooch. From that moment she sparkled with excitement, and it transpired that she had always wanted "a proper diamond brooch with a blue flash".

Hester and I were with her for tea on one of those days in mid-July when the young man from a famous Bond Street shop came with a further selection of brooches for Ivy.

"He was charming," Hester remembers, "and he produced from his pocket, almost like a conjuror, diamond brooch after diamond brooch."

Ivy's eyes shone like the jewels as they were spread on the dining-room table. She quickly pushed aside any set with rose diamonds—to such gems she was completely indifferent—and another handsome piece was also rejected because it appeared incomplete, having once been part of a parure. Two or three brooches—two at least were already in Ivy's temporary keeping— she then pinned in turn high up on her dress, and held her old ivory-backed mirror up in her still beautiful hands to view the result with amused and critical interest. This was an unusual procedure, for Ivy did not often look at herself in the glass. Then she asked us for our opinion. The prettiest of the brooches was very spiky, and Hester begged her not to choose it.

"I knew she sometimes even pinned a brooch on to a little jacket she wore when she had to stay in bed," Hester explains, "and I hated to think of that little chin being scratched by even a blue flash diamond. But Ivy insisted and chose that very one, sending us out of the room like school children while she discussed the price. She loved that brooch, and as I had feared often wore it, even sometimes on her bed-jacket. At other times she kept it by her in a little handbag with a small pearl-studded watch and other treasures and brought it out to show her friends. Little did I think that this diamond brooch, against which I voted so strongly, would before long become mine."

Yet another death of a close friend, Rhienke Zouthart, saddened Ivy's last months. Even in her last days Ivy's tenderness for her friends persisted. Hester fell and injured a knee, and on 12th July Ivy wrote to her in a very shaky hand:

"Dearest Hester,
"The news is so bad that I have hardly faced it, and wish indeed that you could dispose of it in the same way. I fear it will not be a long, but a very long trouble, and I can't get to you and do what I can. But all my love and sympathy.
"Ivy."

Ten days later she sent Francis King one of the last letters of her life:

"July 22, 1969
"My dear Francis,
"You must be fearing I had left the earth; and its binding forces hardly increase. May I ask one question? Has this double

world the same significance as it would have here, or anything approaching it? Just *Yes* or *No*, and we will pass on.

"The book★ is the strongest you have done, and quality seems to break in everywhere, or perhaps rather to break out. You have great gifts, and the present misfortunes† will not alter its inevitable end. You may come to say you are glad it all happened. It is better to be drunk with loss and to beat the ground, than to let the deeper things gradually escape.

"Do come and see me when you can.

"Yours always with love,

"Ivy."

"Now that I re-read the letter," Francis King comments, "her question seems far more enigmatic than it did at the time, when I took it that she was speaking of what is usually meant by 'another world'. Perhaps it was not *about* another world that she was asking—or not what is usually meant by another world. . . . Those last two sentences are magnificent, I think—such beautiful prose and she could write like that because she herself had never 'let the deeper things gradually escape'".

In this letter Ivy wrote her own true epitaph.

During the morning of Wednesday, 29th August, Hester rang me up and told me that Ivy, who had been in bed again with bronchitis for several days, had died early that day. Dr Pasmore was away, but Dr Connolly had arranged for a night nurse to come, although Ivy was in fact alone when she died. The housekeeper had telephoned to Dr Connolly, Herman Schrijver, Hester and Alison Waley. Herman had come and had taken the certificate of death to the Registrar, and Alison had taken the jewellery and the insignia to the bank.

Hester had picked a handful of flowers from those well-known balcony boxes and laid them on the bed beside that small form.

★ *A Domestic Animal.*

† A threatened suit for libel, the withdrawal of the original edition and the subsequent financial loss. The book was republished in 1970 by Longmans.

Yes, how tiny Ivy looked! And how heartbreaking to think that we should never again hear her say, "Come again. I am always here."

Later that long day I was sitting alone in the cool quiet drawing-room. Ivy's armchair was standing just where she had always sat, with her back to the great windows with their pale blinds as ever half drawn. Under a cushion in the corner of the sofa nearest to her chair was the usual jumble of newspapers and chocolate boxes. I remembered how she used often to say after tea, "Will you have a chocolate?", and tell her guest which was the best of the current boxes. "Although chocolates are not what they were. Nothing is." And then she would often gently urge the rummager to be careful. "My little book is there. It has loose pieces and easily gets in a muddle."

From beneath the pile I drew out twelve shabby little exercise books, mutely apologising to the author for my temerity and at the same time blessing her for letting me know where she kept them as they could so easily have been thrown out as rubbish. It was five years since Ivy had begun to write this last unfinished, still untitled book. Miss Greig had several times begged to be allowed to type the script as far as it went, feeling that it would help the author to be able to read a clear copy of what she had written. Ivy, however, refused to have the script touched until it was finished, and warned Miss Greig that it would be "a terrible manuscript, so much crossed out".

Indeed whole pages were crossed out and many passages erased and written over, and the twelfth mutilated and often scarcely legible notebook was not numbered in the usual way but simply marked NEXT. Cicely Greig skilfully deciphered and typed the manuscript, and she and I and Charles Burkhart helped Livia Gollancz to prepare the book for the press, choosing the title *The Last and the First*,★ from its final words, "How the first can be last, and the last first", which she must have written at an earlier date, as the handwriting was well-formed and clear. I contributed a foreword, *A Book in the Making*, and Charles Burkhart wrote *A Critical Epilogue*.

★ Published February, 1971.

As Dolores, in Ivy's first novel, says to the ageing dramatist, Claverhouse, of his latest play:

"There is great good in it. . . . It is not like the work of your prime; but then it is not the work of your prime. It will have its own value for that."

All the familiar ingredients are here, including Eliza Heriot, a formidable tyrant.

"She wielded the power as she thought and meant, wisely and well, but had not escaped its influence. Autocratic by nature, she had become impossibly so, and had come to find criticism a duty, and even an outlet for energy that had no other."

Charles Burkhart, while agreeing that *The Last and the First* is not Ivy's greatest book, ends his epilogue:

"It needs no searching . . . to find the wit, still moral and sane and saving, in this twentieth and last novel; like expert swords, in formal exercise, glittering in the empty air."

That evening Ivy's face appeared on the television screen with the announcement of her death, and the obituary notices were many and distinguished, speaking of I. Compton-Burnett as the most original writer of her generation and one whose books would still be read and discussed a century hence if novels were still read at all.

In her will Ivy's lawyers, Mowll & Mowll, were appointed her executors and no literary executor was named. She left the copyrights and royalties of her published works to her cousin Anthony Compton-Burnett, who is also one of the six residuary legatees, and a large sum of money to her publishers for a new collected edition of her works. To various of her friends she left personal bequests in the form of mirrors, ornaments, jewellery and pieces of furniture which were minutely described in her will. The remaining chattels went to Hester Marsden-Smedley.

Kay Dick describes the events following Ivy's death so vividly that I cannot do better than to quote her.*

"The funeral was an incredibly macabre event, starting with the cremation service at Putney Vale cemetery. There was something unreal, in the Jamesian sense, about the various groupings of family and friends, as people hovered about uneasily, like uncertain ghosts, before shuffling into the chapel. . . ."

There was no outstanding figure, no one to receive the mourners, and a number of Ivy's closest friends met on this occasion for the first time. Her sisters were there but, knowing few people and fewer knowing them, kept in the background. Anthony Compton-Burnett, a schoolmaster at Eton, was there with his wife. He had been summoned to the flat recently by Ivy and was known to none of her friends, although Basil and Hester, both coming of cricketing families, had been told years before with pride by Ivy that she too had a cousin who was a fine cricketer.

"We were told that we were expected to foregather at Ivy's Kensington flat after the service," Kay Dick continues.

"By one of those remarkable yet ever-recurring coincidences, we all went through the front door of Ivy's flat at four sharp—but no gong boomed. Tea (weak as ever) and sherry (indifferent as ever) were served. I believe I held a cup of tea in one hand and a glass of sherry in the other, as did several other people. We were told that we were each to take away, that very day, after the tea and sherry, the article that Ivy had bequeathed to us, signing for it in front of Ivy's solicitor."

The reason for this was that the Cornwall Gardens lease would expire in two months' time, so the flat had to be completely cleared as soon as possible.

To return to Kay Dick:

* *Ivy and Stevie.*

"As people left Ivy's flat, lugging their loot down the stairs, I was reminded of the death scene in *Zorba the Greek*. I believe it was Julian Mitchell who wryly said, as he passed me on the stairs, that he felt 'like a criminal'. Indeed, this staggering finale was reducing us all to that level. Possibly the most bizarre touch of all, which really did convince me that Ivy had written the script, was the maidservant standing at the door, thanking each departing guest for coming and asking everyone to come again to tea. This upset some people; they viewed it as disrespect. I found it quite proper and in its place, and assured the maidservant (who was after all merely repeating a formality of Ivy's training) that indeed I would be happy to come again, knowing, of course, that, unhappily, never again would I be invited to tea by Ivy."

On Friday, 24th October, there was a "Commemorative Meeting" at Crosby Hall, this place being chosen as it is the centre for the British Federation of University Women, and Ivy never ceased to be proud of having graduated at Holloway College and also of having been given an Honorary Degree by the University of Leeds.

The meeting was well attended. As one of the oldest friends I had been asked to preside, and after a few preliminary words I called on Raymond Mortimer, the first distinguished reviewer to have recognised Ivy's quality, to be the first to pay her this final tribute from her friends and readers. He was followed by a number of other distinguished writers, speaking for themselves and for others unable to be present.

As *vale* let Margaret Jourdain give Ivy the last bunch of those wild flowers which were, in her own words, "my passion". They come from *An Outdoor Breviary*, written many years before the friends met.

"Beneath the hedge, the dead sorrel spires are dipped in rust, and the black fallen hawthorn leaves, the silver grass stalks bleached by sun and dew, are the background to the pushing up of young grass, and of plantain and primrose crowns, of heart-shaped leaves of the celandine, and trodden chickweed by the gatepost. A dandelion is half open by the roadside, and a pale-coloured half-open speedwell and a pinkish-lilac ragged robin are spreading under the shelter of some bronzed green bramble-leaves, while wild parsley lays its jewel-like green fronds here and there above the sallow grass, and the buff oak leaves that choke the ditch, and the grey-veined mat of ivy."

THE NOVELS OF I. COMPTON-BURNETT

Original publishers and dates of publication are given. As the present book goes to press (1973) all titles are in print. *Dolores* is published by Blackwood, Edinburgh, and all other titles by Gollancz, London. In addition Gollancz have issued a de luxe limited edition of the nineteen mature novels.

DOLORES, Blackwood, 1911.
PASTORS AND MASTERS, Heath Cranton, 1925.
BROTHERS AND SISTERS, Heath Cranton, 1929.
MEN AND WIVES, Heinemann, 1931.
MORE WOMEN THAN MEN, Heinemann, 1933.
A HOUSE AND ITS HEAD, Heinemann, 1935.
DAUGHTERS AND SONS, Gollancz, 1937.
A FAMILY AND A FORTUNE, Gollancz, 1939.
PARENTS AND CHILDREN, Gollancz, 1941.
ELDERS AND BETTERS, Gollancz, 1944
MANSERVANT AND MAIDSERVANT, Gollancz, 1947 (issued in the U.S.A. under the title BULLIVANT AND THE LAMBS)
TWO WORLDS AND THEIR WAYS, Gollancz, 1949.
DARKNESS AND DAY, Gollancz, 1950.
THE PRESENT AND THE PAST, Gollancz, 1953.
MOTHER AND SON, Gollancz, 1955.
A FATHER AND HIS FATE, Gollancz, 1957.
A HERITAGE AND ITS HISTORY, Gollancz, 1959. Dramatised version by Julian Mitchell, published 1966.
THE MIGHTY AND THEIR FALL, Gollancz, 1961.
A GOD AND HIS GIFTS, Gollancz, 1963.
THE LAST AND THE FIRST, Gollancz, 1971 (published posthumously)

INDEX

Index

MANNERS

GOOD MANNERS ARE NEVER PASSÉ.

—*Slim Aarons*

395

SIMON & SCHUSTER

NEW YORK   LONDON   TORONTO   SYDNEY

always gracious,
sometimes irreverent

MANNERS

BY

Kate Spade

edited by Ruth Peltason and Julia Leach

illustrations by Virginia Johnson

HAVE YOU EVER WONDERED...?

*For your birthday your sister gave you a bright yellow coat.
You adore her and would never want to hurt her feelings, but the yellow
makes your skin look sallow and the coat is a bit snug. Can you re-gift?*

Re-gifting is one of the most delicate etiquette topics. If
your sister will notice the coat's disappearance, then
hang it in your closet. If your sister lives 2,000 miles away,
consider giving the coat to a friend. First and foremost,
keep in mind the feelings of the original gift-giver.

*You're taking the red-eye from LA to New York, and the young man
sitting next to you has brought his own midnight snack. Orange peels
and half of a bologna sandwich remain on his tray well into
the in-flight movie. Do you have to grin and bear it?*

There is more than one use for the air sickness bag.
With a warm smile, gently gesture toward the tray and volunteer
to scoop up the orange peels. This direct, yet kind hint should catch
his attention and prompt quick disposal of the offending items.

*You're treating business clients to their favorite lunch at the
Grand Central Oyster Bar. One person lifts the shell and slurps
the oyster right into his mouth. Should you follow suit?*

Apparently, your colleague last enjoyed oysters
at a beachfront bar. Unless you're in a casual place,
oysters should be eaten with a shellfish fork.
And never, ever attempt to cut these delicate treats.

HAVE YOU EVER WONDERED . . . ?

Spending a weekend at a friend's country house can be completely relaxing. Often, however, one experiences mild pangs of angst. Your friend and her husband are sleeping in, yet you've been up since 7 AM and are craving a cup of coffee. Is it okay to brew a pot?

Consider your relationship with your hosts. If you've been coming to their home for years, then by all means make some coffee, but take care not to wake them. If you're visiting new friends, don't overstep your bounds in their home; instead, distract yourself with the morning paper.

You're hosting a festive dinner party and learn the afternoon of the gathering that your brother will be bringing his new girlfriend. She's wonderful, charming, and she's a vegan. How can you quickly prepare to meet her culinary needs?

Presumably at this late hour, the shrimp is marinating, and it's likely that salad, which should be appealing to your brother's girlfriend, is already on the menu. During cocktails, set out some fresh fruit; when dinner is ready, refresh the fruit plate and keep it on the table. Most importantly, make your vegan guest feel at ease and avoid referring to her dietary preferences.

For the past few months you have been working on a big project and have overlooked some personal matters, large and small. One of them is a letter you intended to send to your aunt, thanking her for the floral shirt she gave you at Christmas. Now that it's April, is it too late to send a note?

It's never too late to send a thank-you note. Your aunt, who may be disappointed by your lack of communication, will be glad to hear from you and know that all is well. In the future, keep a box of thank-you's handy (pre-stamped if your schedule is that frantic) and remember that the ten minutes it takes to express your thanks will be time well spent.

HAVE YOU EVER WONDERED...?

*A business colleague is hosting dinner for fifteen.
What can you give that would be most appreciated?*

Although wine is a customary hostess gift, it's likely that she's already selected a red and a white. Since flowers are always a crowd pleaser, this is a safe token. Arriving with them is always thoughtful; better still, send the flowers early the day of the gathering.

Traveling to Japan for the first time on business, you receive an invitation to a formal tea ceremony. What can you expect and how should you behave?

Simply prepare to eat, drink, and be (quietly) merry. The host has spent a great deal of time preparing the food, flowers, and scrolls, and as a guest your most important responsibility is to compliment her or him on each of these elements. Be sure to write a thank-you note within three days of the ceremony. This is known as *korei*, "thanking afterwards."

You're at your in-laws for Thanksgiving dinner and have been asked to set the table. They have twice as many forks than you usually use, as well as extra spoons. What are the basics of setting formal flatware?

If the plates will be on the table when guests are seated, place the napkin to the left of (not under) the first-course, main-course, and salad forks. Knives, with blades facing the plate, and the soupspoon are placed to the right of the plate. The dessert fork and spoon are placed above the plate, the spoon on top facing left, and the fork underneath with tines facing right.

H A V E   Y O U   E V E R   W O N D E R E D . . . ?

You're a bridesmaid in your brother's summer wedding in Nantucket. His fiancée has chosen dresses that are vaguely nautical, but your personal style is Comme des Garçons. Are you obliged to wear the dress during the reception?

With any luck, your brother will get married only once. So while boating insignia may not reflect your personal taste, in the spirit of the event wear the dress with a smile. Unless they've encouraged everyone in the party to change clothes, stay the course, enjoy the evening, and toast to the lovely couple's future.

At the end of a long evening, you're helping a close friend straighten up. While neatening the couch, you knock a vase off the console and it crashes to the floor. You know she brought it home from her honeymoon in Greece. What to do?

Some situations are inherently unpleasant, and this is one of them. It's incumbent on you to offer a sincere apology and understand that the broken vase may cause your friend considerable dismay. If the break was clean, gently insist on arranging to have a specialist handle the repair. If the vase shattered, don't get overly emotional—leave that to your friend. In either case, the next day follow up with a note of apology and a small bouquet.

You and a friend are enjoying happy hour when the bartender sets down a tequila sunrise from the man across the bar. Do you accept? Show interest? Whose move is it?

Protocol suggests that the ball is in your court. While you're not obligated to accept the cocktail, rejecting it sends a firm message. If you're interested in moving beyond significant eye contact, a subtle smile and lingering gaze should get him up off his barstool.

CONTENTS

THE WORLD IS ROUND, AND MANNERS AREN'T SQUARE

"Etiquette means behaving yourself a little better than is absolutely necessary."

—*Will Cuppy*

Yankee pride, Southern charm, California laissez-faire, Texan hospitality, and Midwestern manners—all are phrases we use to communicate a certain welcoming quality and friendly state-of-mind. When I meet people and tell them I'm from Kansas City, they assume I'm going to behave well and with kindness. It's a Midwestern "thing," they say, that down-home quality bred in the American heartland. In my opinion, as far as manners go, the true American heartland extends from coast to coast and points in between. Much of my work involves travel, and I have been fortunate to meet nice people all over the country.

So why a book about manners? And are we just preaching to the choir? My husband, Andy, and I believe that good manners are the essence of communication. For years we've had a tradition in our office that each new employee is welcomed with a copy of Emily Post's etiquette book. Consider Mrs. Post's words, wise when first written eighty years ago, and still meaningful today: "Charm cannot exist without good manners—meaning by this, not so much manners that precisely follow particular rules, as manners that have been made smooth and polished by the continuous practice of kind impulses." What a perfect definition of a caring and cultured society!

I've been inspired by Emily Post for years, as well as by many people in my own life who have in their unique way demonstrated the bounty that good etiquette brings. Now, in *Manners*, I've tried to cover topics that seem part of the way we live today—the overnight guest, cell phone behavior, even the etiquette of bicycling on city streets. Americans have long had a love affair with food and with dining out, and to that end I have included some of my observations on table manners, including those for children. (On the subject of manners at the table, I would like to add that you may feed your dog table scraps *as long as no guests are present*. That seems fair to me. And to my dog, Henry.) You'll find recommendations on tipping, both during the year and at holidays, and suggestions for being a good traveler, whether at home or abroad. For those of you who are globe-trotters, the international welcome mat should be respected. The key is learning the rules of being a goodwill ambassador wherever you go.

Of course, life isn't perfect—someone calls you by the wrong name, your wine spills, an invitation never arrives, or you're an hour early for cocktails or a week late for an appointment. It happens, and for every social disaster, gracious recovery is available. There are examples of things we've all experienced, which I hope will help you grapple with the occasional social stumbling block. But for all the specific advice in the world, I can say that nothing beats humor and graciousness as antidotes to nearly any social faux pas. The last section of *Manners* touches upon a miscellany of topics—lending books, double dipping, borrowing clothes from a friend, the night-owl neighbor, re-gifting, and money (an endless source of consternation).

My hope is that *Manners* helps to ensure what Emily Post called "the continuous practice of kind impulses." Life is a bowl of cherries—as long as you know what to do with the pits.

Kate Spade
New York City, 2003

SECTION ONE

Exercising Your Manners, 365 Days a Year

THE DAILY LIFE OF MANNERS

MODERN-DAY ETIQUETTE

10 GENTLE REMINDERS

Making others feel at ease is the essence
of etiquette, yesterday and today.

There are few words more elementary or
more welcomed than *please* and *thank you.*

Good moods are contagious.
Hopefully, yours will be pleasantly catching.

Be aware and considerate of personal
space—physical, visual, and aural.

Showing respect is a gift, one that costs
nothing and is endlessly appreciated.

Think of your tone of voice as a telegraph.
To the listener, it speaks volumes.

A short fuse does nothing but burn. Should
you find yourself with one, steer clear of others.

Never underestimate the message
that's sent by your poise and your posture.

Clothes count. Appropriate attire is
not only respectful, it's refreshing.

Let common sense be your guide
and graciousness your goal.

AT HOME, YOURS OR OTHERS

Hospitality is first learned at home, where *good morning* and *good night* are first expressed, and where the common experiences of everyday life are discussed. Being a team player and showing consideration of others are essential around family and close friends. Once you learn the ABCs of good behavior at home, you'll also become everyone's favorite guest.

THE 9-TO-5

The planet called "your office" is where you spend more time each week than anywhere else (except perhaps in your bed, sleeping). Doing your work well and being collegial are assets that will stay with you throughout your career, and in whatever field you pursue.

TABLE MANNERS

Which fork or how many glasses, and ways to navigate a forkful of peas are rudimentary lessons of being *à table* without calling attention to yourself. Table manners are a skill that once mastered last a lifetime, and will take you from the picnic table to White House receptions (should you be invited).

MANNERS ON THE MOVE

Plains, trains, and automobiles may take you from Point A to Point B, but bear in mind that you're often in the company of hundreds of strangers. The more you both "speak the same language," the smoother the ride.

DRESS ETIQUETTE

Nothing's wrong with your shirt tail out—if you're gardening. Showing an appreciation for time and place are reflected first in your appearance; it's often what leaves a lasting impression, as well. Personal grooming and style are your calling card wherever you go.

IN THE PUBLIC EYE

Do you hold the door for someone older? How generous should you be with holiday tips? These are questions often raised when considering manners at large. Of course popcorn and movies are ideal mates, but not everyone agrees, so best to chew quietly.

AT HOME, YOURS OR OTHERS

"If you were at my house, your comfort would matter most to me. So I'd try to think of ways to make you feel at ease, or do my best to anticipate what you might want."

BEFORE YOUR GUESTS ARRIVE...

A welcoming household takes work, and behind-the-scenes preparations will make your company feel relaxed.

Sweep the front walk and turn on the lights. Nothing suggests an inviting home more than the friendly glow from lights seen upon arriving.

Fluff the couch pillows, but don't overly "style" them—after all, your guest is in your home, not in a hotel lobby.

Have snacks prepared, as well as white and red wine, soda, and juice.

If it's wintertime, have logs on hand for a fire.

Set out fresh flowers. If house lights say "welcome," then flowers offer a warm smile.

A bathroom being shared with your company should be cleared of overly personal effects. Be sure to put out a fresh bar of soap and guest towels, and a scented candle.

If you have children, scoop up errant toys and games from public spaces.

And be ready before your company arrives. Nothing's more awkward for the guest than watching her host run around tidying up.

WHEN YOU WELCOMED YOUR GUESTS, THE SUN WAS SHINING...

Have umbrellas handy for any departing guests who would otherwise get soaked getting from your front door to their car or to a cab.

IDEALS TO ASPIRE TO...

"The ideal guest is an equally ideal hostess; the principle of both is the same: a ready smile, a quick sympathy, a happy outlook, [and] consideration for others...."

— Emily Post, *Etiquette*

"Basically, I think the kitchen is off-limits to guests. However, if one of my close friends who loves to cook wants to help, then I'm thrilled."

WHEN YOU'RE THE GUEST...

Don't stand on ceremony, and don't sit on the arms of chairs and couches, either—Be natural but not overly familiar.

Be a team player—Whether your hosts suggest watching *King Kong*, playing Scrabble, or sitting on the porch (even though it's chilly), be eager and accommodating.

Exercise restraint—Feet belong on the floor, not on the furniture; don't assume a bowl of fresh raspberries has only your name on it; and if your host doesn't sleep in, then neither should you.

Be prepared—If your hosts are tennis players or they're having friends in for cocktails, then plan ahead and bring the proper clothes.

Want to be invited back?—If you've stayed for the weekend and didn't arrive with a hostess gift, be sure to send a note and a small gift, ideally no more than two weeks after your visit.

"I always prefer to take care of cleaning up after everyone has gone home—sometimes even the next day. As a guest, I find it distracting to hear the *clinkety-clink* of dishes coming from the kitchen. Besides, there's no faster way to kill a party atmosphere than to start rounding up glasses and so forth. The point is for you and your guests to relax and enjoy yourselves."

"IT WAS A DELIGHTFUL VISIT—PERFECT, IN BEING MUCH TOO SHORT."
—JANE AUSTEN, *EMMA*

TABLE MANNERS

"I don't think that table manners are passé. Since everyone is in plain sight of everyone else, it's pretty obvious if you slurp your soup or hoard the bread basket. Does anyone enjoy being at a table with a loud mouth or messy eater?"

The dining table is intended for china, glassware, utensils, and linens. Key chains, lipstick, the mail, and children's toys are best placed elsewhere at mealtime.

"AS THE SHIPS SAIL OUT TO SEA, I SPOON MY SOUP AWAY FROM ME."

"Higher emotions are what separate us from the lower orders of life . . . higher emotions, and table manners."

—Deanna Troi,
from *Star Trek: The Next Generation*

COLOR THAT LASTS

There's a practical explanation for the word *lipstick* —the color actually does *stick*, so before a meal don't overdo it and leave behind a trail of red on your dinner napkin. If you want to touch up your lipstick after a meal, it's best to excuse yourself from the table. (But lip balm, used discreetly, is permissible at the table.)

BODY LANGUAGE

You might need to lean on your elbows if you're dining out and are seated at a small table in a crowded restaurant. But at home, where the table is ample and ambient sound is comfortable, avoid placing your elbows on the table. (And never hunch over and "hug" your plate.)

FINGER BOWLS

"I love when little finger bowls are used, especially after eating ribs or shellfish. I find that gives me a chance to clean up without having to excuse myself from the table. And it also saves extra wear on the napkins."

AND DON'T FORGET...

When serving food, be sure that all your guests are taken care of before serving yourself.

Food should always be passed to the right, or counterclockwise.

If the dinner conversation is running long and you're inclined to yawn, either quietly excuse yourself or be clever and camouflage your fatigue.

When you are asked to pass the salt, pass the pepper, too.

NEXT TIME YOU'RE AT THE WHITE HOUSE

When dining with the president of the United States, a guest can respectfully assume that decorum and style are established by him, and, as such, are to be adopted. One evening President Coolidge invited some friends to dinner at the White House. When it came time for coffee, the president poured his into a saucer. So did his guests. Then Coolidge added some cream and sugar. His guests did the same. Then Coolidge leaned over and gave the saucer to the family cat.

"THE REAL TEST OF PERFECT TABLE MANNERS IS NEVER TO OFFEND THE SENSIBILITIES OF OTHERS."
—EMILY POST, *ETIQUETTE*

UTENSILS

THE LANGUAGE OF FLATWARE

Of all the traditional guidelines for handling a fork, knife, and spoon, two are especially useful. If you pause during the meal, set your fork on the left side of your plate, with the tines down, and the knife on the right, with the sharp edge facing in. When you're done, set your knife and fork beside one another on the right side of your plate, fork tines facing up or down.

YES, YOU CAN CUT YOUR SALAD...

If you find that your chopsticks are becoming more like pickup sticks in your hands, don't be shy: ask for a fork.

The lingering resistance dates back to the time when knife blades were made of silver, which interacted with the vinegar in the dressing. Today, since most flatware is stainless steel, cutting your salad is a matter of personal preference.

NAPKINS

After being seated, wait until your host has joined the table and lifted his or her napkin, then place yours neatly on your lap.

When excusing yourself from the table between courses, place your napkin on your seat or the arm of your chair. (And leave the table napkin-free.)

If you have an especially large or oversize napkin, first fold it in half and then place it on your lap.

BEFORE YOU LEAVE THE TABLE

When you're done with the meal, simply rest your napkin to the left of the place setting. If the plates have already been cleared, then place it neatly on the table in front of you, but not as originally folded.

PORTIONS

Unless you've just bicycled fifty miles and are ravenous, start with moderate portions. You can always take seconds when they're offered, but when you do be sure to compliment the cook.

Leaving food on your plate is not a sign of good manners. But eating what you've served yourself is.

Take small portions of everything. Overcooked, undercooked, burnt, and zealously spiced are not good reasons to pass up a dish—unless, of course, you're allergic!

DRINKS

WHEN SERVING WINE...

QUANTITY—For a dinner party, estimate one bottle of wine for every two people. Even if you wind up with extra, it's better than not having enough.

WINEGLASSES—Set out glasses for each type of wine you plan to serve.

THE SEQUENCE—White before red, and dry before sweet is traditional.

HOLD THE GLASS JUST SO...

For room-temperature wines, hold wineglasses or goblets under the bowl. Chilled wines (whites and rosés) should be held by the stem of the glass. As for champagne, choose the base or the stem, depending on your glassware.

"Mrs. Givings, sitting tense as a coiled snake on the edge of the sofa, gently closed her eyes and wanted to die. Sherry in a highball glass!"

—Richard Yates, *Revolutionary Road*

FINGER FOODS

Hors d'oeuvres are one of the few foods that adults are encouraged to eat with their fingers. That said, there are pitfalls to avoid. In addition to certain hors d'oeuvres, there are more common foods that require a bit of dexterous handling, such as the proverbial "hot dog with everything" at the ball game.

CHERRY TOMATOES—This is a one-bite food, so choose your tomato wisely.

BUFFALO CHICKEN WINGS AND SPARERIBS—It's assumed that spicy wings and ribs are finger food, so enjoy yourself. But be sure to have a "bone bucket" on hand before digging in.

PIZZA—Even the common "slice" can be eaten with grace. Hold the pizza with your fingers and curl the sides so that the topping doesn't slide.

RADISHES AND CELERY—If garnishes are passed at dinner, spoon them onto your butter or cocktail plate. If the radishes aren't neatly trimmed and the celery still has its "feathers," make as discreet and tidy a pile as possible on the side of your plate.

SHRIMP—One dip and two bites are recommended. The tail should be disposed of as quickly as is convenient.

CORN ON THE COB—Whether you eat yours typewriter style (across) or around, the cleanest way to eat fresh corn is to salt and butter it as you go. On the other hand, if you're among close friends or family, you may not need to be as tidy—so long as you don't let familiarity breed poor manners.

DEVILED EGGS—This always delicious food is also always messy. No one expects you to eat this in one bite (unless you want beaver cheeks), so use a napkin and be as tidy as possible.

CAVIAR—Use the serving spoon to put some caviar on your plate, and your own knife or spoon to gently prepare your portion. Take care not to overload your cracker or toast point with the sieved chopped egg and caviar. Nothing is worse (and more wasteful) than little grains of expensive caviar falling onto the carpet.

ASPARAGUS—Although not traditionally considered a finger food, there are times when you can pick up the asparagus and eat a single stalk. It's easier to plate this vegetable and use a knife and fork.

FRENCH FRIES—No fork ever made French fries taste better. Use your fingers and enjoy yourself.

TROUBLE FOODS

Some foods can be described as "trouble foods" because they pose a problem: what do you do with leftover shells and bones? What's a discreet way to bite into a triple-decker club sandwich? And what about fruit pits and banana peels? Nothing is more awkward than trying to take a spoonful of French onion soup au gratin and winding up with a skein of cheese a foot long. (If it happens, twirl the cheese around your soupspoon.)

FRUITS, JUICY AND OTHERWISE—Fruits that are juicy are best peeled and eaten with a knife and fork. So-called dry fruits, such as apples and pears, may be sliced and eaten with your fingers. Peeling is optional.

DISTASTEFUL FOOD—Have courage and camouflage your displeasure. Have a sip of water or wine to help mitigate the problem.

OVERSIZE SANDWICHES—This is not a contest between you and the sandwich. Triple-deckers or megasize roast beef sandwiches are best cut into smaller, more manageable pieces. Always use a knife and fork to eat an open-faced sandwich.

PEAS—These are always a challenge for the Artful Eater. You might need a pusher, such as a piece of bread or your knife, to help get the peas onto your fork. The alternatives: gently spear the peas with your fork tines or abstain.

ICE CREAM CONE AT THE BEACH—Even though children beg for it, sand and sun are the natural enemies of ice cream. It's not such a good idea, unless you're a very speedy eater or sitting on the boardwalk.

FRUIT AND OLIVE PITS
These do not go into your napkin, but are best placed in the cup of your hand and set on the side of your plate. This applies to watermelon seeds, too.

FISH BONES
Never, ever swallow. Instead, remove the bones from your mouth as discreetly as possible and place them on the side of your plate.

DARE I EAT A PEACH?

"If you are able to eat a peach in your fingers and not smear your face, let juice run down, or make a sucking noise, you are the one in a thousand who *may*, and with utmost propriety, continue the feat."

—Emily Post, *Etiquette*

EMBARRASSMENT MANEUVERS

Your soup dribbles down your shirtfront, you accidentally squirt your seatmate when you squeeze lemon on your salmon, or the table leg you kicked turns out to be the person directly across from you. These are among the hazards that can befall even the most conscientious diner. Fortunately, for every accident there truly is a remedy.

NAVIGATING TROUBLE AT THE TABLE...

HOT FOOD AND BEVERAGES—If you've taken a sip of your coffee or soup and it's too hot, quickly swallow some water. The same holds true for very hot food. Whatever you do, don't spit it out.

"WAITER, THERE'S A FLY IN MY SOUP!"

"KEEP IT DOWN, SIR, OR THEY'LL ALL BE WANTING ONE."

THE UNEXPECTED "GARNISH"—Insects and food may be part of nature, but they don't belong together in a dish, whether at home or in a restaurant. If you're at someone's home, quietly tell your hostess about the problem; she should remove the offending dish with the utmost discretion. (Take care not to embarrass or offend anyone.) If you're at a restaurant, discretion is still called for, and yes, you're within your rights to expect an apology.

TOOTHSOME TIDBITS—Despite the best intentions, little particles of food will nest in between your teeth, especially poppy and sesame seeds, salads, and corn. Their removal requires diplomacy and tact; whether a friend tells you or you become aware of the problem yourself, excuse yourself briefly from the table. Take care of the problem in private and away from others.

GESUNDHEIT!—First you feel a little itch in your nose, and then before you can reach for a handkerchief or tissue, you sneeze. It's the most human of incidents, but when it happens at the table be sure to turn your head away from the food and the guests. After the fact, a tissue (or your napkin) is nonetheless a reassuring gesture, but when you blow, don't honk!

"SPINACH BETWEEN YOUR TEETH IS NOT CONSIDERED AN ACCESSORY."

BABIES, CHILDREN, AND TEENAGERS AT THE TABLE

Unless your company is your family, babies are best fed separately from the adults. Most young children find a roomful of adults about as much fun as heat rash, so unless you wish to see your children squirm and fidget, excuse them from dining with grown-ups. But teenagers toe the line between childhood and adulthood, and as such are ripe subjects for table manners.

A FEW WORDS OF ADVICE...

SEATING—To thwart an outbreak of giggles or other shenanigans, avoid clustering children together, especially siblings.

PICK YOUR BATTLES—For teenagers, pulling in their chairs, remembering their napkins, and taking reasonable portions is multi-tasking of the highest order. Be grateful for efforts large and small.

BE TOLERANT—Accept that children and adults at the table operate with different sets of standards. This includes laughter, too. After all, you're a parent, not a policeman, and you're both there to enjoy yourselves.

Tiffany's Table Manners for Teenagers dispenses sound advice with insouciant wit and charm...

"You don't have to wait for your hostess to start eating, but don't leap at your food like an Irish wolfhound."

"Don't put too much in your mouth at once. It looks as if you were brought up in a kennel."

"Remember that a dinner party is not a funeral that your hostess has invited you to because she thinks you are in dire need of food. You're there to be entertaining. Be gay. Do your part. Don't be a gloom."

THE GOOPS

The Goops they lick their fingers,
And the Goops they lick their knives;
They spill their broth on the tablecloth—
Oh, they lead disgusting lives!
The Goops they talk while eating,
And loud and fast they chew;
And that is why I'm glad that I
Am not a Goop—are you?

— Gelett Burgess

MY IDEA OF THE 9-TO-5

"We like to think of ourselves as having a modern office, and we believe it makes perfect sense to give each new employee a copy of Emily Post's etiquette book. To me, Emily Post is generous and cheerful. Much of her advice is good common sense, and I like that she has such a positive outlook and a dry sense of humor."

kansas city   new york   paris

TIMELINES

Repeated tardy arrivals, early departures, or excessive doctor's appointments during the workday actually do affect your coworkers. The clock on the wall is there to help you pace the day, not skip out on it.

PERFUME AT WORK

If there's one thing people can disagree about, it's perfume and cologne. If you want to wear a scent, take a modest approach and choose something with subtle notes. Strong or cheap perfumes may cause offense and are inappropriate.

Perhaps no office equipment is more abused than the telephone. All the more reason to bear in mind a few caveats when placing or receiving calls: your tone should be professional but friendly; be concise and straightforward; return calls and voice mail messages within a day; and reserve the speakerphone for only the most appropriate occasions.

ODOR-AMA

You've been putting in long hours, you're trying to finish a presentation, and you can't find time for a proper lunch hour. So you order in a hamburger. Or a pizza with pepperoni. Or Kung Pao Chicken. Result? Your colleagues feel the need to fumigate their offices and yours. A little self-policing and abstinence will not only keep the air fresher, but your office relationships won't suffer. Even Busy People need to be considerate.

BEING A GOOD CITIZEN

A good test of citizenship comes into play when you work in an office. Be responsible and replace the used coffee filter, invite a new colleague to lunch, or volunteer to help organize the office holiday party. Be fair. Be nice. Be loyal.

THE MANICURIST WILL (NOT) SEE YOU NOW

Whether you have a closed office or a cubicle, there is nothing professional about doing your nails at your desk. If you think you must, then you need to plan your time more carefully.

After all the care you put into the clothes you wear to the office, don't forget that your office needs to look presentable too.

ROMANCE IN THE OFFICE

If only more people heard this phrase and thought "oxymoron!," because so many of these sparks smolder, sputter, and leave singed feelings. The office romance that ends in marriage is rare. Be smart: do work in the office and romance on your own time.

IN A MANNER OF SPEAKING...NOSY PARKER

A busybody or snoop. Opinion varies as to the origin of the phrase, but the most applicable refers to English parkskeepers ("parkers") who liked to keep tabs on amorous dalliances in Hyde Park. "Funny thing about Callie: every time you saw her at the water cooler, she was deep in an Important Conversation with another colleague. No surprise she was nicknamed the nosy parker in the office."

IN THE PUBLIC EYE

"First impressions, and how you handle being out in public, are serious considerations for everyone. I'm reluctant to impose myself, so to me making a discrete entrance is a pretty safe approach. And it never hurts to have a warm smile ready. I think it makes other people feel relaxed."

For quick purchases and transactions, have your money or credit card ready. Both the cashier and the people behind you will appreciate this. (Avoid searching for loose change in the bottom of your purse, too.)

PEDESTRIAN YEAS AND NAYS

Walking on a sidewalk should be a harmless activity, but unless you live in a small town, you know that potential hazards await you on any city street.

THE PASSING LANE—Walk to the right, pass on the left. Adjust your pace and don't "tailgate" the person in front of you, either. Obey traffic lights and signs. As for jaywalking, it just isn't safe.

SIDEWALK ROLLERBLADERS AND CYCLISTS—No ambiguity here: wheels and city sidewalks are not meant to mix. Only baby strollers allowed.

SAUNTERERS AND SHOPPERS—The wild card of pedestrians. They stop and start unexpectedly; they switch "lanes" absentmindedly; and they're rarely in sync with the normal flow. The remedy: pass them. If you're the slow walker, enjoy your stroll, but be aware of the surrounding pace.

YOUR UMBRELLA, WET OR DRY—When passing someone tall, lower your umbrella to avoid grazing their eye; conversely, raise your umbrella over anyone shorter than you. Accept that some negotiation of sidewalk space will be necessary and adjust your umbrella accordingly. Once it stops raining, carry your umbrella on a vertical slant, tip facing down.

SIDEWALK GRATES—Only hazardous if you're wearing high heels!

WHAT FLOOR, PLEASE?
WHEN IN THE ELEVATOR...

Turn off portable CD players.

Remove your hat.

Passengers should allow those entering unblocked access.
For those entering, step in and to the side or back.

When your floor is approaching,
try to be close to the doors for exiting.

ROUND AND ROUND SHE GOES...

Whereas a man commonly opens a door for a woman to enter
first, the situation is reversed with a revolving door. In this case,
the man goes first and pushes the door for the woman, or else
he pushes it forward from the side and allows her to enter first.

ESCALATORS

The English win hands down when it comes to escalator etiquette:
keep to the right and leave the left side free for passing. Short
of that, do your best not to block or impede others, and if you're
the one doing the passing, remember to say "excuse me."

IT'S A GROCERY CART, NOT A GO-CART

There are a few tales of people meeting in the aisle of a grocery
store and falling in love, but most people who "bump" into
others in the aisles come closer to fisticuffs than romance.

AISLE ETIQUETTE—When you park your cart, hug the wall, not the center of the aisle;
before you turn a corner, look ahead to see if the lane is clear.

AT THE DELI COUNTER—Wherever there is a line of people waiting to be served, assume there
is a ticket machine and wait your turn; you can reasonably expect others to do likewise.

CHECKOUT LINE—The tension of waiting on line to pay up is worse than horses straining to
break at the gate: for some reason, at this point all people want is *out*. Patience truly is a virtue
in this case. If there is an express lane for ten items or fewer, do the math the old-fashioned
way—each item counts.

RANDOM ACTS OF KINDNESS—If the person behind you only has only one or two items
and you have several, be gracious and let him or her go first.

TIPPING

Not only is tipping a customary way of showing your appreciation for services, often the people you're tipping are those most in need of extra money. One school of thought is that you should tip regardless of the quality of the service; others feel that a tip is a direct reflection of good service, and thus is earned. Also consider the personal relationship you might have with someone, such as the waiter at your neighborhood diner. In the end, be generous yet fair.

FOOD AND DRINK
Restaurant check: 15% to 20%
Gratuity is usually included for groups of six or more.

Bartender: $1 per drink

Food delivery: 10% (in bad weather, 15%)

Hotel room service: 15% of the check

DAY OF BEAUTY
Hairdresser: 15% to 20%

Manicurist and pedicurist: 10% to 20%

Masseuse: 10% to 20%

MISCELLANY
Coat check: $1 to $2 per item

Ladies' room attendant: $1

Usher at the ball game (if shown to your seat): 50 cents to $1

Valet parking: $2 to $3

TRAVEL
Airport skycap: $1 or more per bag

Bellhop: $1 per bag

Taxi or hired car: 15% to 20%

HOLIDAY TIPPING

The gift of a holiday tip is a way of thanking certain people for taking care of you during the year. Depending on what you're able to spend and how many people are on your list, it's a good idea to plan ahead by putting money aside from time to time. It's also useful to keep track of who you tip and what you give each year.

APARTMENT BUILDING STAFF

In general, the cash you give is thanks for the help you've received during the year and is a reflection of the type of building and city you live in.

Doorman: $25 to $100

Superintendant: $30 to $100

Custodian: $20 to $30

Handyman: $10 to $30

HAIRDRESSER

The cost of a regular session (plus a small gift). Again, this depends on your relationship, the salon, and how frequently you have your hair cut.

BABYSITTER

The equivalent of two nights' pay (plus a small gift)

HEALTH CLUB

Locker room attendant: $5 to $10

Trainer: $50 (or more)

And don't forget the dry cleaner, housekeeper, dog groomer, lawn crew, and parking garage attendant.

RESTAURANTS

Among the pleasures of daily life is dining out. You don't have to cook or clean up, and you get to eat exactly what you want. The price you pay for this luxury isn't just for the food; it's for the relationship between you and the restaurant, and between you and your waiter.

RESPECT YOUR RESTAURANT

Arrive five to ten minutes
prior to your reservation.

Wait your turn to greet the hostess.

Dress in keeping with the
style and ambience of the restaurant.

Have the proper form of payment
("cash only" is usually non-negotiable).

DINING DILEMMAS—"LET'S HAVE DINNER"

Other than politics and sports teams, nothing has the potential to
cause more angst among friends and couples than the question,
"who pays?" If it's just you and a close friend, split the check or
alternate paying for the whole tab. If one has invited the other, the
expectation is that the invitee is being treated. (Some fair exceptions:
a significant age difference requires senior to pay for junior;
if it's a business meal, regardless of who issued the invite the bill
is paid by the person who stands to gain more from the meal.)

"THER OUGHT T'BE SOME WAY T'EAT CELERY SO IT WOULDN'T SOUND LIKE YOU WUZ STEPPIN' ON A BASKET."
—KIN HUBBARD

The waitstaff (waiter, waitress, waitron) are trained to accommodate you—to a point. Be cordial and concise, and expect the same in kind. Service in a diner is different from service in a four-star restaurant, and you'll enjoy yourself more if you adjust your expectations accordingly.

MOVIES

Inexplicably, when the lights go down in a movie theater, bad behavior has a way of sneaking in. Forethought and sensitivity to those around you will help keep the experience enjoyable.

When you enter a row, face the people already seated.

Your coat belongs on your chair—not on one beside or in front of you.

Turn off cell phones and pagers.

If you must talk to your companion, do so infrequently and keep your voice very low.

Wait until the credits are rolling before standing up to leave.

POPCORN is one of the pleasures of moviegoing, but it can also be annoying to those around you. Chew but don't chomp, and be sure to take any leftover popcorn with you when the movie's over.

Candy with CRINKLY WRAPPERS and plastic bags should be opened before the movie begins, especially if it's a serious story.

Unhappy about someone else kicking your seat or CHATTING too loudly? Stay calm, be friendly, and address the problem as quietly as possible.

HEIGHT MATTERS

It seems so obvious, but it bears repeating: short people truly can't see over the heads of tall people. When you choose a seat, consider if the person behind you will be able to see. Be sure to remove your hat, whether it's a wide brim or a baseball cap.

"THE PEOPLE IN THE MOVIE SHOULD DO THE TALKING, NOT THE PEOPLE IN THE AUDIENCE."

MANNERS ON THE MOVE
IN A CAR, ON A TRAIN, PLANE, OR SUBWAY

As long as you observe some basic guidelines, traveling with hundreds of strangers on open highways or in close quarters can bring unexpected pleasures.

AUTO ABC'S...

When you're driving, use your horn less and your patience more. Running traffic lights, tailgating, and trying to outfox another driver won't really save you time, and it may endanger others around you. Perhaps there should be a refresher course in drivers' education from time to time, along with a checklist of common courtesies.

Your car is for driving, not storing—Keep your car clean of debris, kids' toys, your dry cleaning, and so forth. No one wants to ride in a messy car.

Music—Be congenial and don't impose your music (and the volume) on your passengers.

Sensible stowaways—Maps, tissues or napkins, paper and pen, and bottled water for long trips.

Headlights—Use your bright lights responsibly, not selfishly.

Road rage—Anger management is essential for safe driving, for both you and others. If you become incensed, pull over until you have calmed down.

BINGO!

The telltale green board with its plastic colored sliding windows has been amusing children in cars since 1960, when Auto Bingo (also known as Car Bingo) was first made by Regal Games. Today you can also play Find-a-Car Bingo, Traffic Safety Bingo, and Interstate Highway Bingo.

SUBWAY MOVIES

The Taking of Pelham One, Two, Three (1974)
The Last Metro (1980); *Sliding Doors* (1998)

ETIQUETTE GOES UNDERGROUND—THE SUBWAY

Subway etiquette has its own unique parameters, though being cordial remains the best tactic. Let others get off before entering a subway car; allow one seat per person (that includes any packages as well); if you bump into someone getting on or off the subway, smile and apologize; keep your voice down (ditto for portable musical devices); offer your seat to an older person, someone who is disabled, or a pregnant woman. One other point: a subway car is not a dining car.

AIRPLANE ADVICE

Sharing the armrest and forced conversation are among the irksome social perils of airplane travel. What are your options?

The armrest—One to a customer, and if you're in the center seat, choose one side and stick to it.

Being kicked from behind—For most children, an airplane is even worse than being buckled into the backseat of the family car. If a child is repeatedly kicking the back of your seat, politely speak to the parents.

Making conversation (or not)—Reading a book is enjoyable and sends a signal to the would-be talkative seatmate that you prefer silence to conversation.

The pleasure of your own company—If you really want to sit back and tune out, listen to your portable CD player (with the volume turned down), put on your sunglasses, and sleep.

BICYCLING FOR GROWN-UPS

If you're going to ride alongside cars, you need to follow the standard rules of the road.

Obey traffic signs and signals.

Ride with the traffic.

If there's a designated bike lane, use it.

Use proper hand signals when turning and passing.

Ride defensively, and in consideration of your fellow riders. Be on the lookout for potholes and grates, pedestrians and stray animals, cars suddenly stopping and car doors opening. Be smart and wear a whistle around your neck.

Wear a helmet, and don't worry about looking foolish. It's not a beauty contest.

AIRPLANE MOVIES

Casablanca (1942)
The V.I.P.s (1963)
Goldfinger (1964)
Airplane! (1980)
Love, Actually (2003)

"THE TRUE TRAVELER IS HE WHO GOES ON FOOT, AND EVEN THEN, HE SITS DOWN A LOT OF THE TIME."

—COLETTE, *PARIS FROM MY WINDOW*

VACATION TRAVEL

For the peripatetic, a little trip is always satisfying. The spa retreat, the art excursion, and the gustatory adventure are all worth a timeout from your day to day life.

RESET YOUR WATCH—Get on vacation time and don't bother about the time "back home."

BE IN THE PRESENT—Why talk about the office when you're horseback riding in Aspen?

GOING OVERSEAS?—Make sure your passport is current, and that you arrive at your destination with enough foreign currency to get from the airport to your hotel and buy a coffee and a pastry.

BEFORE THE TRIP YOU WERE THE BEST OF FRIENDS...

If you travel with a friend, plan to take roughly the same amount of luggage; that way neither one of you will potentially slow down the other.

Agree on a budget beforehand.

Discuss your expectations and your privacy preferences.

If things become rocky, realize it's temporary and that sometimes it's wisest to agree to disagree.

Keep a sense of humor!

PARLEZ-VOUS FRANÇAIS?

When you travel to a foreign country, bring your manners with you. What you wear, how long you bathe, even how you address shopkeepers are important. You'll enjoy yourself more when you respect the local customs and do your best to follow them. If you ask for ice water and the waiter adds only a cube or two, don't bemoan it, accept it. Better still, switch to wine.

"SPLENDID MANNERS—IN THE AMERICAN STYLE."

—HENRY JAMES, *PORTRAIT OF A LADY*

AT YOUR HOTEL

Welcome to your home away from home, where the room is always neat, the bed freshly made, and the bathroom squeaky clean. The price for this retreat is a simple understanding of the protocol between you and the staff.

Your hotel concierge is there to make your stay as pleasant as possible and is your primary general contact during your stay. You may rely on him or her to provide you with information and to cheerfully resolve any possible problems. When you ask for special care, be polite and flexible; grandstanding is not only unattractive, it is often self-defeating.

THE HOTEL SOUVENIR

You might think that the hotel ashtray or bath mat would look quaint in your home, but the hotel feels otherwise. Most good hotels, however, will gladly allow you to purchase a signature bathrobe, for example, and they'll be happy to send you home with some bath toiletries and stationery.

PERSONAL PECCADILLOES

Seasoned travelers are not only savvy about the type of room they prefer, they're specific about what they travel with to ratchet up their temporary comfort zones. The range of items is broad (from scented travel candles and pillows to flower vases and little lamp shades), but the selection is always very personal. That said, don't expect the housekeeper to refresh your flowers or clean up spilled candle wax without a personal request and appropriate gratuity.

ROOM 728

If your room is less than ideal, don't ask the bellhop to find you another room (and don't berate him, either). Contact the concierge and discuss your needs. When the bellhop moves you to a more satisfactory room, be sure to double his tip; after all, he has now carried your bags twice.

DRESS ETIQUETTE
FROM MORNING . . .

"I don't think anyone expects you to be in the same mood seven days
a week, and that goes for how you dress, too. Just the same, I do believe
that certain conventions call out for certain attire. To me, this applies equally to
a major executive or to a young woman working at a little shop. Dressing with
a regard for others is a sign of respect."

"IS MY DESIRE TO DRESS APPROPRIATELY FOR SPECIAL OCCASIONS AS DATED AS A LIME RICKEY?"

OUT AND ABOUT: DRESSING UP, DOWN, AND GOING YOUR OWN WAY

The two pillars of appropriate attire are a true sense of your
own style and an appreciation for the occasion or time of day.

HAIR—Develop a style that best flatters you 24/7. Your hair
should complement, not overwhelm, your appearance.

MAKEUP—It's always fun to buy a new tube of lipstick, but
for daytime keep it simple. A fresh look is an all-around winner.

JEWELRY—When it comes to wearing jewelry during the day,
understatement is the goal unless you are naturally given to
overdrive in your appearance. A couple of choice pieces always
look good.

NAILS—Clean and natural are the operative words here. Anything
else is *de trop* for daytime.

CLOTHES—The ideal wardrobe allows a woman to select clothes
that are suitable for lunch with friends, going to the office, or
doing errands.

. . . UNTIL NIGHT

"Selecting my wardrobe when Andy and I are headed someplace special is when I get to indulge myself. I love wearing beautiful things and sparkly jewelry, and a night on the town cries out for adornment."

8:00 CURTAIN

Think about where you're going, not just about what you'll be doing. If it's to see La Bohème at the Metropolitan Opera House, make the extra effort. Wear a dress that *radiates*. Remember that lighting in restaurants or at concert halls tends to soften features and add mystery. Dress to thrill.

"AS FAR AS I'M CONCERNED, 'PLAYING DRESS UP' BEGINS AT THE AGE OF FIVE AND NEVER TRULY ENDS."

"Like the elegant décor of the Plaza, the splendor of a theater deserves an audience with attire to match—and I've always been one for matching."

IN A MANNER OF SPEAKING . . . PUT ON THE DOG

To dress with flair; first used in 1871. "Nothing so delighted Claire and Whit like an evening at the Philharmonic. Claire was resplendent in plumes of coral silk chiffon and Whit put on the dog with his bespoke gray pinstripe suit and Asprey cufflinks."

DRESSING DISASTERS:
SLIPS, RIPS, AND BROKEN HEELS

When it comes to dressing, even the best-laid plans can go awry. Just the same, you still have options: be pragmatic, resourceful, and do your best to look upon the incident as *incidental*. Above all, never be self-deprecatory as a way of passing off a sartorial blip.

"Who hasn't had a heel snap or a button burst?
Any time you go out, myriad things can go wrong.
My advice about the unexpected is pretty simple:
laugh, throw back your shoulders, and move on."

A FEW SURPRISES WE'VE ALL EXPERIENCED...

The blouse with the missing button—You noticed this during a business lunch. *If you're wearing a blazer, draw it closer; otherwise, pull up your napkin to cover the offending wink of skin.*

A hole in one—You walk into a room, sit down, and realize you've got a large run in your stocking. *Excuse yourself and remove the stockings. Even on a cold day a bare leg is preferable.*

Great dress, wrong bra—When you put on your sleeveless dress it didn't occur to you to check that no straps showed in back. *If you have a shawl or sweater, drape it over your shoulders, or ask a friend to borrow hers.*

You're stepping out of the car and whoops—the heel on your shoe breaks off. *Ask yourself which looks funnier—one bare foot with one shoe, or two bare feet? Sometimes it makes more sense to jettison both shoes.*

The one time you borrow clothes from your best friend, disaster strikes—the zipper breaks, buttons burst, or you become a magnet for mustard. *The sooner you can change, the better. Afterward, be honest and tell your friend what happened; inform her you'll have the garment repaired and dry cleaned. Return it with a short note and a small token expressing your appreciation.*

You missed the fine print: you're the only one in formal wear. *Slip off your jewelry, unpin your hair, and quickly wipe off excess "party" makeup. Then flag down the nearest waiter with the champagne tray.*

You thought the restaurant was casual, when in fact it's dressy, as are all the people already there. *Comb your hair, apply lipstick, and don a confident smile, then glide to your table as though you were in ermine (and pray for a banquette seat). Once the table's pushed in, who will know you're in jeans?*

Your date sees the tags you forgot to remove hanging inside of your new coat. *Laugh it off, then quickly get into your coat and head out the door.*

"HAVE YOU EVER SEEN AN 80-YEAR-OLD WOMAN LOOK GREAT WITH A TATTOO?"
—ANDY SPADE

You thought you were being smart by wearing Band-Aids with your new sandals—until you looked down and 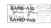 saw them poking out. *There's no denying the relief from* *this little strip of adhesive and gauze, but having your Band-Aids show is not unlike your slip or bra strap showing. Before you go out, make sure they're well tucked away. As backup, it's always smart to carry a few emergency Band-Aids in your wallet.*

SOCIAL SPILLS AND GRACIOUS RECOVERIES

It's one thing to get mail with your last name misspelled and quite another when an acquaintance continually does the same thing (and mispronounces your name as well). What can you do? How can you be gracious without embarrassing your friend?

A FEW SOCIAL SPILLS WE'VE ALL WITNESSED (OR COMMITTED) . . .

Squirting your seatmate when you crack open a lobster
Offer your bib, if you have one, another napkin, and maybe even a piece of your lobster if it was from the claw.

Arriving a week early for a party
Humor is really the only way out of this one. Explain that you're on a campaign to improve your tardiness and that you seem to have gone slightly overboard in the other direction.

Inquiring after someone's spouse and learning that they're no longer married
It's apparent that this is more of an acquaintance than a close friend, so offer a brief but sincere apology. Don't, however, take license and ask why the marriage ended.

Wearing the same dress as the hostess of an event
This is a case of the Frozen Smile Solution. Doubtless, neither of you is amused by the coincidence, but outwardly make light of it and let it pass.

Spilling a Sea Breeze down the front of your white summer dress
Someone else spilling a Sea Breeze down the front of your white summer dress
Both spills were accidental, and thus it doesn't matter how the cocktail got on your dress. Excuse yourself, find some club soda, and do what you can in the short term to minimize the problem.

And that most unpredictable of bathroom boo-boos: a stubborn toilet
Who said life's fair?

THE NAME GAME

Social faux pas are often committed in the misspelling or mispronunciation of a name. Contrary to the belief that you should grin and bear it, it's actually a kindness to correct the person right then, rather than wait until a later time. Sometimes a delay adds to someone's embarrassment rather than mitigates it. When you do inform someone of your correct name, do so in a friendly and casual manner.

SOME COMMON AND UNCOMMON SPELLINGS

Alice, Alyce	Leah, Lia
Ana, Anna	Lesley, Leslie
Claire, Clare	Lisa, Liza
Eileen, Ilene	LouLou, Lulu
Elise, Elyse	Maira, Maria, Maura, Moira
Elizabeth, Elisabeth, Lisbeth	Sara, Sarah
Joanna, JoAnne	Susan, Suzanne
Karen, Karyn, Caryn	Zoë, Zoey

BLUNDERS...

MISPRONUNCIATION OF A FOREIGN WORD

To the trained ear, it's like fingernails on a blackboard listening to someone mispronounce a foreign word. If you aren't especially facile at foreign languages, opt for the commonly translated title of a film or food (unless of course, *linguini alla vongole* simply sounds better than saying pasta with clams). Also, take care not to salt your words with a bon mot when a good word will work just as well.

WHAT DO YOU DO WHEN...

You're at an interview before a building's co-op board and you get the hiccups?
Ask for some water and try to brush it off by saying you must be a little nervous. If possible, avoid having to excuse yourself from the interview.

You're taking your best friend out for a fancy birthday lunch only to learn after the check arrives that it's cash only—and you have about $20?
You're caught in the middle. You don't want to ask your friend for money, but you can't expect the restaurant to break their rule just for you. However, in a pinch, a restaurant might help you save face if you let them hold your credit card as security while you go to the nearest ATM.

You've recently arrived in Tokyo for a business trip and you're strolling with important clients when you accidentally step on a wad of gum?
First of all, it's always wise to read up on the customs and manners of a country you'll be visiting. In some cases, England can be as "foreign" to an American as Japan. Lacking any specific information, do your best to ignore the problem until you're somewhere you can excuse yourself and remove the gum in private. (But if you're about to enter someone's home, then you do need to take care of the problem beforehand.)

You're talking to the company vice president and you realize that his fly is open?
You have a couple of options, and you should select what's most appropriate to your relationship with this person. You can be direct and simply tell him, or you can ignore it and hope some other Good Samaritan will let him know.

You're at a picnic with a bunch of friends and their children when eight-year-old Sam roughhouses and lands a swift kick to your shin?
Apply ice and grab a beer.

IN A MANNER OF SPEAKING...
BETWEEN A ROCK AND A HARD PLACE

To be forced to choose between two unsatisfactory
options. A modern variant of the phrase "between
Scylla and Charybdis," from *The Odyssey*. "Lucy was
trying to enjoy herself at a dinner party, but the man
across from her was occasionally kicking her. If she
said something, she risked offending him, but if she
kept quiet, she'd end up with a considerable bruise."

THINGS THAT GO BUMP IN THE NIGHT...

Out of the corner of your eye, you sense movement, or
perhaps you hear a little scratching sound. Maybe there's
no warning; maybe the critter or bug simply appears.
Nothing packs a shot of adrenaline more than discovering
an outdoors animal or insect *indoors*. For the houseguest
who's squeamish or mouse phobic, this is NO FUN.
Mosquitoes, mice, even chipmunks skittering about are best
tolerated and require that you be the Stoic Houseguest, at
least until morning. Then you can decide whether to speak
to your hosts about your night, or write it off to a bad dream.

WHEN STUART LITTLE COMES CALLING...

It's 1 A.M. and you're just about to turn out the light when you see a mouse in
your room. You shriek, the mouse runs, your hosts continue sleeping. Calm
down—the mouse is twenty times more scared than you. The little mouse will
definitely not jump on your covers, though you might want to leave the door
to the hallway open a crack, just in case he wants to go exploring elsewhere.

SECTION TWO

From Me to You:
The Gentle Art of Communicating

Artful Conversation

Telephones, Cell Phones, and Secondhand Chat

Written Correspondence

Invitations, RSVPs, Thank-You Notes

Letters I Love · Letter Trivia

ARTFUL CONVERSATION

"Frankly, I like to talk, so I rarely find myself without something to say. But there is a difference between just *talking* and really thinking about what would interest the other person. Nothing is more embarrassing than possibly boring someone. If I feel stumped when I'm talking with someone, I try to widen the group and pull in more people. Sometimes that's the perfect solution."

"GOOD FENCES MAKE GOOD NEIGHBORS."

—ROBERT FROST, "MENDING WALL"

"Talk to somebody, for Christ's sakes, honey, talk to somebody. If she catches you standing here not talking to anybody, she'll take us off her invitation list, and I love these parties."

—John Cheever,
"The Enormous Radio"

WORDS TO ARTFULLY DODGE...

In mixed company, some words are best left unsaid, such as *short, bald, fat, skinny, still single,* and *unemployed.*

IN A MANNER OF SPEAKING...SPOONERISM

The accidental but often hilarious transposition of initial sounds. The term was named after William A. Spooner, who made many such faux pas. Among his best known: "Son, it is kisstomery to cuss the bride."

SOME TIMELESS ADVICE ON MAKING CONVERSATION

Be a good listener—A sympathetic listener makes others comfortable.

Good conversation is all about give and take—Excel at each.

Being naturally shy is okay—Most of the sins of bad conversation are made by talking too much, not too little.

Think before you speak—What's said can't be taken back.

Less is more—No need to tell all.

Silence is acceptable—Don't feel obliged to fill up airtime.

Your age—If you're going to lie, skip the subject altogether.

Think about the topic—Seek common ground and build from there.

Give praise when relevant, but don't go overboard—Too much blunts sincerity and credibility.

Consider what *not* to talk about—Unless you know the person well, it's wiser to avoid sensitive subjects such as politics, child raising, money, or the Mets.

When talking about your children, easy does it—Touting your child's skills or appearance can be offputting to your listener. The same holds true for pets.

The weather—Uniquely boring.

Boasting is boring, too.

Be tactful—Most people don't care to be reminded about growing older. (Would you?)

Humor is healthy—Sarcasm and malice are not.

Don't worry about being clever—Be genuine, be yourself.

"CYNICISM IS INTELLECTUAL DANDYISM, BUT GRACIOUSNESS IN SPEECH IS AN APHRODISIAC."

—ANDY SPADE

PARDON MY FRENCH...

Sugar, *merde!*, drat, crikey, fudge, cor blimey, jiminy Christmas, balderdash, son of a gun, dang it, for crying out loud, bull pucky, jiminy cricket, baloney, *schiss*, *zut alors!*

TELEPHONES, CELL PHONES, AND SECONDHAND CHAT

"I rarely have time for social calls during the day, and we're often out at night, so I try to fit in my phone calling when I'm on my way to a meeting, or perhaps heading out to the airport on a business trip."

HOW TO GIVE GOOD PHONE...

WHEN YOU CALL—Most calls should be placed between 8 A.M. and 10 P.M. on weekdays; 10 A.M. and 10 P.M. on Saturdays; and noon and 10 P.M. on Sundays.

CALL WAITING—Unless you're expecting a call, let the second call go into voice mail. If, however, you decide to answer a call, it should be done only to inform Caller #2 that you will return the call. If you are in the middle of a serious conversation, don't pick up call waiting.

RETURNING CALLS—Personal calls should be returned the same day or within twenty-four hours.

"I'M NOT AFRAID TO ADMIT I LIKE TALKING ON THE PHONE. WEEKENDS ARE BEST OF ALL, WHEN I'M RELAXED AND HAVE A CHANCE TO CATCH UP WITH MY FRIENDS AND MY FAMILY."

CELL PHONE DO'S...

For economy and convenience.

When you're on the go and need to confirm or change appointments, reservations, film schedules.

Keep the conversation friendly.

When you enter a restaurant, a shop, or a museum, set your phone to vibrate; better still, if it's not essential, turn it off.

Children and babysitters—Being reachable is a worthy use of the cell phone.

For an emergency—This goes without saying.

AND DON'TS...

Don't use a cell phone as a panacea for boredom.

Don't use a cell phone to talk in public about personal or professional problems, financial woes, health worries.

Don't swear or conduct an argument on a cell phone in public. Nothing excuses such behavior.

Don't assume it's okay to speak loudly because you think what you're saying is impressive to those around you. Keep your voice low at all times.

Don't assume it's okay to speak at length while on a train or in an airplane.

Deep-six cell phones
in restaurants.

SECONDHAND CHAT

Secondhand chat is right up there with secondhand smoke. By the time you've finished looking in a boutique, chances are that if someone is on a cell phone, you'll wind up knowing her shoe size, what she's shopping for, and her budget. You'll probably even know the name of her date. This is selfish and boring. Please, don't blow smoke in our face or talk in our ear.

CELL HELL

"I have a like/dislike relationship with my cell phone. The ease and freedom it gives are great, but like a lot of people, I'm not used to being 'connected' so frequently. When people use cell phones in public, such as on the street, while shopping, or in a doctor's office, I wish they would use more discretion and be considerate of others around them."

WRITTEN CORRESPONDENCE

"I love stationery, so I can never have enough beautiful writing papers around. If I were a lady of leisure, I'd find it peaceful to spend my mornings at a proper writing desk, sending off little notes to people. As it is, I never have that kind of morning (or day, for that matter). Who doesn't enjoy receiving a note in the mail?"

LETTERS

"You deserve a longer letter than this; but it is my unhappy fate seldom to treat people so well as they deserve."

—Jane Austen

FORMAL SALUTATIONS

We may live in a more casual society, but a little decorum is still called for in proper letters. It never hurts to err on the side of politesse, and if you think you should use a surname in a thank-you letter, then begin your note with the salutation "Ms.," "Mrs.," or "Mr." Switch to a first-name basis once you have established a mutual rapport.

"ALWAYS HANDWRITE A FORMAL SOCIAL NOTE."

NEATNESS COUNTS

Not all penmanship is created equal, but you can control the overall look of a letter. Spilled coffee, a bent piece of paper, and words crossed out are all telltale indications of a letter best left unsent. For the recipient, the appearance of your letter is a stand-in for you.

"DO NOT BE TEMPTED BY A TWENTY-DOLLAR WORD WHEN THERE IS A TEN-CENTER HANDY, READY, AND ABLE."

—WILLIAM STRUNK, JR., AND E. B. WHITE, *THE ELEMENTS OF STYLE*

Nowadays, house stationery is a restitution of more traditional times. Some people choose to have house stationery if they own a second, or country, home.

BE NATURAL

For personal correspondence use natural language and avoid sounding mannered or formal. Feel free to use contractions, such as *it's* and *I'm*, which echo our everyday speech.

IN A MANNER OF SPEAKING...CLICHÉS

There are scores of clichés from all over the world, and many of them have as their source either the Bible or Shakespeare. It's easy as pie to use a cliché, but in correspondence, remember that a little goes a long way, so take the following phrases with a pinch of salt: two peas in a pod; dancing on the head of a pin; bib and tucker; grin like a Cheshire cat; knock the socks off; two left feet; birds of a feather flock together; and life is a bowl of cherries.

"BREVITY IS THE SOUL OF WIT."

—SHAKESPEARE

ENVELOPE SIZES	
ENVELOPE	SIZE
A2	$4^{3}/_{8}$ by $5^{3}/_{4}$"
A6	$4^{3}/_{4}$ by $6^{1}/_{2}$"
A7	$5^{1}/_{4}$ by $7^{1}/_{4}$"
A8	$5^{1}/_{2}$ by $8^{1}/_{8}$"
A10	6 by $9^{1}/_{2}$"
$6^{1}/_{4}$"	$3^{1}/_{2}$ by 6"
$6^{3}/_{4}$"	$3^{5}/_{8}$ by $6^{1}/_{2}$"
$7^{3}/_{4}$"	$3^{7}/_{8}$ by $7^{1}/_{2}$"
$8^{5}/_{8}$"	$3^{5}/_{8}$ by $8^{5}/_{8}$"
9"	$3^{7}/_{8}$ by $8^{7}/_{8}$"
10"	$4^{1}/_{8}$ by $9^{1}/_{2}$"
11"	$4^{1}/_{2}$ by $10^{3}/_{8}$"

PAPER SIZES	
PAPER	SIZE
MONARCH	$7^{1}/_{4}$ x $10^{1}/_{2}$"
HALF	$5^{1}/_{4}$ x $3^{3}/_{4}$"
BUSINESS	$8^{1}/_{2}$ x 11"
LETTER	$5^{1}/_{4}$ x $7^{1}/_{2}$"
CHIT	$5^{3}/_{8}$ x $4^{1}/_{8}$"
POSTCARD	4 x 6"

IN A MANNER OF SPEAKING...BROWNIE POINTS

Indicating favor or kudos. "Hallie had always been a reliable correspondent, but she earned brownie points from her parents for the frequent and endearing letters she sent them while in the south of France. Perhaps it was the sea air."

GREAT DIARISTS

Dr. Johnson

Anne Frank

Samuel Pepys

Katharine Graham

Tibor Kalman

Henry Stimson

Cecil Beaton

Eleanor Roosevelt

Virginia Woolf

Andy Warhol

Bridget Jones

> "I HAVE MADE THIS LETTER LONGER, BECAUSE
> I HAVE NOT HAD THE TIME TO MAKE IT SHORTER."
>
> —BLAISE PASCAL

CORRESPONDENCE THAT NEVER GOES OUT OF STYLE

General invitations

Wedding invitations

Birth announcements

Place cards

Thank-you notes

"Dear John" letters

Love letters

Vacation postcards

Fan mail

Moving or new home announcements

THE STATIONERY WARDROBE

"when we began our company, we were so small (there were just four of us and not that many handbags) that we decided all of our correspondence should be lowercase as a reflection of our size. whether a letter was typed, whether it was someone's name or the beginning of a sentence, we used lowercase. we took it very seriously. i suppose we've grown up because now we use uppercase and lowercase."

BUSINESS STATIONERY

LETTERHEAD	DESCRIPTION: Includes company name, name, title, address, phone, fax, and e-mail. Folds in thirds to fit inside an envelope. 8½ x 11" ENVELOPE: Company name and address on either the face or the back flap. USES: For formal communication and to project the image of the company. Letterhead with the sender's name and company information should be used only by that person and only for business matters—never personal.
MONARCH	DESCRIPTION: Typically includes individual's name and title. Folds in thirds to fit inside an envelope. 7¼ by 10½" ENVELOPE: Sender's name and company printed on the back flap. USES: For more collegial business letters; when you are on a first-name basis with the recipient. Informal communiqués.
CORRESPONDENCE CARDS	DESCRIPTION: Heavy paper stock with the name of the individual. 4¼ by 6¼" ENVELOPE: Sender's name and address on the back flap. USES: For brief, handwritten notes.
BUSINESS CARDS	DESCRIPTION: Heavy card stock, preferably. May be printed, engraved, with or without special border treatment. Often the most creatively designed element in the business stationery repertoire. 3½ by 2" (standard), with customized variations. USES: Capsule version of the corporate identity.

Ways to close a business letter: *Sincerely; Sincerely yours; Very truly yours; Yours truly; Gratefully*

SOCIAL STATIONERY

LETTER SHEETS	DESCRIPTION: Name and address, or only address. Folds in half to fit inside an envelope. ENVELOPE: Name and address, or only address. USES: For more general correspondence or for a lengthy note.
FOLD-OVER NOTES	DESCRIPTION: So called because they fold along the left side or top. May be printed or engraved with your full name, a monogram, or one initial on the cover page. Write on pages 1, 3, and 2, in that order. The back side should remain blank. Folds in half to fit inside an envelope. $5\frac{1}{4}$ by $7\frac{1}{2}$" ENVELOPE: Name and address, or only address. USES: The most formal of social stationery. As a reply to a formal invitation, sympathy note.
HALF-SHEET	DESCRIPTION: Named because they are half the size of a letter sheet. May have only a name, a name and address, or be monogrammed. The second sheet is unembellished. $5\frac{1}{4}$ by $3\frac{3}{4}$" ENVELOPE: Name and address, or only address. USES: For general correspondence.
CORRESPONDENCE CARDS (also known as "informals")	DESCRIPTION: More informal than a letter but regarded as the principal form of social stationery. Heavy card stock, with optional monogramming or name across the top. May be plain or bordered. No fold. Write only on the front side. $6\frac{3}{4}$ x $4\frac{1}{4}$" ENVELOPE: Address on two lines on back of envelope. USES: The most versatile of all social stationery—as a thank-you note, or turned into an invitation, or stamped and sent as a postcard.
CALLING CARDS	DESCRIPTION: Heavy paper stock. May include only the name, name and phone, or the name and address. The address is typically in the lower right-hand corner. $2\frac{7}{8}$ by 2" (if single) or $3\frac{1}{8}$ by $2\frac{1}{4}$" (if married) USES: Mainly as gift enclosures or for social purposes.

Ways to close a social letter: *Warmly; Warm regards; Best; Fondly; Affectionately; Appreciatively; Yours*

BUSINESS LETTERS

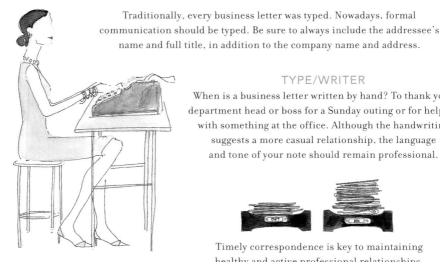

Traditionally, every business letter was typed. Nowadays, formal communication should be typed. Be sure to always include the addressee's name and full title, in addition to the company name and address.

TYPE/WRITER

When is a business letter written by hand? To thank your department head or boss for a Sunday outing or for helping with something at the office. Although the handwriting suggests a more casual relationship, the language and tone of your note should remain professional.

Timely correspondence is key to maintaining healthy and active professional relationships.

BUSINESSESE IS A FOREIGN LANGUAGE

Be direct and use plain language; keep to the point; be specific; use active verbs; state your expectations of the recipient; be professional, be human.

REPETITIVE REDUNDANCIES

Final conclusion

Mix together

Basic fundamentals

Specifically customized

Very urgent

Very unique (now, that is special!)

WINDBAG WORDS

Some language and phrases are inherently clunky, obtuse, or deadly dull. Do your best to avoid the following . . .

Enclosed herewith
Here is

Due to the fact that
Because

Per your request/Further to your request
As you mentioned

As to when/Until such time
When

"I DON'T WRITE MANY FORMAL LETTERS, BUT ANYTHING WITH MY SIGNATURE IS ALWAYS HANDWRITTEN."

E-MAIL AND FAXES

"I'm a Luddite when it comes to e-mail. I love writing letters too much to think that e-mail should be anything but a convenience. But of course I understand its usefulness at work."

E-mail is so easy and fast that it's possible to overlook the courtesies naturally associated with more conventional forms of communication.

IN THE OFFICE—E-mail should always be professional, regardless of the brevity or frequency of your correspondence with another colleague. The "send" button is powerful; don't send an e-mail when you're angry. Be discreet: any e-mails sent within a company may be forwarded to others, and may also be reviewed at any time by management.

AT HOME—As with any personal correspondence, remember that your character is represented by what you write. Don't waste other people's time by forwarding a joke or graphic to everyone in your address book. If you're upset or angry, then e-mail is best avoided, for you and the recipient.

> "EVERYBODY GETS SO MUCH
> INFORMATION ALL DAY LONG THAT
> THEY LOSE THEIR COMMON SENSE."
>
> —GERTRUDE STEIN

While the fax machine beats snail mail in terms of speed, bear in mind a few pointers:

Sending a confidential fax is inherently risky, so take necessary precautions.

Never read a fax intended for someone else.

Don't send pages and pages of a document by fax unless cleared beforehand with the recipient; it can tie up or jam a machine. (Consider a messenger, express mail, or e-mail.)

Time of day—The safest time to fax is daytime, yours and the recipient's. Never send a fax during the night to someone's home.

INVITATIONS

"Andy and I love to give parties, and whether they're casual gatherings or big blowouts, half the fun is creating the invitation. I love the formal presentation of a proper invitation, and Andy always helps with the imagery and the words. His injections of humor are priceless."

"IF YOU MUST INVITE A CHATTERBOX, TRY TO DILUTE HER WITH COMPANY."
—ANONYMOUS

Invitations are usually written in the third person
and are best sent two weeks ahead of time.

WHEN YOU SEND AN INVITATION,

please be sure to add all the essentials:

Event

Date

Time

Place

Style of dress, if relevant

RSVP

If an occasion is informal, then you can phone your friends, though in the end you may find it's not the best way to keep careful tabs on everyone. *Bear in mind: never issue an invitation to someone in front of others, and once you have extended invites, they should be recalled for only the most compelling of reasons.*

IN A MANNER OF SPEAKING . . . FIELD DAY

To have an enjoyable time. The phrase derives from the time when circuses and fairs typically set up in fields. "Although secretly she'd dreaded turning forty, Ruby had a field day at the party her close friends gave. The Japanese hanging lanterns, the scent of wisteria, and Bellinis were all such thoughtful, personal touches."

RSVPS

This is one French expression that just about everyone who has ever gone to a special event knows. In the world of etiquette, it's right up there with *please* and *thank you*.

WHEN AN RSVP IS UNNECESSARY

Formal or informal invitations to cocktail parties or teas don't require an acceptance unless an RSVP is included. For these events, many hostesses may even indicate "regrets only" as a way of keeping a rough head count.

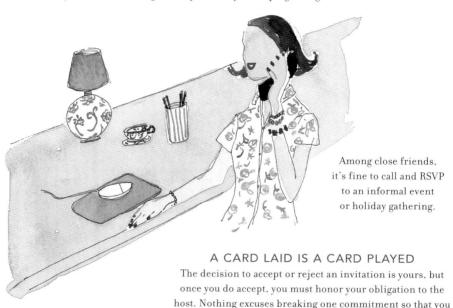

Among close friends, it's fine to call and RSVP to an informal event or holiday gathering.

A CARD LAID IS A CARD PLAYED

The decision to accept or reject an invitation is yours, but once you do accept, you must honor your obligation to the host. Nothing excuses breaking one commitment so that you can attend another event. (It would be very embarrassing if word got back to the original host that your "headache" had cleared and you were seen at another party.)

A reply to a formal invitation should be made within two days.

WHEN YOU ACCEPT—Repeat the event, date, and time.

WHEN YOU DECLINE—Repeat the event and date, and include a brief reason for your regret.

THANK-YOU NOTES

"Thank-you notes make all the difference between *feeling* grateful and *showing* your gratitude. You're not a bad person if you don't send off a note of thanks, and certainly I understand how busy everyone is, but I do believe that it's better to send the card than to agonize over not having warmly thanked someone."

When you send a note, refer to the actual gift, event, or even the conversation that you're acknowledging.

The "Three-Day Rule" applies to sending a thank-you note as well as responding to a written invitation with an RSVP.

"THE WORST INDIGNITY DOES NOT EXCUSE YOU FROM WRITING A DELIRIOUS LETTER THANKING YOUR HOSTESS FOR A *HEAVENLY* WEEK-END."

—ALICE-LEONE MOATS

"Dear Judith and Evan: This is an unpardonable time for a b&b . . . not to mention a few other Common Courtesies like saving my reason if not my life when I could not get across Third and 50th. I know you understand my laxness. Whether you condone it is another matter. . . ."

— To Judith and Evan Jones,
May 29, 1971, from M.F.K. Fisher

IN A MANNER OF SPEAKING . . . A BREAD-AND-BUTTER LETTER

A note of thanks acknowledging someone's hospitality, originally following a weekend as a houseguest. "Amy meant to send off a bread-and-butter letter right away thanking Meg for the marathon tennis weekend, but what with the two babies and new home, she was a week or so behind." Better late than never.

CHILDREN AND THANK-YOU NOTES

Until a child can make some scribbles of his or her own, thank-you notes should come from you. But please, write on behalf of your child, not in the first person as your child, which only moves the dial from cute to cutesy. Around the age of five or so, however, encourage your child to write a sentence or two. Don't worry about the results: the recipient will be charmed by the wayward handwriting and whatever is written. Over time, the act of sending a note will take root; expect full growth by the age of fourteen.

Sometimes just the words *thank you* and a bottle of wine send the perfect message.

"An engraved or printed thank-you card, no matter how attractive its design, cannot take the place of a personally written message of thanks."

—Emily Post

THE TARDY THANK-YOU NOTE

It happens: even with the best of intentions, your note is weeks late. What to do? Write it and send it along anyway. You may need to be a bit clever in your note, but there is no need to belabor its tardiness. Concentrate on the gift or affair itself. As with any note of this kind, be sincere.

LETTERS I LOVE

"Great letter writing is an art that I admire and which I hope never disappears, especially with so many more people sending faxes and e-mail. A courtship in letters is priceless, and a letter with wit is an achievement."

Mozart once wrote to his wife, Constanze,
Catch! An astonishing number of kisses are flying about.
The deuce! I see a whole crowd of them!
Ha! Ha! I have just caught three. They are delicious.

John Lennon was awarded an MBE (Member of the Order of the British Empire), which he initially accepted and later turned down, for political reasons. His telegram to Queen Elizabeth:

YOUR MAJESTY, I AM RETURNING THIS MBE IN PROTEST AGAINST BRITAIN'S INVOLVEMENT IN THE NIGERIA-BIAFRA SCENE, AGAINST OUR SUPPORT OF AMERICA IN VIETNAM AND AGAINST COLD TURKEY SLIPPING DOWN THE CHARTS.

WITH LOVE, JOHN LENNON

Zelda Sayre to F. Scott Fitzgerald, Spring 1919:

Don't you think I was made for you? I feel like you had me ordered—and I was delivered to you—to be worn—I want you to wear me, like a watch—charm or a button hole bouquet—to the world.

Letter from Jack Kerouac to Joyce Johnson, June 27, 1957:

Dear Joyce, Disregard last letter, I think exaggerated conditions here in gloomy mood.... Go ahead as planned, I'll be with you all the way... all the way to Mexico, eventually, I have an idea... and you must write a novel about Mexico too!

Love
Jack

Letters between Winston Churchill and his wife, Clementine, are valuable for the insight they give us into their 57-year marriage and as a record of a remarkable time in history. Hers was written in 1909, and his in August 1914.

My Darling

I gave the P.K. her bath to-night—Hodgy Podgy says I did it quite nicely & I want to do it always now, & she, H.P., is quite jealous—

I have found a lovely new ride for us on Saturday—

I hope you will have a nice dinner party to-night—I do wish I was there. . . .

Good-night my darling Pug—I must have lessons in Kat-drawing as your pugs are so much better than my Kats

Your loving
Clementine

Cat—dear—

It is all up. Germany has quenched the last hopes of peace by declaring war on Russia, & the declaration against France is momentarily expected.

I profoundly understand your views—But the world is gone mad—& we must look after ourselves—& our friends. It wd be good of you to come for a day or two next week. I miss you much—Your influence when guiding & not contrary is of the utmost use to me.

Sweet Kat—my tender love—

Your devoted
W

Kiss the kittens

David O. Selznick was one of the all-time great Hollywood producers (Dinner at Eight, A Star Is Born, Gone With the Wind) and was famous for his prodigious correspondence on matters large and small. The telegram is from Selznick to Katharine Brown, of Selznick International, in 1939, regarding Ingrid Bergman in the forthcoming Intermezzo, her first American-made film:

I NOTE BERGMAN IS 69¼ INCHES TALL. IS IT POSSIBLE SHE IS ACTUALLY THIS HIGH, AND DO YOU THINK WE WILL HAVE TO USE STEPLADDERS WITH LESLIE HOWARD?

Letter from E. B. White in 1951 to the head of the ASPCA, who
had accused him of not paying taxes on his dog in Maine:

*You asked about Minnie's name, sex, breed, and phone number. She doesn't
answer the phone. She is a dachshund and can't reach it, but she
wouldn't answer it even if she could, as she has no interest in outside calls.*

When the humorist Robert
Benchley visited Venice for the
first time, he sent a friend
the following telegram:

*STREETS FULL OF WATER.
PLEASE ADVISE.*

WESTERN UNION
TELEGRAM

1920
GOOD MORNING ZELDA YOU KNOW
I DO SCOTT

Telegram from F. Scott Fitzgerald
to Zelda Fitzgerald, 1920

James Thurber's drawings and stories delighted readers of *The New Yorker*
for years. As it turns out, his personal letters were also a revelation
of wit and heart, as is this one to his daughter, Rosemary, in 1947:

*Pansies have always been one of my favorite flowers and I shall put this
one between the pages of the album containing your baby pictures, including
the one of you strangling the snake which made us think that you were going
to turn out to be the first woman president of the United States. . . . Helen
and I are delighted by the increase in your correspondence and the darn
swell letters you write. What are you trying to do, be better than me?*

Love and kisses from us both.
Daddy

Telegram from Harpo Marx to then Senator John F. Kennedy, congratulating Kennedy on receiving the Democratic nomination for president, July 1960:

FIRST—CONGRATULATIONS.
SECOND—DO YOU NEED A HARP PLAYER IN YOUR CABINET.
THIRD—MY BEST TO YOUR MA AND PA.

John Donne to Sir Henry Wotton:

Sir, more than kisses,

Letters mingle souls;

For, thus absent friends speak.

With his customary droll humor, S. J. Perelman replied to a young designer who had sent him a fan letter but had misspelled his name:

The next time you issue a demand for anything, honey, whether it's a spoonful of farina or a Christmas card, examine the name of the person you're asking and spell it correctly. Now wipe the egg off your face and have a happy New Year.

LETTER TRIVIA

"Like so many girls, I had a pen pal when I was a teenager, and I was always thrilled to get mail. My sisters and I were also pulled into writing chain letters, which probably got us into the habit of what is now called correspondence. And though I'm not a serious stamp collector, I do think it's a wonderful hobby, and I love when Andy picks up the occasional old stamp with flowers on it at the flea market."

"DEAR JOHN"

Not every romance survived the prolonged separation when men went off to fight in World War II. For the woman who had chosen to leave the marriage, the news was conveyed to her overseas serviceman by letter. "John" was the name for any soldier (going back to the refrain in a song from 1917, "Over There").

WATERMARKS

A watermark is typically a discreet indication of the maker of the stationery. It is translucent in effect and most visible when held up to the light. Over its seven-hundred-year history, the watermark has been a symbolic way of encoding a message, proprietary (a papal cross, a crown), or a reference to the quality of the paper used. Today, a watermark is centered toward the bottom of a sheet of paper, though it was originally centered in the body of the paper. A watermark may be letters or numerals, be geometric, or depict a scene.

"DEAR CLASSMATES"

The 1903 graduating class of Goucher College, in Baltimore, participated in a fifty-year round-robin of letter writing. More than 35 women from a class of 54 wrote to one another about marriage and children, education, work, both world wars, the depression, travel, and getting older.

FETCH!

More than 100 dog breeds have been featured on stamps
in countries all over the world. For would-be collectors
and dog fanciers, that's a lot of letters to fetch.

Bernese Mountain Dog—Ajman, Bhutan

Border Collie—New Zealand

Borzoi—Abkhazia and Buriatia, both in Russia

French Bulldog—Bhutan

Irish Water Spaniel—Ireland

King Charles Spaniel—Great Britain

Scottish Terrier—Antigua and Barbuda

IN A MANNER OF SPEAKING...CATCH-22

Of the many phrases and sayings that abound, this one has a relatively young but literary
pedigree. Joseph Heller coined the phrase in his novel by the same name in 1961. Then, as now,
it indicated a dilemma in which the choice creates another problem, equally unsatisfactory.
"Barbara was seriously crazy about chocolate, and her latest passion was tiny dark chocolate
nuggets. Now she was down to her last six, and that was always the catch-22: eating them
was a delicious proposition, but if she ate them all, then she wouldn't have any left to eat."

"Neither snow, nor rain, nor heat, nor gloom of night stays these
couriers from the swift completion of their appointed rounds."

*This phrase was proudly chiseled above the entrance to the
General Post Office in New York City more than 50 years ago.*

IN SCRABBLE, LANGUAGE IS AN EIGHT-LETTER WORD, UP, DOWN, OR SIDEWAYS

JAZY—The highest score for a four-letter word. It means "a worsted wig" and at face value is worth 23 points.

ETAERIO—The most likely seven-letter word to appear on the game rack. It means "an aggregate fruit."

An enterprising architect named Alfred Butts devised this word game in 1948 as a way to combine vocabulary skills and chance. He called it Criss-Cross Words, but with his partner changed it to Scrabble, which means "to grope frantically." Of the many rules and important terms for Scrabble players to know, perhaps the most damning is "coffeehousing," which means distracting your opponent from the play at hand. This is strictly forbidden.

SOME KEY DATES...

1450 Gutenberg prints his massive Bible

1638 First printing press set up in America, in Cambridge, Mass.

1780 Earliest use of the steel-nib pen

1798 Invention of lithography

1847 First postage stamps in America

1868 The typewriter is patented

1880 Invention of monotype and linotype

INTRODUCING MR. ZIP...

On July 1, 1963 the U.S. Post Office introduced Mr. Zip to the American public. Mr. Zip's surname is an acronym for Zone Improvement Plan.

MOVIES AND LETTERS

The Postman Always Rings Twice —
Lana Turner, John Garfield

The Scarlet Letter —
Lillian Gish, Lars Hanson

The Letter —
Bette Davis, Herbert Marshall

Cyrano de Bergerac —
Gérard Depardieu, Anne Brochet

Shakespeare in Love —
Gwyneth Paltrow, Joseph Fiennes

You've Got Mail —
Tom Hanks, Meg Ryan

QWERTY SKILLS

The longest words that can be typed with the left hand
are *desegregated, reverberated, stewardesses, watercress.*

The longest words that can be typed with the right hand
are *homophony, nonillion, pollinium, polyphony.*

The longest word than can be typed on the top row is *rupturewort;*
and the longest words from the middle row are *Hadassah* and *alfalfa.*

SECTION THREE

A Manners Miscellany

BOB & CAROL & TED & ALICE

MAKING INTRODUCTIONS—For every matchmaker, there's someone else who thinks fate should do the introductions. If you're a "people" person, someone who enjoys being with people and introducing others, then follow your natural inclination. But once you've introduced a man and a woman, it's best to remove yourself. Otherwise, that all-too-knowing expression "shoot the messenger" might be applied to you.

SWAK—Does anyone know what a first date is anymore? Maybe not, but one thing is unchanged, and that's a kiss. Whether you've been taken to a four-star French restaurant or you've gone together to a bookstore and then out for coffee, there is no rule that says your date must be sealed with a kiss. Or even with an air kiss, or just a handshake.

THE PAST IS PROLOGUE, NOT DIALOGUE—It's a slippery slope when either person on a date talks about an ex. Stay in the present, look to the future.

"I LOVE MICKEY MOUSE MORE THAN ANY WOMAN I HAVE EVER KNOWN."

—WALT DISNEY

IN A MANNER OF SPEAKING . . . THE BEE'S KNEES

The best, or of high quality, derived from the fact that when bees carry pollen, it's in little sacs on their legs. "What more could she ask for? He sent flowers, they had a weekend of marathon movies, he dressed well, and he was funny. In sum, and as far as Donna was concerned, Tom was the bee's knees."

ALL IN THE FAMILY

HOLIDAYS—For the half-dozen or so times a family gets together to celebrate a holiday, it's incumbent on everyone to be on their best behavior. These are the occasions when you can look around the room and appreciate that of the hundreds of people you know, this group is the nearest to your heart and the people who care most about you.

COMMON COURTESIES—Among the members of your family, don't make the mistake of assuming that you can be late without phoning ahead, cancel a visit, or borrow something without asking (even your mother's pruning shears).

WET TOWELS—Sharing the bathroom is sort of adorable when children are small and you can control how many times they hop in and out of the tub. After that, the bathroom can become territory even Napoleon could covet. Who likes stepping on a soggy bathmat? Or finding someone else's wet towel on your dry one? Like every common room in the home, this is one place where continual courtesies are always appreciated.

THIS, TOO, SHALL PASS—Warfare in the form of sibling rivalry is first learned at home, some of it physical (two brothers playing swords); some of it mental (a sister outfoxing her brother for the last piece of cake); and some of it hierarchical (the oldest gets first use of the family car but is expected to pick up the younger ones at school). Blessedly, most of these childhood torments fall away after adolescence and result in familial friendships. As the parent, practice patience and bear in mind that this, too, shall pass.

> "A FAMILY IS A UNIT COMPOSED NOT ONLY OF CHILDREN BUT OF MEN, WOMEN, AN OCCASIONAL ANIMAL, AND THE COMMON COLD."
>
> —OGDEN NASH

IN A MANNER OF SPEAKING . . . BLACK SHEEP

To be regarded as the renegade or outcast. Long ago, shepherds believed that black sheep frightened the white sheep in the herd, hence they were cast out of the flock. "No matter how you looked at it, Julian was the black sheep of the family: of the three boys, he was the one who stayed out past his curfew, lost his allowance (or spent it too quickly), and was late coming to the table for dinner most nights. Just the same, to his mother he was a darling."

people with "arachibutyrophobia" get hysterical when peanut butter sticks to the roof of their mouths · 75

SOCIAL GRACES, MINOR ANNOYANCES

MAY I AIR-KISS YOU? The handshake of yesterday is the air kiss of today. If you'd rather shake hands, then be swift and extend your hand in greeting before someone leans over to plant a kiss. Depending on where you live, the social air kiss can vary: in some cities, one kiss will do it; in others it's European style, with a buss to both sides. If you each turn so that you accidentally kiss on the lips, make light of it.

TO HUG OR NOT TO HUG—If you're friends, then yes. If it's a business colleague or client, with whom there is a genuine rapport, then yes. If you're meeting up with a group that includes good friends and near-acquaintances, then hugging everyone is optional—but so time-consuming!

SORRY, BUT WHAT'S YOUR NAME?—You're in a swoon, you and your new amour kiss, and he calls you by someone else's name. What to do—step on his foot? Vow never to go out with him again? Or call him by a wrong name? If you care, then bring it to his attention, but don't let it keep you up at night.

WE MUST DO LUNCH

Sincerity is the cornerstone of good manners, so if you suggest lunch or a drink to someone, be sure to mean it. Follow up with a phone call or written invite within two days' time.

BYOP—You've just settled down into your seat for a movie and dug into your popcorn, which . . . is greasy and stale. And cost you $7, thank you very much. Should you get up and go back on line? No, but next time bring your own.

DOUBLE DIPPING—It's not sanitary, it's certainly not appetizing to witness, yet just about everybody does it. If you're passing hors d'oeuvres, you can help prevent this by immediately offering someone a napkin or toothpick. You can't reform all of the folks all of the time, but no harm comes from trying.

THE CELL PHONE REDUX—Don't use the availability of a friend or colleague on her cell phone as an excuse for being late for a date or an appointment.

THE ART OF THE TOOTHPICK
Actually, there is no art to using a toothpick. When you feel the need for a little dentistry, excuse yourself and take care of the problem in private.

IN A MANNER OF SPEAKING . . . MIND YOUR P'S AND Q'S
To be on your best behavior and mindful of your language. When all type was set by hand, typesetters needed to be particularly careful not to confuse their *p*'s with their *q*'s. "Tim, who was known to guffaw at the most inappropriate of times, did his best to mind his p's and q's when visiting his conservative godparents."

TARDINESS—Some people are inherently tardy, no matter how hard they try; others are always early. With understanding, both kinds of people can be accommodated. What isn't excusable, however, is calling someone at the exact time you're supposed to meet and saying that you'll be anywhere from 15 to 30 minutes late. Calling ahead shows respect for the other person.

SAMPLE SALES—Everybody loves a bargain, and for the Constant Shopper, a sample sale is right up there next to heaven. But don't let this feeding frenzy make *you* frenzied. Tugging and pulling, and griping and glaring are beneath you. After all, just because a two-ply cashmere sweater in your favorite color has been reduced from $395 to $125, doesn't mean that you should have it. Or does it?

WHISPERING, GOSSIPING, AND YELLING

Whispering once or twice in a movie or during a performance is justifiable, and yelling on a baseball field is also understandable. But gossiping is as reckless as riding in a car without a seat belt. Buckle up, button up, zip it, sshhhh.

IN A MANNER OF SPEAKING...MAD MONEY

Money that a lady carries should the date end in a quarrel (Webster's, 1922). "Dianne had long been trained to carry around a little mad money with her, just in case something went wonky on a date. But she hadn't expected that would ever happen when she was out with John. Alas, it did."

MANICURES ON THE GO—Some habits die hard, such as filing or clipping one's nails in public, and yet nothing is more inappropriate. On a long bus ride, while sitting on a park bench, or (heaven forbid!) while waiting for your date in a restaurant are all manicure no-no's. When it comes to lavishing care on your hands and feet, please visit a nail salon, or do your beautifying at home.

IT'S NOT MUSIC TO MY EARS—If it's your portable CD player, a few reminders will prevent others from wanting to pull the plug, so to speak. When you're at the beach, consider that the couple reading ten yards away prefers the sound of the waves to the sound of your hip-hop. At the office, follow company protocol. If playing music is acceptable and considered inspiring, be considerate of your coworkers and adjust the volume. If playing music is frowned upon during the day, then save your tunes for after-hours work.

TO ERR IS HUMAN,
TO FORGIVE DIVINE.

GUM IS Y/GUMMY

A piece of gum is refreshing and a quick fix if you're hungry, thirsty, or bored. In public, please don't smack your chops, blow bubbles, or snap your gum when you chew. And if you're with others, then offer gum all around. Of course some circumstances are inherently gum free, such as a job interview, baby christening, or romantic dinner for two.

UNGRACIOUS GIGGLES

"My church giggles grew louder and louder, and the more I tried to tame them, the worse they got, until the Church of England must have had doubts about my prospects for salvation."
—Sarah Ferguson

HOSPITALITY AND FOOD

MAKE MINE A BAGEL WITH COFFEE—If you're having family or friends for the weekend, especially if they're from out of town, be thoughtful and ask if there are special food requests. In particular, most people have a set routine when it comes to breakfast and they'll be grateful if you can accommodate them.

THE INTOXICATED GUEST—"A girlfriend of Kate's stayed up late with us one evening and we all decided it would be a good idea for her to spend the night. I gave her one of my T-shirts, a toothbrush, water, and said good-night. When we woke the next morning she was gone, leaving a thank-you note with apologies. A few days later she sent a package. Inside was a T-shirt printed with the words *inebriated guest T-shirt for sleeping over.*" —Andy Spade

I have eaten
the plums
that were in
the icebox

and which
you were probably
saving
for breakfast

Forgive me
they were delicious
so sweet
and so cold

—William Carlos Williams,
"This Is Just to Say"

"HERE'S YOUR HAT, WHAT'S YOUR HURRY."
—OLD AMERICAN SAYING

IN A MANNER OF SPEAKING...DUTCH TREAT

Paying your own way. From the seventeenth century, when the Dutch were regarded by the English as their rivals. ("Going Dutch" is an Americanism, dating to 1914.) "For all the years they'd been friends, Sophie and Sarah went Dutch treat when it came to dining out. It simplified the whole who-pays-for-what dilemma."

IN A MANNER OF SPEAKING...GRATUITY

Meaning graciousness or favor. From the French *gratuité* or medieval Latin *gratuitas* for "thankful." "Susan and Adrian were regulars at their corner French bistro, where they liked to bring their own wine. The waiters never minded, although a supplemental gratuity was added to their bill."

WHAT'S MINE IS MINE

ON LENDING AND BORROWING BOOKS—It's been six
months since a newish friend has borrowed a book of yours.
Can you ask for it back without seeming impolite or embarrassing the friend?
Yes. It's never wrong to ask for what is yours. However, if someone asks to
borrow a book that you care about, then you're better off suggesting some
other book instead.

LENDING CLOTHES—In gambling, the token guideline is that you should
never gamble what you can't afford to lose. Ditto when it comes to your clothes.
If you're the borrower, make sure to have the garment cleaned after wearing
and return it to its owner, preferably in better condition than you received it,
and within a week's time.

OFFICE MATES—Although a friend or colleague would never come into your
home and walk off with your dictionary or calculator, trespasses of this nature
occur in offices with surprising frequency. And with no discernible sign of
embarrassment, either. The rules of borrowing still apply: don't take anything
without asking. Everyone has a favorite something, even if it's only a pencil.

HOME LOANS

It's Friday night, you've packed the car
with groceries, your swimsuit, and the dog,
and you're headed to the country house.
Someone else's country house. When
friends graciously lend you the use of their
home, take care not to overstep your
boundaries in their absence. Don't assume
you can cut their lilacs and put them in your
room or run the air conditioner willy-nilly.
Ask them for any guidelines before
you arrive, and remember, what's theirs
remains theirs, even in absentia.

GIFTS, GIFTING, RE-GIFTING

"RE-GIFTING IS AN ART FORM. BUT
BEWARE: IF YOU RE-GIFT TO OTHERS,
THEY MAY RE-GIFT UNTO YOU."

—ANDY SPADE

WHEN THE GIFT'S NOT RIGHT—Nothing is ever to be gained from parsing the truth, but flat-out honesty isn't always the best solution, either, when you've received a gift that doesn't fit, isn't your style, or would look out of place in your home. The grin-and-bear-it approach works only some of the time. What if, for example, the gift is a dress that is overly tight, or yards too big? Step up to the plate and offer a warm thanks. And depending on the relationship and the object, diplomatically state the problem. After all, who wants to spend money on something that is never used?

BABY #3—Should you give another baby gift if you've already done so for babies one and two? Common sense is a good guide here. The point of a baby shower is to help the new mother feather her nest with clothes, stroller, and other paraphernalia. The hand-me-down machinery should then kick in for any successive brood.

THE GIFT OF MONEY—It may be tempting to ask for money instead of an object as a gift, but forswear the desire. Gifts should be freely given, not solicited. Be grateful for whatever someone has thought to give you.

EXCHANGING WITH A FRIEND OF MEANS—Clearly money wasn't the reason you two became friends, so don't let it become a matter of concern when exchanging gifts. You should spend only what you want, or are able to. This is not a contest.

RE-GIFTING—The quiet truth is that people do re-gift. Re-gifting is done with gifts that don't fit, aren't to your liking, or aren't returnable. Don't re-gift as a way of cleaning out your closet or saving money. As with any gift, the selection should be suited to the recipient.

MUSEUMS AND GALLERIES

NE TOUCHEZ PAS!—When you were a child, how many times did your mother tell you not to touch things in a store? The reprisal for such misbehavior in a museum or gallery is taken seriously, and is an inflexible rule worldwide. (Standing close to the art only works if you're not blocking anyone else's view.)

THE ART EXPERT—You know the type: he or she tends to recite at length (and loudly) on the artist, the brushstroke, the attention to detail, the quality of the print, or almost anything so as to convey Knowledge. But might doesn't equal right, so to all ad hoc experts and lecturers please don't pontificate on the paint. Lecture halls have seats; museums and galleries don't.

THE OUT-OF-TOWNERS—For many tourists, a visit almost anywhere isn't complete without the obligatory stop at the museum. Culture in any form is a blessing, so next time you find yourself looking at Egyptian hieroglyphs, enjoy the art, but please refrain from chatting about where you'll be having dinner. (Duane Hanson, where are you when we need you?)

MY CHILD COULD HAVE DRAWN THAT— This is a distinction only a privileged group can say, among them Picasso's mother, Matisse's father, de Kooning's parents.

IN A MUSEUM
SOLO VIEWING IS BLISS.

ANIMAL LOVERS

PET ALLERGIES—Being considerate of someone who's allergic to house pets is not simply a manners issue; often, it can be a serious concern for the person who has allergies. If you have pets, it's your obligation to let any first-time visitors know in advance. For some people, it's easy enough to take an allergy pill, but they will be less uncomfortable if you vacuum and dust before they arrive.

IT'S A CAT, NOT A KID—A painful point but true: Kenya, Gray Bear, Jasper, pretty-boy Frankie, and baby-cakes Sophie are not in the genus Homo sapiens. They're animals. So when you want to talk about your "children" around non-animal owners, have a heart and don't test their patience by talking at length about your little *snuggums*.

YOU LOVE DOGS, BUT...

When a friend's dog won't stop jumping on you and is not reprimanded by your friend, keep in mind that your response will be heard with biased ears. (The same thing applies to someone else's children.) Try to be friendly and make a joke, such as "This is the third dog today who's jumped on me. Dogs must love the color orange!" Dog owners everywhere, take note: the incorrigible pooch who yips, jumps, and sniffs is like a child in one basic way . . . in need of manners!

IN A MANNER OF SPEAKING...TO LET THE CAT OUT OF THE BAG

To disclose a secret. An old (and not very nice) country trick of substituting a cat for a pig in a burlap sack. If the buyer checked and saw that it was a cat, then the cat was let out of the bag. "People had long suspected that Charlie and his girlfriend might elope; just the same, the cat was let out of the bag when, unable to contain his enthusiasm, Charlie got into a discussion about diamond rings with his sister."

APARTMENT LIVING

IT'S MY PARTY—Everyone is entitled to give a party, and when you decide to have one, get in touch with those neighbors who might be inconvenienced. Sometimes it's nice to invite your neighbors as well, especially if you think they'll enjoy themselves. Weeknights are generally taboo for big or loud gatherings, and depending on where you live, the music should be lowered by 11:30 on the weekend. (No one, however, should have to tolerate a loud, tone-deaf drunk, night or day.)

GOOD KARMA IS A GOOD NEIGHBOR—Unless you have the luxury of a doorman, receiving packages can be an ordeal. If you will sign for a neighbor's package, hold open the elevator, or help walk a dog when it's owner is sick, this is the surest way for all of you to live harmoniously.

THAT'S NO CHILD, IT'S AN ELEPHANT—To a downstairs neighbor, children and high heels sound more like an invasion than a family happily at play. This is why carpets and rugs are the olive branch of high-rise dwellers. Be considerate and help to muffle ambient sound by covering your wood floors.

HAMMERS, FLOODS, AND THE TREADMILL

The idiosyncrasies of apartment living are as random as the people in any given building. There's the night owl who hangs pictures or vacuums at midnight, the absentminded tenant whose tub frequently runs over (and into your living room), and the sports nut whose *thump-thump-thump* at dawn gives you a major headache. Since what can't be tolerated must be changed, pick your battles wisely. Let reason, not bad temper, guide you. Protracted fighting among neighbors is a lose-lose situation.

THE GOOD SPORT

SNOW DAY—When it comes to skiing, nothing tops "safety first." If you're skiing with people less skilled, don't urge them to ski a more difficult slope. Slow down and go at their pace if you decide to join them at a level suited to their abilities. Pleasure and safety aren't mutually exclusive.

THE SUN WAS IN MY EYE—When kids don't turn in their homework, they pull out the proverbial "dog ate my homework" excuse. It never works. And in sports it never works to blame a poor shot on such things as the sun, worn-out tennis balls, someone else talking.

THAT'S MY BOBBY—Just because the little quarterback on the football field is your child, remember that every parent in the bleachers is rooting for their child, too. If you're annoyed when someone else is cheering and back-slapping about their son's victory, there's not much upside in saying something; instead, take a break and get yourself a hot dog. Clearly, one-upsmanship doesn't only occur on the playing field.

THREE GAMES TO LOVE—Kamikaze tennis is neither a civilized sport nor one to be played in mixed doubles. In competitive sports, tennis is one of the most elegant and gracious games, whether you're playing singles or doubles. It's natural to want to win, but win *well*—you and your opponent should be able to enjoy a post-match drink together.

"I'D JUST AS SOON PLAY TENNIS WITH THE NET DOWN."

—ROBERT FROST

TOUCHDOWN!—Victory does taste sweet, but don't let your enthusiasm become your opponent's poison. Learning to be a good sport applies to winning, too.

NO SPLASHING ALLOWED—A bully in the water is no less culpable than a bully on land. Don't splash others; only use a diving board for diving, not pushing; and never dunk or hold anyone under water. Water games are okay (remember "chicken"?), as long as you keep in mind that all of you are there to have *fun*.

KEEP YOUR COOL—The sky is blue, the weather is mild, even your golf shoes are darling, so why are you in a snit? For some players, golf is the ultimate in relaxation, akin to a pure zen moment. For others, though, that little golf ball comes to represent a meta-physical longing that remains relentlessly elusive. When sand traps and inner demons begin to handicap your game, slow down and gaze at the beauty around you. Nothing is more childish than a grown-up throwing a golf club on the green.

"ALWAYS IMITATE THE BEHAVIOR OF
THE WINNERS WHEN YOU LOSE."
—GEORGE MEREDITH

IN A MANNER OF SPEAKING...RAIN CHECK

A ticket stub good for an event or performance deferred on account of rain; to make good on something at a later time. "Isaac had been looking forward to his first visit to the U.S. Open, but that morning it poured and the courts were too wet to play. His mother assured him they'd get a rain check, good for another day during the tournament."

MANNERS GO ABROAD
THANK YOU—MERCI—GRACIAS—DANKE SCHÖN

A generation or more ago, the proper lady and gentleman knew to follow custom in their dress and comportment wherever they traveled. Now, as Cole Porter wrote, "anything goes." Manners abroad, just like manners on your home turf, help life flow more smoothly and pleasantly. All you need are a few pointers.

COMPORTAMENTO EN PÚBLICO—OUT IN PUBLIC

One of the frequent salvos fired at Americans abroad is their overly casual style of dress. It needn't be so. The Louvre, for example, isn't a gymnasium, it's a museum. So leave your sneakers in your hotel room and don't wear sweat pants, either. On the subject of shoes, always remove them before entering a Japanese home or restaurant unless your host informs you otherwise. When you do so, be certain they're facing the door.

PARLA INGLESE?—No one abroad will expect you to speak their language fluently, but it is a sign of respect to learn how to speak some basic phrases. (The well-known exception is in France, especially Paris, where your perfect English is preferred to your broken French.)

TIPPING—POURBOIRE—TRINKGELD

In many parts of Western Europe, a gratuity of ten to twenty percent is automatically included with your bill, what is known as *servis compris*. But if you're in Denmark, don't leave a tip in a restaurant or if you take a taxi. The Fins don't seem to hunker after pocket change, either, preferring instead to include a gratuity in with a restaurant or hotel bill. The friendly Italians will obligingly accept a tip whenever you choose to give one.

WHEN IT'S WISE TO DISCUSS A FEE IN ADVANCE OF SERVICES RENDERED— Next time you're in one of the Arab countries and wish to hire a car, especially one without a meter, confirm the fare with your driver before your journey. Protocol doesn't require you to tip, but if you want to be certain that your fare doesn't mysteriously double at the end of your ride, be sure to offer something.

TABLE MANNERS—VED BORDET

Don't go looking for a BLT sandwich when you're in France, or in Germany, or in Spain, or just about anywhere but in the United States. Culinary exploration and experimentation are what distinguish the gracious visitor from the small-minded tourist. Tapas in Spain, sushi in Japan, fresh herring in Denmark, or *cotoletta di tacchino alla bolognese* in Italy are what separate the rest of the world from the American melting pot. These distinctions are treasures to be savored. When you're in Japan, don't ask your waiter for a napkin—none are ever used. Instead, the Japanese carry around with them a small washcloth for such purposes.

REJSE—TRAVEL—VIAGGIO—VOYAGE

Every country has specific customs, which bear learning before you visit. In Austria, do bring flowers when invited to someone's home for dinner, but be sure they aren't red roses (unless you're feeling romantically inclined). The Germans will heartily shake your hand upon arriving and leaving, the British may proffer you a rather weak one, and the Greeks may embrace you. As for the British, it's considered indiscreet to inquire after someone's profession when first meeting. The French find any direct inquiry potentially inflammatory, so it's best to follow the lead of your host. In Japan, the women send chocolates to men on Valentine's Day; a month later, the favor is returned.

Punctuality is a many varied thing from country to country. Americans straddle the middle road compared to their foreign counterparts, which suggests, like everything else involved with international travel, that when in Rome do as the Romans do.

MONEY MATTERS

NEGOTIATING—There's a reason why some companies hire professional negotiators to mediate contracts; like many things in life, negotiating is an art. Or at the very least, a talent, which some people naturally have. Feel free to haggle at an open-air flea market where chairs and old record albums and silver coasters can be found. You might even be able to shave a few dollars off something at an antique shop where you have a prior relationship with the proprietor. Where should you pay the sticker price without quibble or dissent?—At a vintage clothing shop, farmer's market, your beauty salon.

INAPPROPRIATE CHARGE—Math may be perfect, but for those of us who do the adding and subtracting, there is always room for error. Always check an itemized bill, be it at the grocery store, restaurant, or hotel. If you find you've been overcharged (or undercharged, for which you deserve an A+ for honesty), quietly speak to the person responsible for your bill. Like so many mistakes, this one was unintentional.

WHEN THE BILL COMES—While everyone else was eating shrimp cocktail and hangar steak, you were nibbling on greens with goat cheese. Then the bill comes and your share is $48. Ouch. For those awkward times when you've eaten considerably less than others with whom you're splitting the bill, be prepared to pay up. When it comes to money, "fair" doesn't always come into play.

STICKER SHOCK—You're at the flower shop, and the New Zealand peonies you covet cost $6. Or so you thought until you got to the counter and learned that they are $6 *a stem.* Be honest and make a simple apology (don't go overboard). Settle on snapdragons instead.

DID YOU PAY RETAIL?
There can be a fine line between interest and envy. Before you ask a friend the price of her new dress, ask yourself why you want to know. Frankly, most people are uncomfortable talking about what they paid for something, and among women the subject may make them a wee testy.

"NEITHER A BORROWER NOR A LENDER BE."
—SHAKESPEARE

ANDY'S TRUISMS

It's difficult to look elegant while eating a chili dog.

Making others feel good makes you feel good.

When you insult another, you insult yourself.

Garlic, onions, and kisses simply don't mix.

Wearing a lobster bib doesn't strip a man of his masculinity.

Being kind doesn't equal being meek.

Sleep with the enemy and wake up without friends.

EXCEPTIONS TO EVERY RULE

You may start eating before everyone else if you have
hypoglycemia or another medical condition (besides rudeness.)

You should pay the check if you invited the couple to
dinner as your guests. However, if they slip their credit
card to the waiter first or threaten you with a steak
knife and insist on paying, then let it go.

Patience is a virtue, unless someone is taking advantage of you.

Be alert. We need more lerts.

THANK YOU

It seems that every project I venture upon involves the helping hands of many people, and this book is no exception. Everyone has pitched in—from my husband and colleagues at *kate spade* to my dog, Henry, who earnestly practices good manners everyday.

Julia Leach, who oversees our creative department and is a longtime friend of Andy's and mine, has truly shouldered the responsibility of putting this book together. I don't know how she manages to have so much energy and such grace under pressure, but she is a god-send. Working in tandem with Julia is our editor and new friend, Ruth Peltason, whose enthusiasm and expertise has helped all of us make this book special. They were joined in their efforts by Virginia Johnson, our gifted illustrator; designer Alberta Testanero, who gave the book its overall look; and Ana Rogers, who took the vision for this book and brought it to life.

Our business partners, Elyce Arons and Pamela Bell, and I were friends long before we started this company, and they have been greatly supportive of this project. Their suggestions, their own experiences, and those we've shared have all contributed to *Manners*. So has the friendship and encouragement extended by Robin Marino, president of *kate spade*. I'm also grateful to Marybeth Schmitt, who has skillfully navigated our publicity efforts. Also at our office I would like to thank Susan Anthony, Barbara Kolsun, Stacy Van Praagh, Meg Touborg, and everyone in our creative department—Biz Zast , Lawren Howell, Jenifer Ruske, Cheree Berry, Naseem Niaraki, and Anthony Coombs. Christine Muhlke, who provided the research, was also invaluable for her natural smarts and good ideas.

For years I've looked to Emily Post for guidance and wisdom. Of the many women who have been challenged by the task of guiding Americans along the course of good manners, Emily Post has done so with charm, grace, and good humor. Her advice on so many subjects remains the best advice to be found, and even though *Etiquette* was published more than eighty years ago, Emily Post still sounds natural and unaffected. She's my idea of a national treasure.

The business of publishing a book is new to me, and I am grateful that our agent, Ira Silverberg, has been so wonderfully wise. I have been fortunate to work with the devoted crew at Simon & Schuster, including David Rosenthal, executive vice president and publisher, whose enthusiasm wowed us all; Amanda Murray, our patient in-house editor; Walter L. Weintz; Michael Selleck; Tracey Guest; Peter McCulloch; and Sybil Pincus. Thank you, thank you.

And then there's my husband, Andy, who first gave me the courage to go into business more than a decade ago and now into books. "We already have so many books and we both love to read," I told him, "do you really think it's a good idea to try being an author?" Well, his answer is before you. Humor and kindness are high on my list of important qualities in a person, and I'm fortunate to have found in Andy a rare combination of both. His ideas and his infectious spirit and voice are in *Manners*, page for page. So, too, is Andy's encouragement, his humor, and his love. I am indeed blessed.

Kate Spade

SELECT
BIBLIOGRAPHY

Axtell, Richard, ed. *Do's and Taboos Around the World.* Comp., The Parker Pen Company. New York: John Wiley & Sons, Inc. 1993.

Baldridge, Letitia. *Letitia Baldridge's Complete Guide to the New Manners for the '90s.* New York: Rawson Associates (div. of Macmillan Publishing), 1990.

Barr, Norah K., Marsha Moran, and Patrick Moran, comp. *M.F.K. Fisher: A Life in Letters.* Washington, D.C.: Counterpoint, 1998.

Benton, Frances, with the General Foundation of Women's Clubs. *Etiquette: The Complete Modern Guide for Day-to-Day Living the Correct Way.* New York: Random House, 1956.

Esar, Evan. *20,000 Quips & Quotes: A Treasury of Witty Remarks, Comic Proverbs, Wisecracks, and Epigrams.* New York: Barnes & Noble Books, 1995.

Feinberg, Steven L. *Crane's Blue Book of Stationery.* Foreword by Stanley Marcus. New York: Doubleday, 1989.

Martin, Judith. *Miss Manners' Guide to Excruciatingly Correct Behavior.* New York: Galahad Books, 1982.

Moats, Alice-Leone. *No Nice Girl Swears.* Foreword by Edna Woolman Chase. New York: Blue Ribbon Books, Inc., 1934.

Morris, William and Mary Morris. *Morris Dictionary of Words and Phrase Origins.* 2nd ed. Foreword by Isaac Asimov. New York: HarperCollins Publishers, 1988.

Osgood, Charles. *Funny Letters from Famous People.* New York: Broadway Books, 2003.

Post, Emily. *Etiquette: The Blue Book of Social Usage.* New York: Funk & Wagnalls Co., Publishers, 1945. Reprint 1949.

Post, Peter. *Essential Manners for Men: What to Do, When to Do It, and Why.* New York: HarperResource, 2003.

Rosenkrantz, Linda. *Telegram!* New York: Henry Holt and Company, 2003.

Soames, Mary, ed. *Winston and Clementine: The Personal Letters of the Churchills.* Boston: Mariner Books, 2001.

Tiffany's Table Manners for Teenagers. Introduction by Walter Hoving. Illustrations by Joe Eula. New York: Ives Washburn, Inc., 1961.

Tiger, Caroline. *How to Behave: A Guide to Modern Manners for the Socially Challenged.* Philadelphia: Quirk Books, 2003.

THE POLITE TRAVELER GOES ABROAD

FRENCH
I'd like to check my raincoat and small dog, Edna.

J'aimerais laisser mon imperméable et ma petite chienne Edna au vestiaire.

NORWEGIAN
Pardon me, sir, could you please help me open my Lime Rickey?

Unskyld meg, min herre, kan de vaere så snill å hjelpe meg åpne min "lime rickey"?

ITALIAN
I need to thank our hostess for taking us to the opera, even though it was six hours long.

Devo ringraziare il nostro ospite per averci portato all' opera, anche se e' durata per sei ore.

PORTUGUESE
Operator, could you please connect me to BUtterfield-8?

Telefonista, por favor me transfira para a "BUtterfield-8?"

Editors: Ruth A. Peltason, for Bespoke Books
             Julia Leach, for kate spade

Designers: Ana Rogers
             Alberta Testanero, for kate spade

The author and publisher gratefully acknowledge those writers whose works contributed to this book.

"This Is Just to Say" by William Carlos Williams, from *Collected Poems: 1909–1939, Volume 1,* copyright © 1938 by New Directions Publishing Corp. Reprinted by permission of New Directions Publishing Corp.

SIMON & SCHUSTER
Rockefeller Center
1230 Avenue of the Americas
New York, NY 10020

For information regarding special discounts for bulk purchases, please contact
Simon & Schuster Special Sales at 1-800-456-6798 or business@simonandschuster.com

Manufactured in Italy

10 9 8 7 6 5 4 3 2 1

Library of Congress Cataloging-in-Publication Data

Spade, Kate.
   Manners : always gracious, sometimes irreverent / by Kate Spade ; edited by Ruth
 Peltason and Julia Leach ; illustrations by Virginia Johnson.
       p. cm.
   Includes bibliographical references.
   1. Etiquette. I. Peltason, Ruth A. II. Leach, Julia (Julia E.) III. Title.

BJ1853.S67 2004
395—dc22

                                                                    2003062970

ISBN 0-7432-5066-4